The bumper Ukulele playlist
Gold Edition

© 2014 by Faber Music Ltd
First published in 2014 by Faber Music Ltd
Bloomsbury House
74–77 Great Russell Street
London WC1B 3DA

Arranged by Alex Davis
Edited by Lucy Holliday

Designed by Sue Clarke
Photography by Ben Turner

Printed in England by Caligraving Ltd
All rights reserved

ISBN10: 0-571-53840-1
EAN13: 978-0-571-53840-9

Reproducing this music in any form is illegal
and forbidden by the Copyright, Designs
and Patents Act, 1988

To buy Faber Music publications or to find out about
the full range of titles available, please contact your
local music retailer or Faber Music sales enquiries:

Faber Music Ltd, Burnt Mill, Elizabeth Way,
Harlow, CM20 2HX England

Tel: +44(0)1279 82 89 82
Fax: +44(0)1279 82 89 83

sales@fabermusic.com
fabermusicstore.com

contents

Aloha Oe	Traditional	05
Amazing Grace	Traditional	06
American Idiot	Green Day	07
Anything Goes	Cole Porter	10
Auld Lang Syne	Traditional	12
Bad Moon Rising	Creedence Clearwater Revival	14
The Bare Necessities	From 'The Jungle Book'	16
Bewitched	Doris Day	18
Can You Feel The Love Tonight	From 'The Lion King'	20
Creep	Radiohead	22
Cry Me A River	Julie London	24
Daisy Bell	Harry Dacre	26
Danny Boy	Traditional	13
Dear Darlin'	Olly Murs	28
Do They Know It's Christmas?	Band Aid	31
Early One Morning	Traditional	38
Edge Of Glory	Lady Gaga	34
Fisherman's Blues	The Waterboys	39
Food, Glorious Food	From 'Oliver'	42
Frosty The Snowman	The Ronettes	44
Grease	Frankie Valli	46
Greased Lightnin'	John Travolta	52
Great Balls Of Fire	Jerry Lee Lewis	54
Green Green Grass Of Home	Tom Jones	56
Grenade	Bruno Mars	49
Have You Met Miss Jones?	Robbie Williams	58
Hello Dolly	From 'Hello Dolly'	60
Hey There Delilah	Plain White T's	66
The Hippopotamus Song	Flanders & Swann	62
How Much Is That Doggie In The Window	Patti Page	64
I Got Rhythm	George & Ira Gershwin	72
I Got You Babe	Sonny & Cher	69
I Only Want To Be With You	Dusty Springfield	74
I'll Never Fall In Love Again	Dionne Warwick	76
I'm Gonna Be (500 Miles)	The Proclaimers	78
It's A Beautiful Day	Michael Bublé	82
It's A Long Way To Tipperary	Judy Garland	81
Jingle Bells	Traditional	86
Kiss Me	Sixpence None The Richer	87
Kum Ba Yah	Spiritual	90
Last Nite	The Strokes	91
Lego House	Ed Sheeran	94

Title	Artist	Page
Let There Be Love	Nat 'King' Cole	100
Life On Mars?	David Bowie	97
Little Brown Jug	Traditional	106
Losing My Religion	R.E.M.	102
Moondance	Van Morrison	108
Morning Has Broken	Traditional	107
My Grandfather's Clock	Traditional	110
My Old Man's A Dustman	Lonnie Donegan	112
Never Tear Us Apart	INXS	114
Of The Night	Bastille	118
On The Street Where You Live	From 'My Fair Lady'	116
Patience	Take That	124
Price Tag	Jessie J	121
Puff The Magic Dragon	Peter, Paul & Mary	126
Raindrops Keep Fallin' On My Head	Burt Bacharach	128
Ring Of Fire	Johnny Cash	130
Rockin' Robin	Bobby Day	132
Scarborough Fair	Traditional	134
Sheena Is A Punk Rocker	The Ramones	138
Spirit In The Sky	Doctor & The Medics	135
A Spoonful Of Sugar	From 'Mary Poppins'	144
Stormy Weather	Etta James	140
Summertime	From 'Porgy & Bess'	142
Tainted Love	Soft Cell	148
There Is A Light That Never Goes Out	The Smiths	150
(They Long To Be) Close To You	The Carpenters	152
This Land Is Your Land	Woodie Guthrie	154
Touch The Sky	Julie Fowlis	145
Tragedy	The Bee Gees	156
Umbrella	Rihanna	158
Waltzing Matilda	Traditional	166
Waterloo Sunset	The Kinks	160
The Way You Look Tonight	Frank Sinatra	162
What A Wonderful World	Louis Armstrong	164
What Shall We Do With The Drunken Sailor?	Traditional	167
Whiskey In The Jar	The Dubliners	168
The White Cliffs Of Dover	Vera Lynn	170
Wild Mountain Thyme	Traditional	169
The Wild Rover	Traditional	176
You're The First, The Last, My Everything	Barry White	172
You've Got A Friend In Me	Randy Newman	174

Reading Chord Boxes

A chord box is basically a diagram of how a chord is played on the neck of the Ukulele. It shows you which string to play, where to put your fingers and whereabouts on the neck the chord is played.

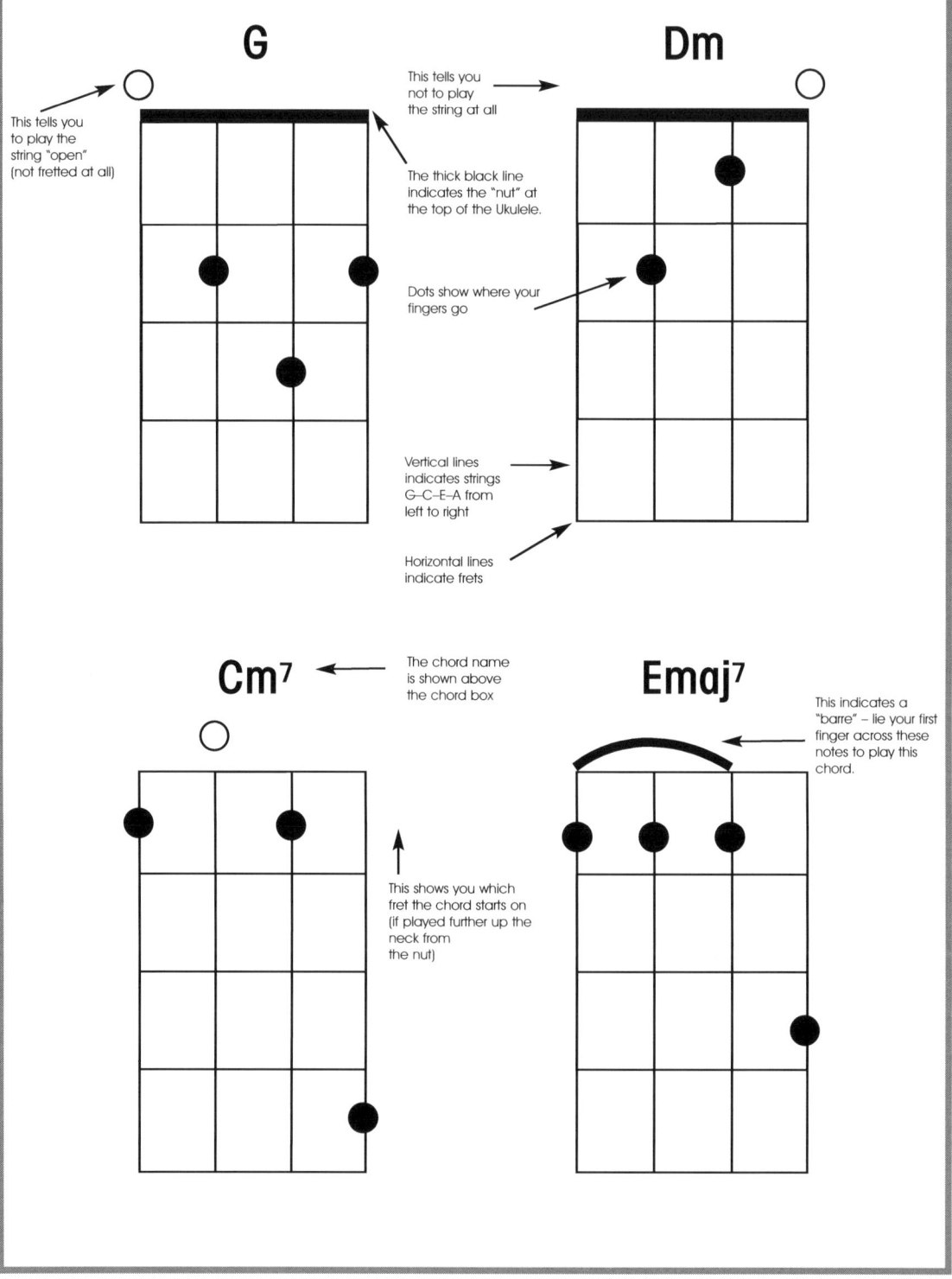

Traditional

Aloha Oe
Words and Music Traditional

Verse

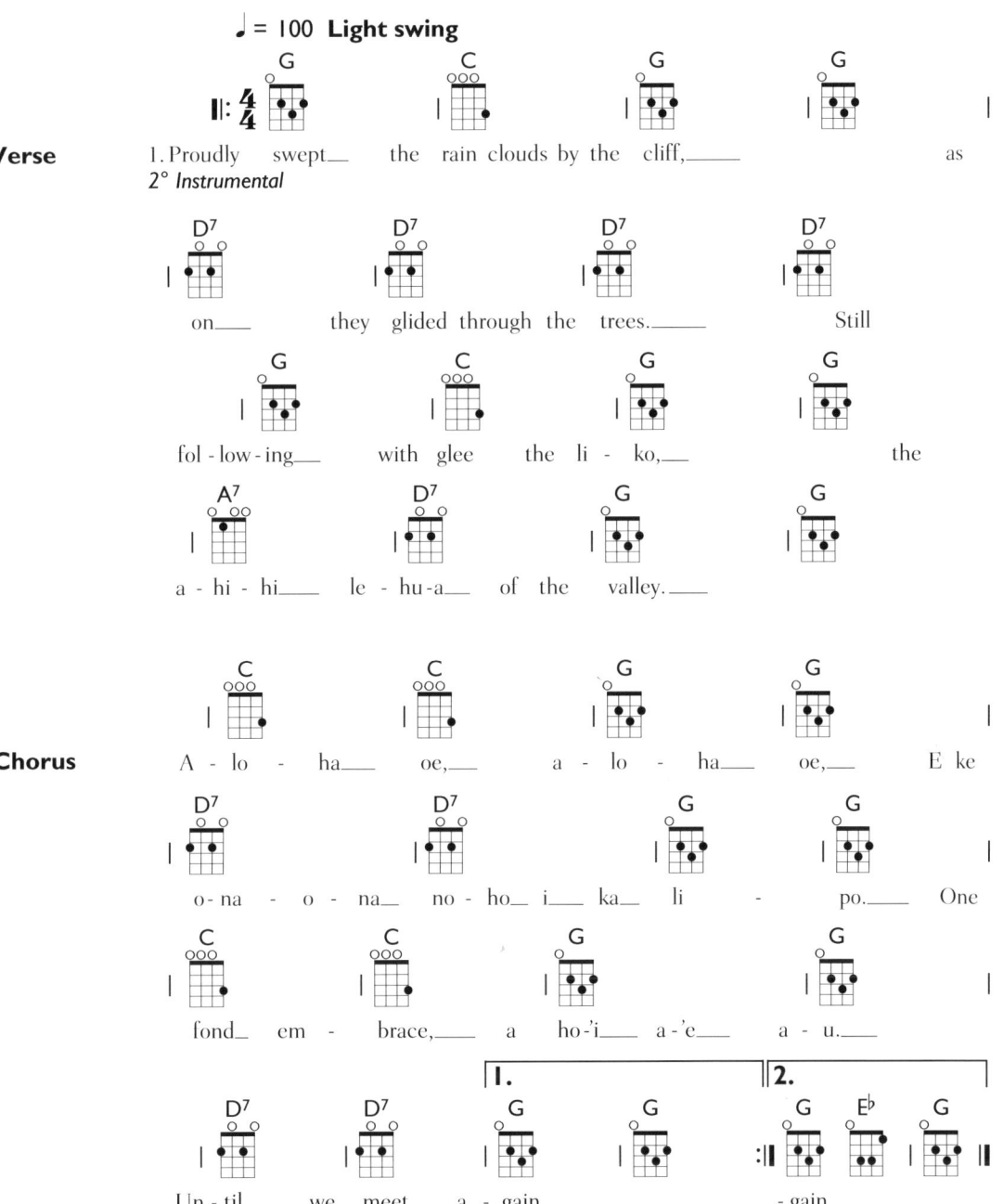

Amazing Grace

Words and Music Traditional

Traditional

♩ = 70

Verses

C	C	F	C
1. A - ma - zing grace,	how sweet	the sound	that
2. 'Twas grace that taught	my heart	to fear	and
3. Through ma - ny dan - gers, toils	and snares	I
4. When we've been there a thou -	sand years	bright

C	Am	G	G7
saved a wretch	like me.		I
grace my fears	re - lieved,		how
have al - rea - - dy	come,		'twas
shi - ning as	the sun,		we've

C	C7	F	C
once was lost,	but now	am found,	was
pre - cious did	that grace	ap - pear,	the
grace that led	me safe	thus far,	and
no less days	to sing	God's praise	than

C	G	G7 C	C
blind but now	first	I see.	
hour I will	bring	be - lieved.	
grace we first		me home.	
when		be - gun.	

© 2014 Faber Music Ltd
All Rights Reserved.

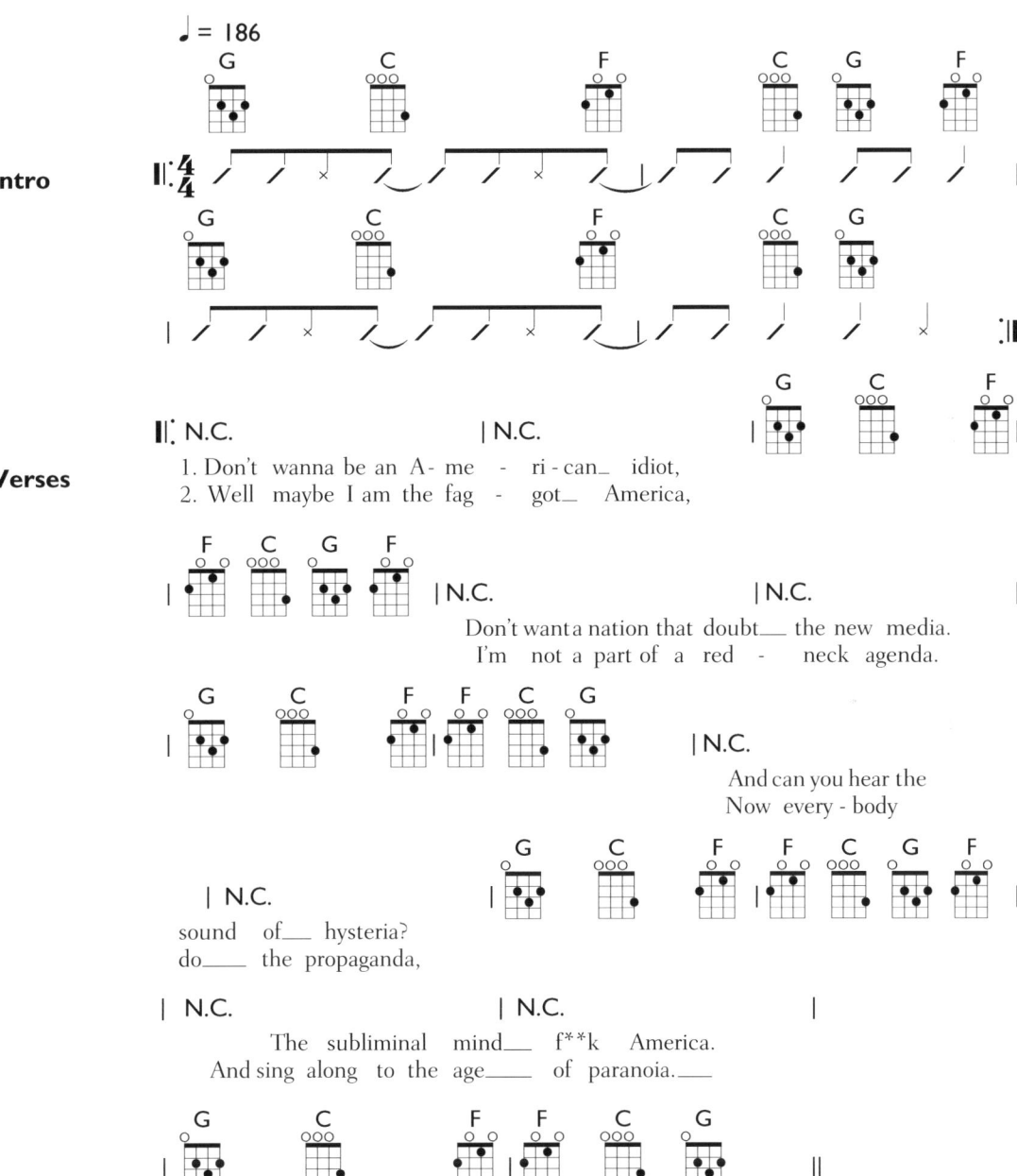

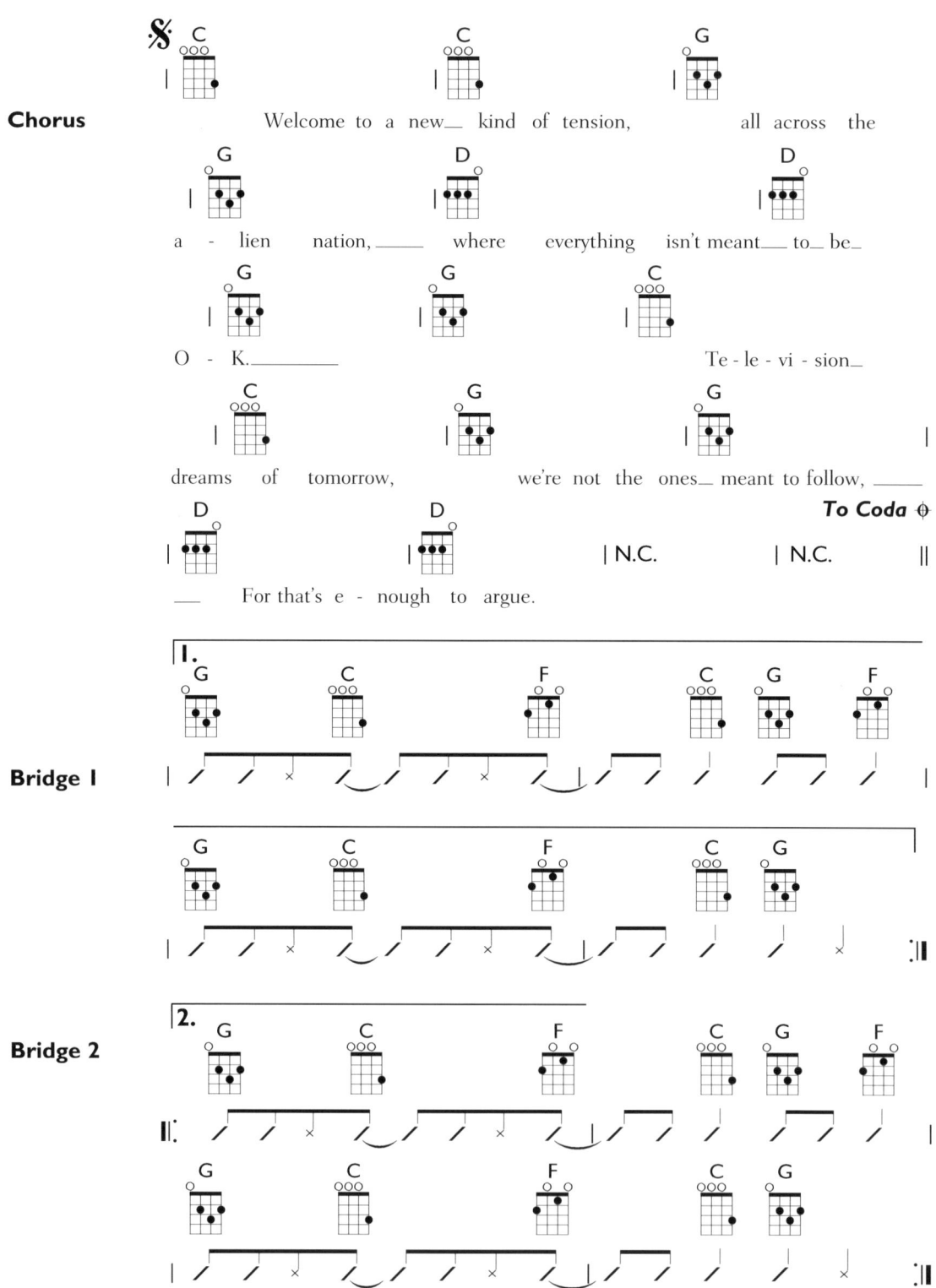

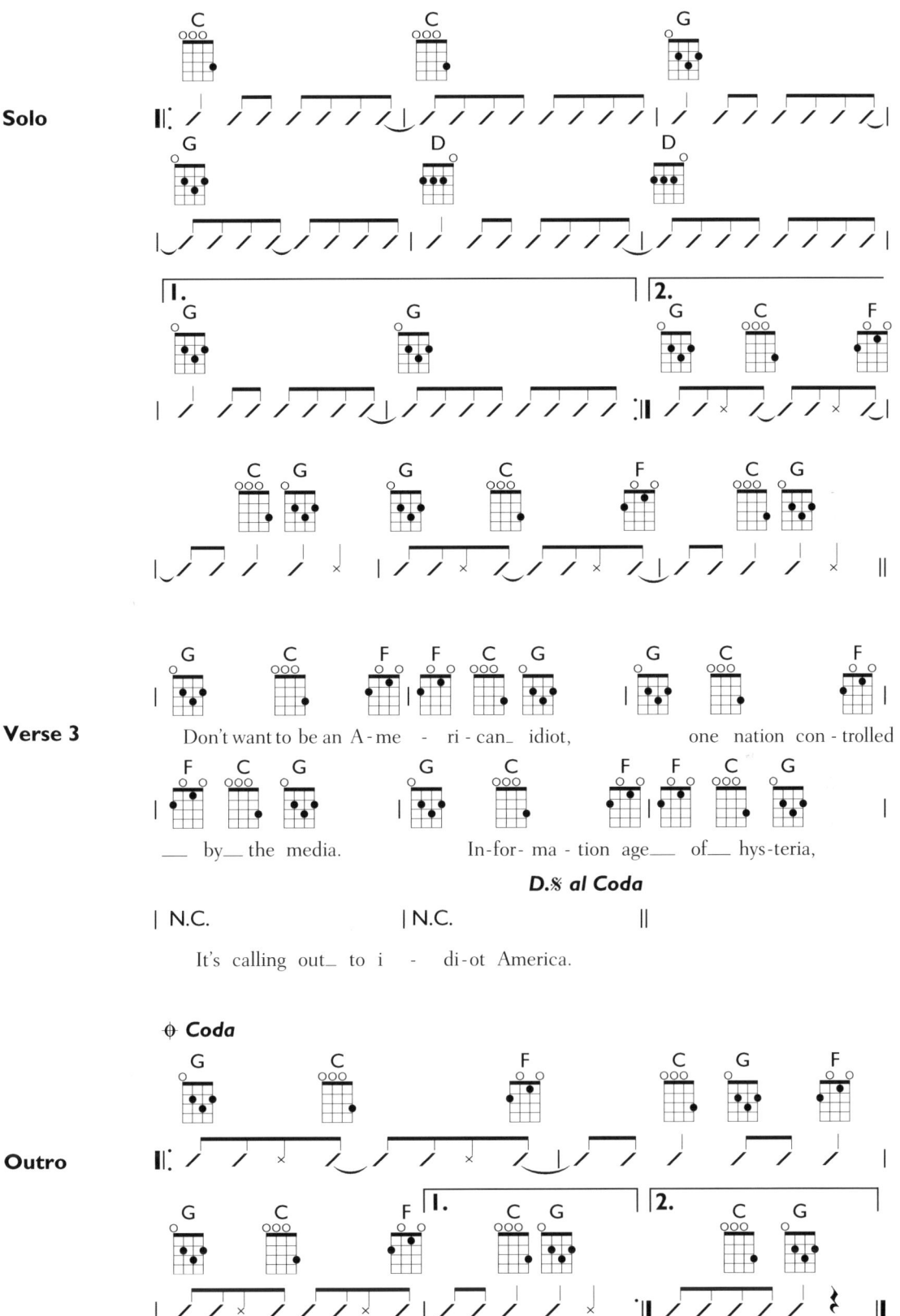

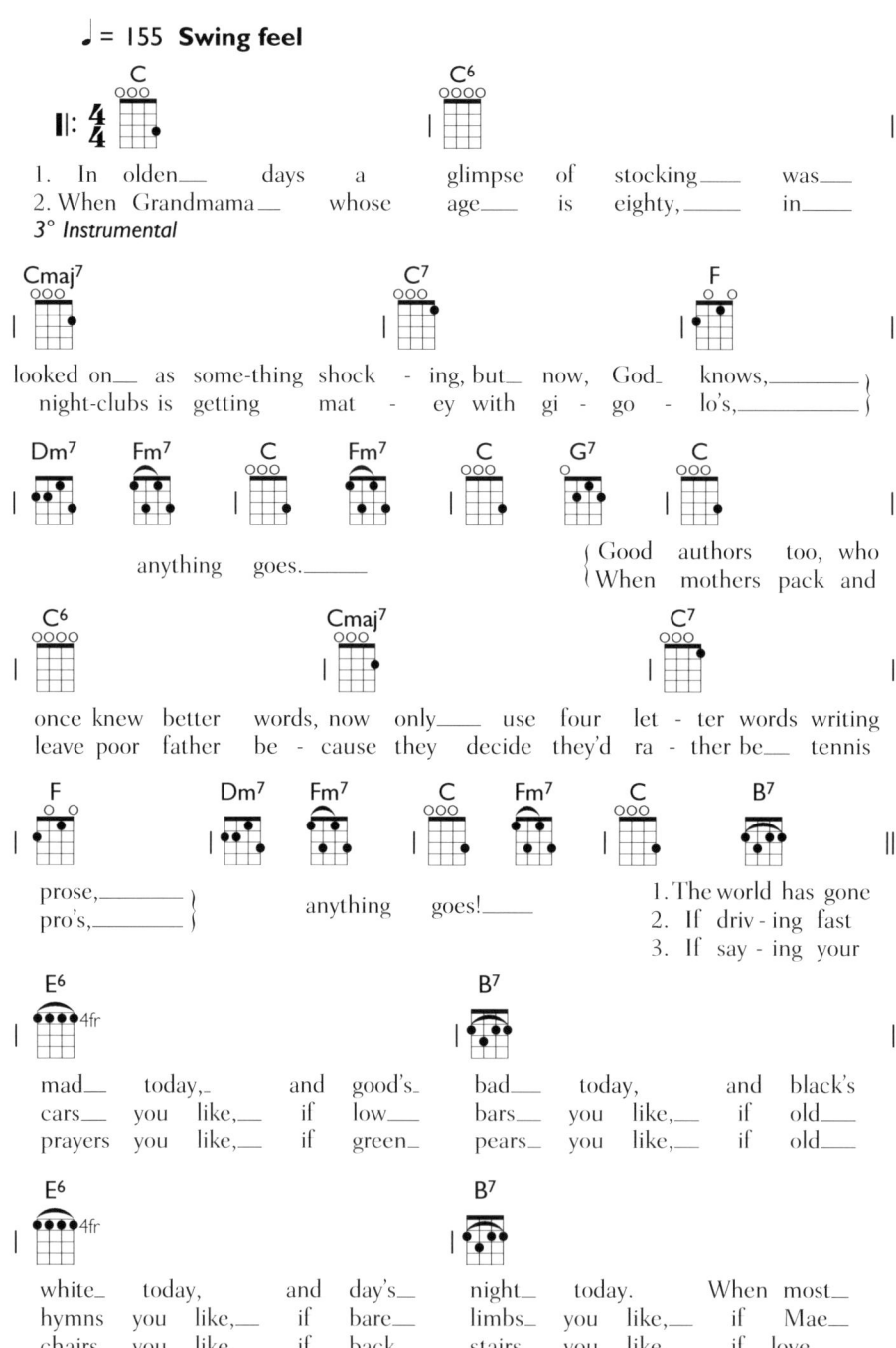

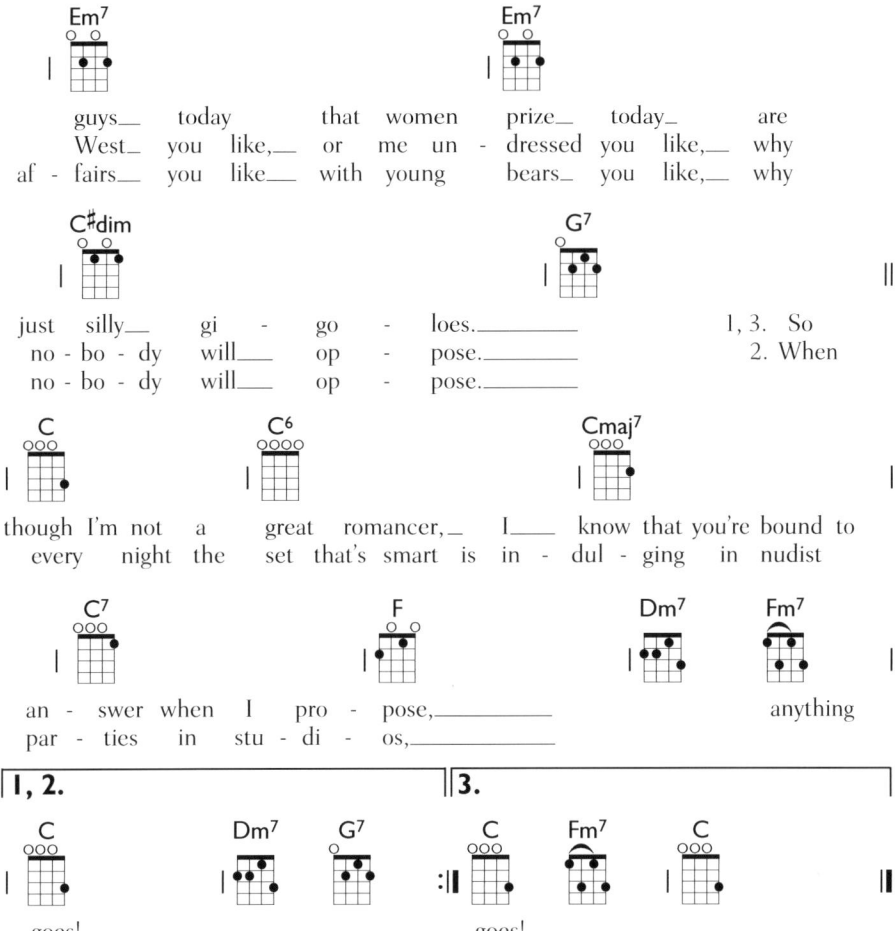

Traditional

Auld Lang Syne
Words and Music Traditional

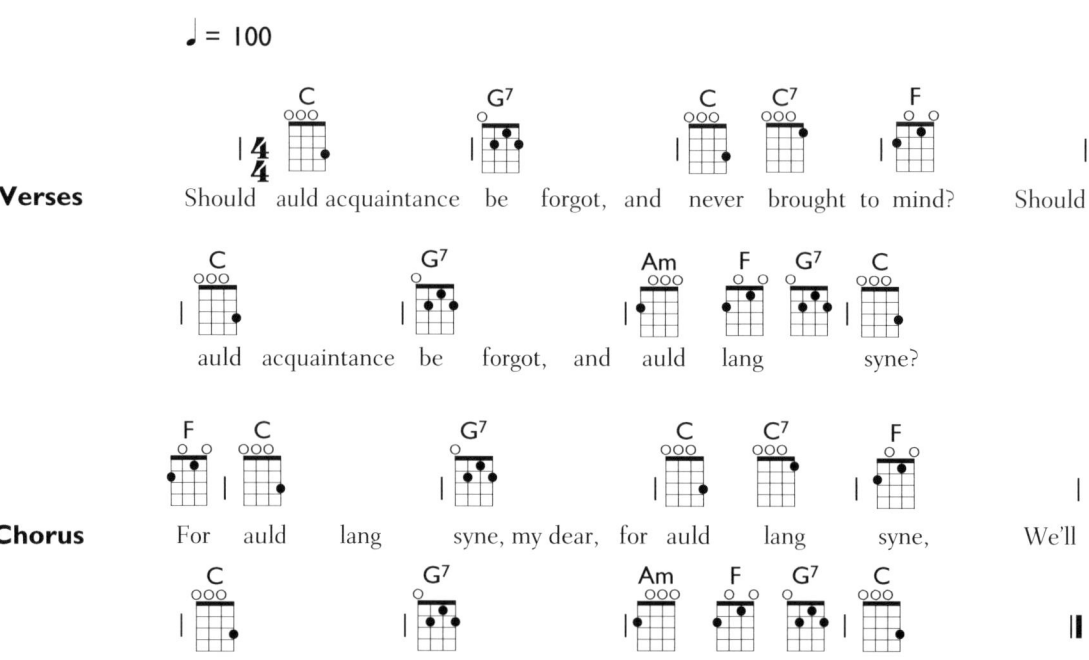

Verse 2
And surely ye'll be your pint-stowp,
And surely I'll be mine
And we'll take a cup o kindness yet,
For auld lang syne.

Verse 3
We two have run about the braes
And pulled the gowans fine,
But we've wandered many a weary foot
Since auld lang syne.

Verse 4
We two hae paddled in the burn
From morning sun till dine
But seas between us braid have roared
Since auld lang syne.

Verse 5
And there's a hand my trusty friend
And gie's a hand o thine
And we'll take a right good willy waught
For auld lang syne.

© 2014 Faber Music Ltd
All Rights Reserved.

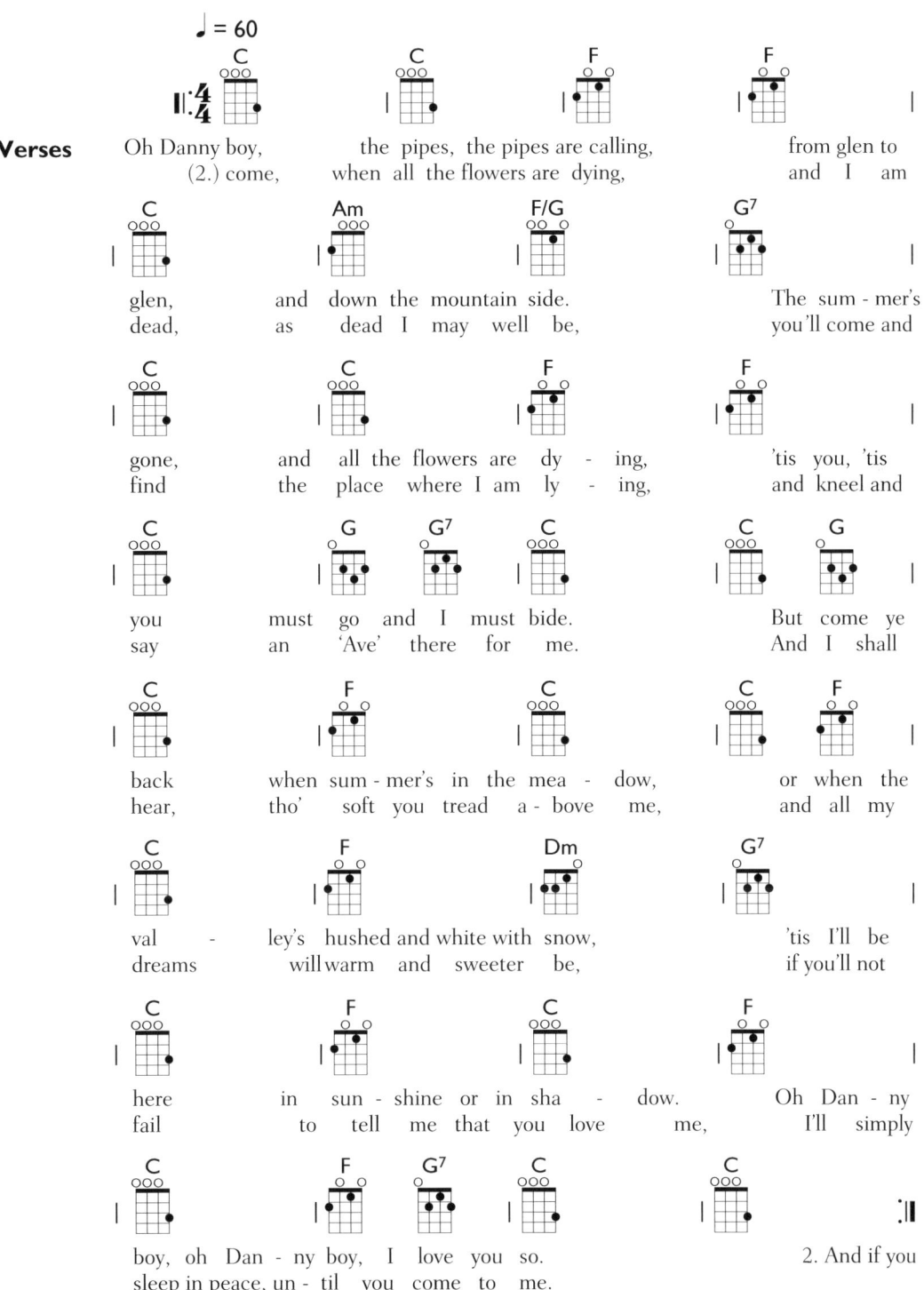

Bad Moon Rising

Creedence Clearwater Revival

Words and Music by John Fogerty

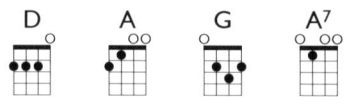

♩ = 90

Intro | D A G D |

Verse 1
| D   A⁷ G *Strumming ad-lib. sim.* | D | D   A⁷ G | D |
  I see the bad moon a-rising,   I see trouble on the way.
| D   A⁷ G | D | D   A⁷ G | D ||
  I see earthquakes and lightnin',   I see bad times today.

Chorus 1
| G | D |
  Don't go around tonight,   well it's bound to take your life,
| A⁷   G | D ||
  There's a bad moon   on the rise.

Verse 2
| D   A⁷ G | D | D   A⁷ G | D |
  I hear hurricanes a blowin',   I know the end is comin' soon.
| D   A⁷ G | D | D   A⁷ G | D ||
  I fear rivers overflowin',   I hear the voice of rage and ruin.

Chorus 2   As Chorus 1

© 1964 Jondora Music
Burlington Music Co Ltd
All Rights Reserved.

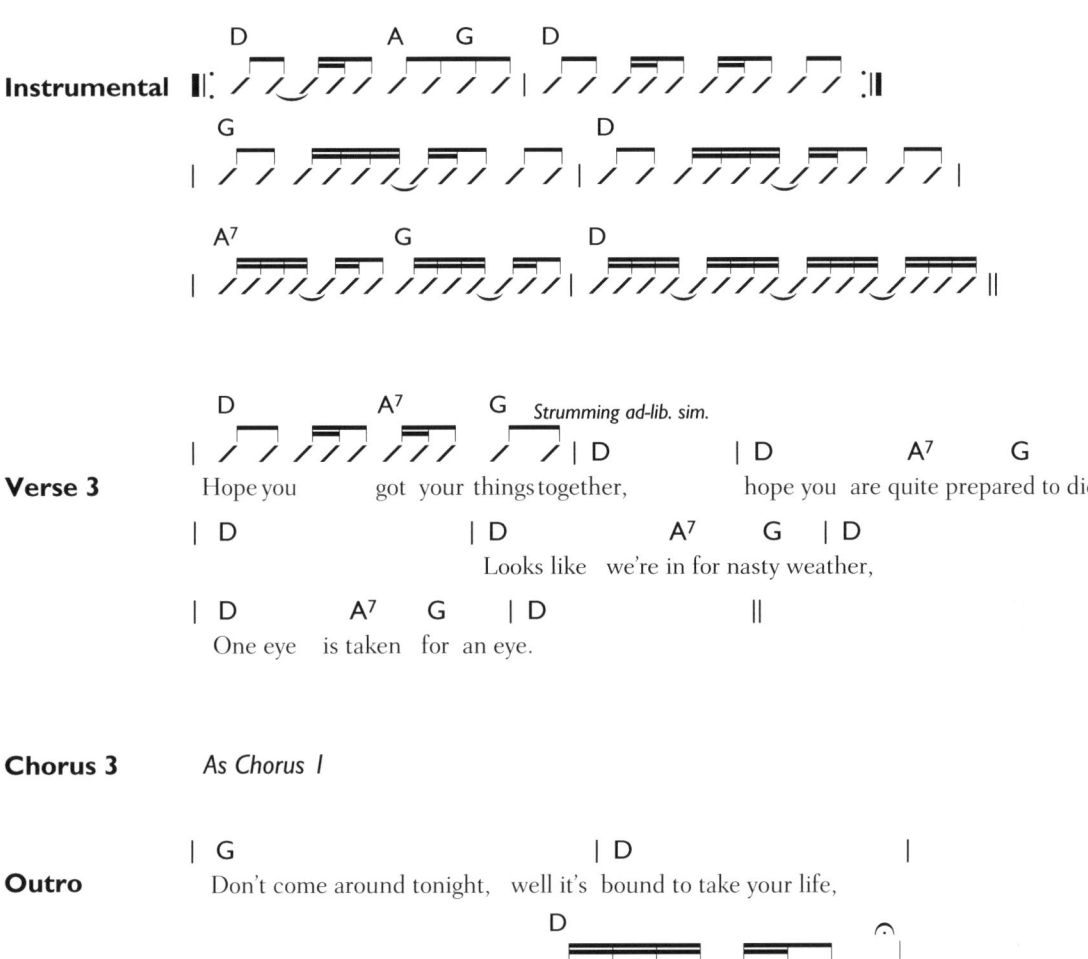

The Bare Necessities

From 'The Jungle Book'

Words and Music by Terry Gilkyson

♩ = 200 **Fast Swing**

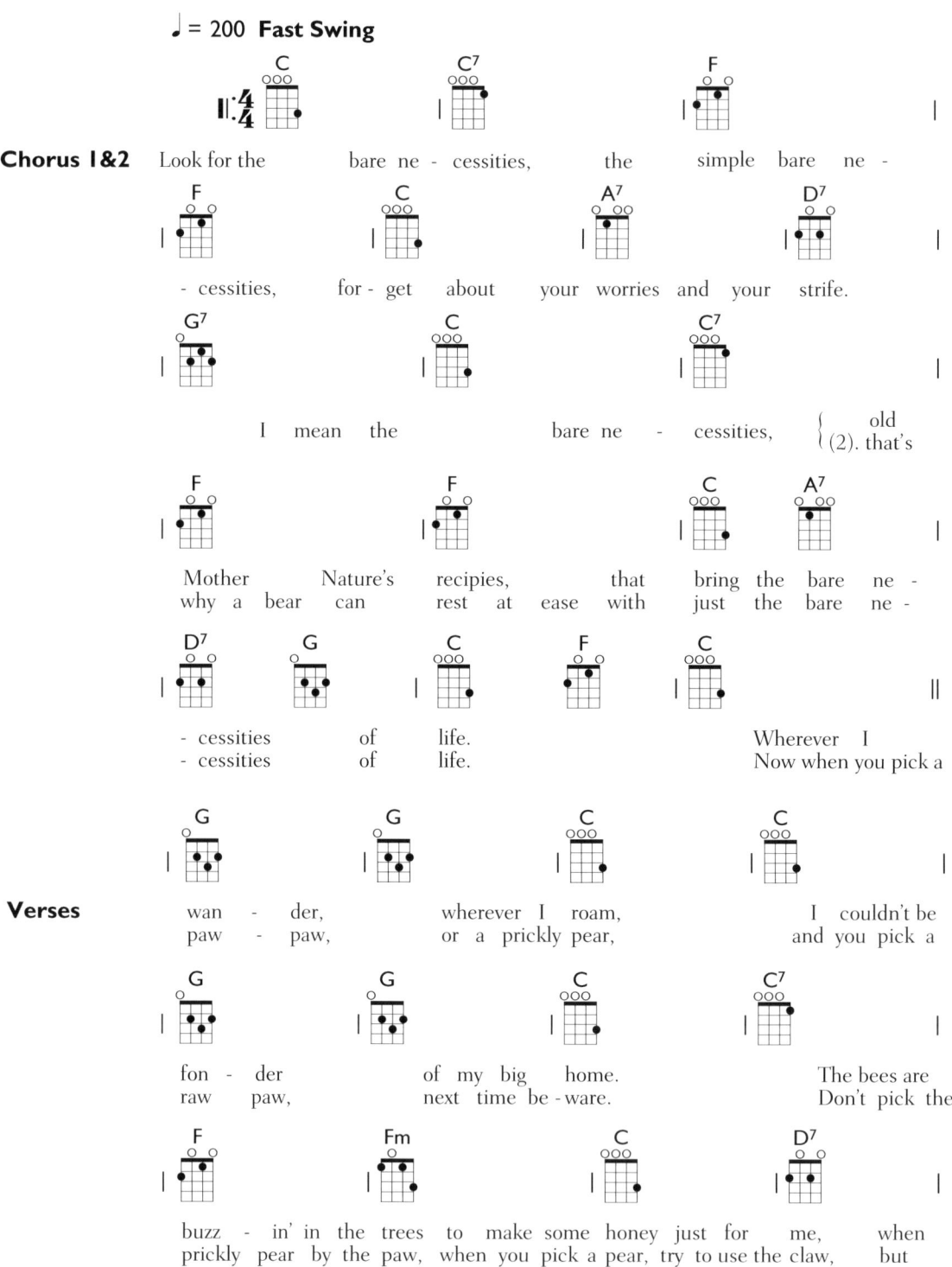

© 1967 Wonderland Music Company Inc administered by Artemis Muziekuitgeverij B.V.
Warner/Chappell Artemis Music Ltd
All Rights Reserved.

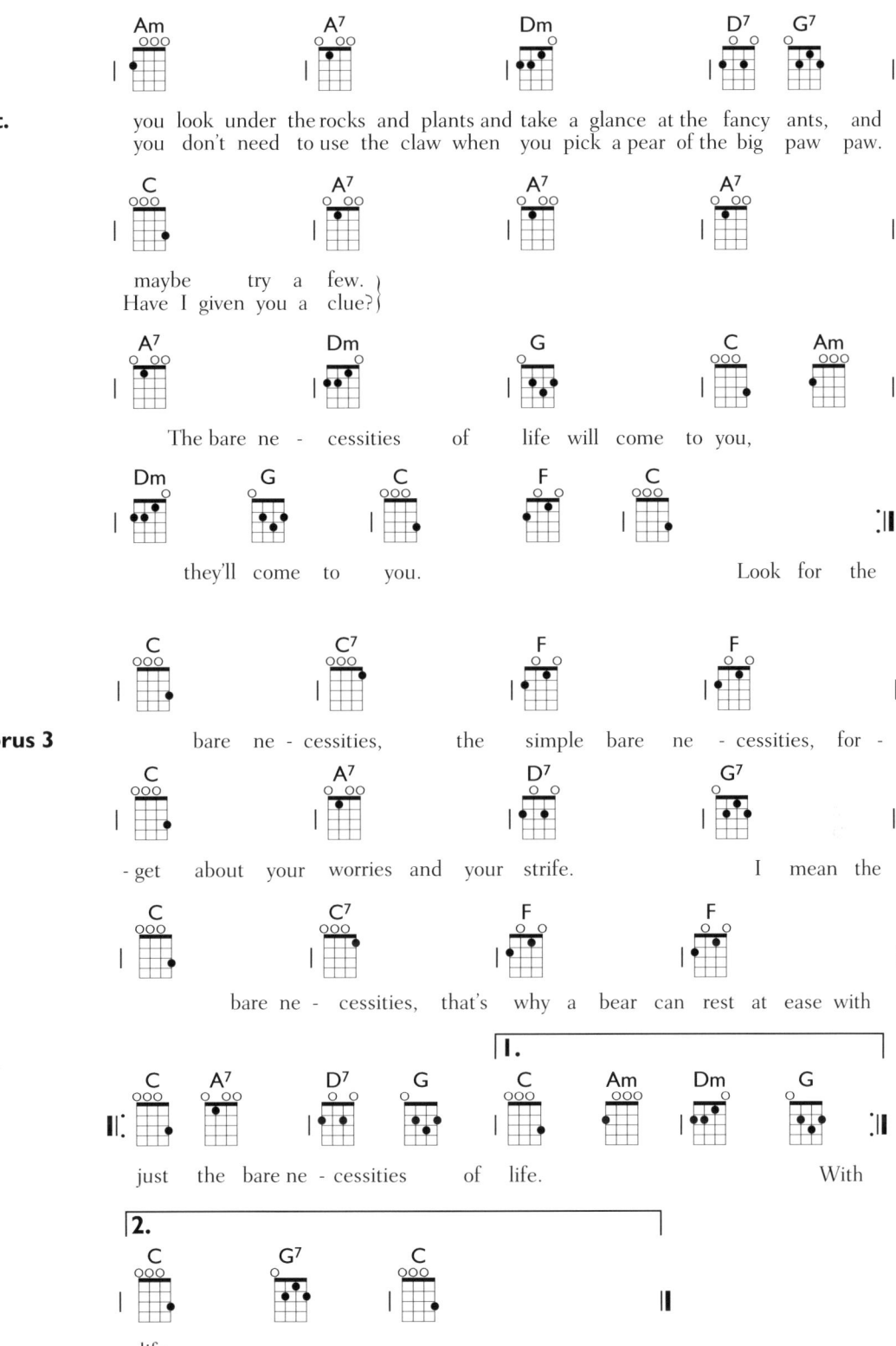

Bewitched
(from "Pal Joey")

Words by Lorenz Hart
Music by Richard Rodgers

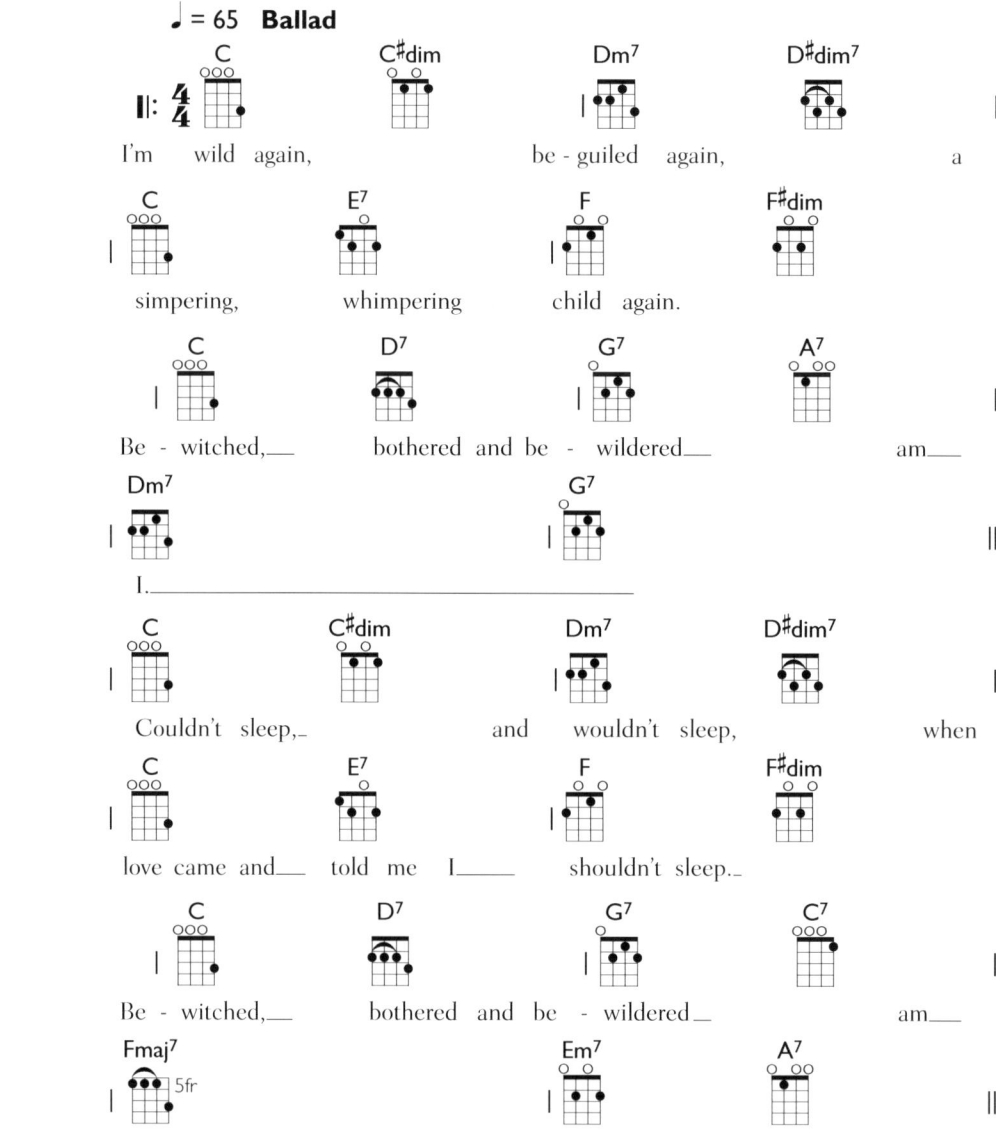

© 1941 (Renewed) Warner/Chappell Music Ltd and Williamson Music Company,
a Division of Rodgers & Hammerstein: an Imagem Company
This arrangement © 2014 Warner/Chappell Music Ltd and Williamson Music Company,
a Division of Rodgers & Hammerstein: an Imagem Company
Warner/Chappell Music Ltd and Imagem Music
International Copyright Secured All Rights Reserved
Reprinted by Permission of Hal Leonard Corporation

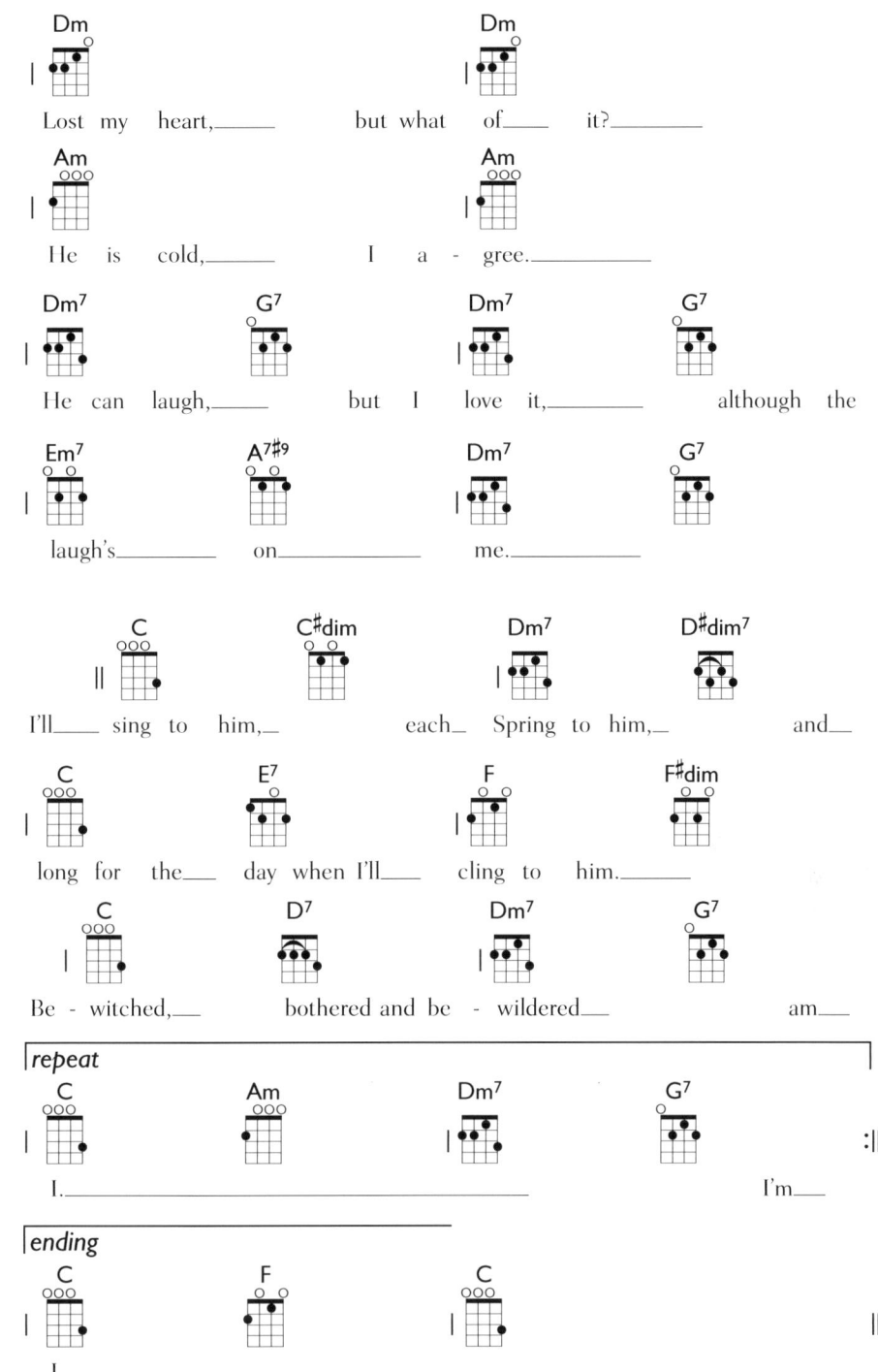

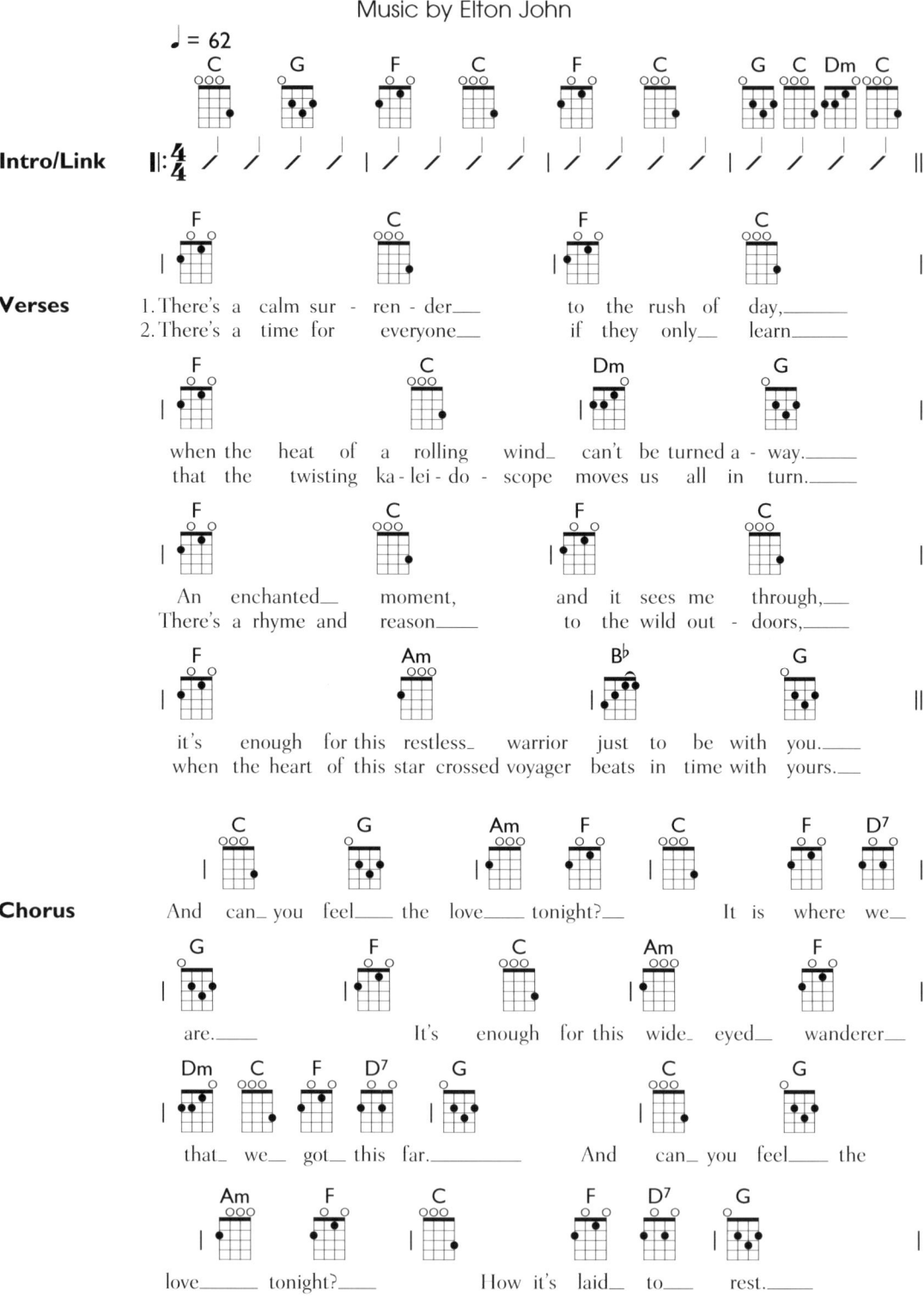

cont.

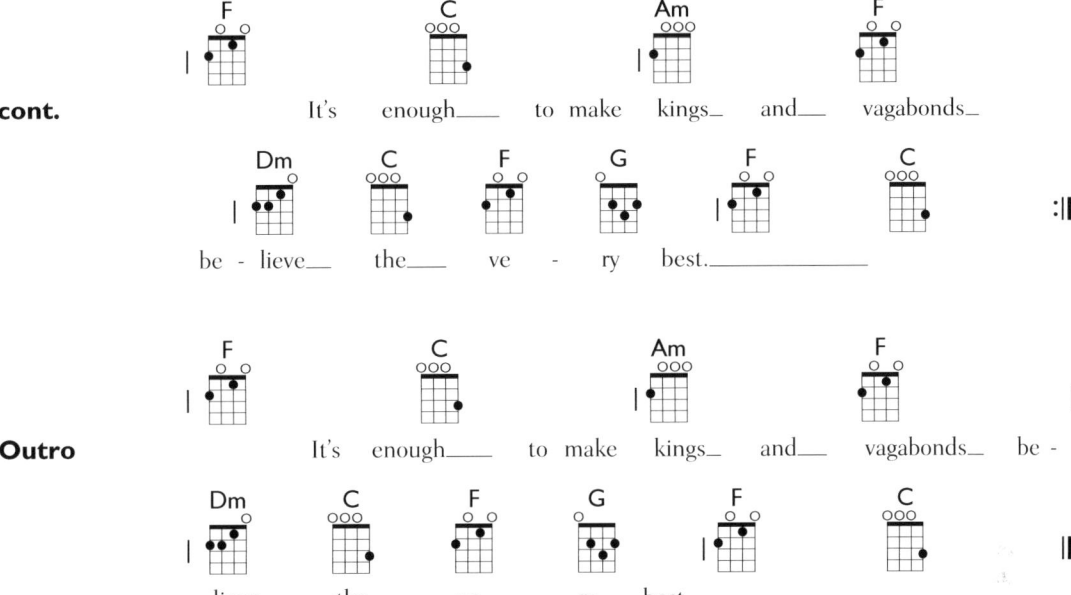

It's enough to make kings and vagabonds be-lieve the ve-ry best.

Outro

It's enough to make kings and vagabonds be-lieve the ve-ry best.

Creep

Words and Music by Thomas Yorke, Jonathan Greenwood, Colin Greenwood, Edward O'Brien, Philip Selway, Albert Hammond and Mike Hazelwood

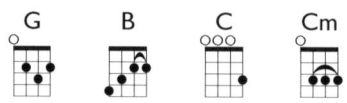

♩ = 92

Intro

| G | | B | |
| C | | Cm | *Strumming cont. sim.* |

Verse 1

|| G | | G | | B | |
When you were here before, couldn't look you in the eye,

| B | | C | | C | |
You're just like an an - gel, your skin makes me cry.

| Cm | | Cm | | G | | G | |
You float like a fea - ther in a beautiful world.

| B | | B | | C | | C | |
I wish I was spe - cial. You're so very

Cm
spe - cial. But I'm a creep,

Chorus 1

G *Strumming cont. sim.*
| G | | B | | B | |
I'm a weir - do. What the hell am I doing

| C | | C | | Cm | Cm |
here? I don't belong here.

Verse 2

Strumming as per verse 1

| G | | G | | B | |
I don't care if it hurts. I want to have control.

| B | | C | | C | | Cm |
I want a perfect bo - dy, I want a perfect soul.

© 1992 Warner/Chappell Music Ltd and Imagem Songs Limited
(This song contains elements from "The Air That I Breathe" by Hammond/Hazlewood © Imagem Songs Limited)
All Rights Reserved.

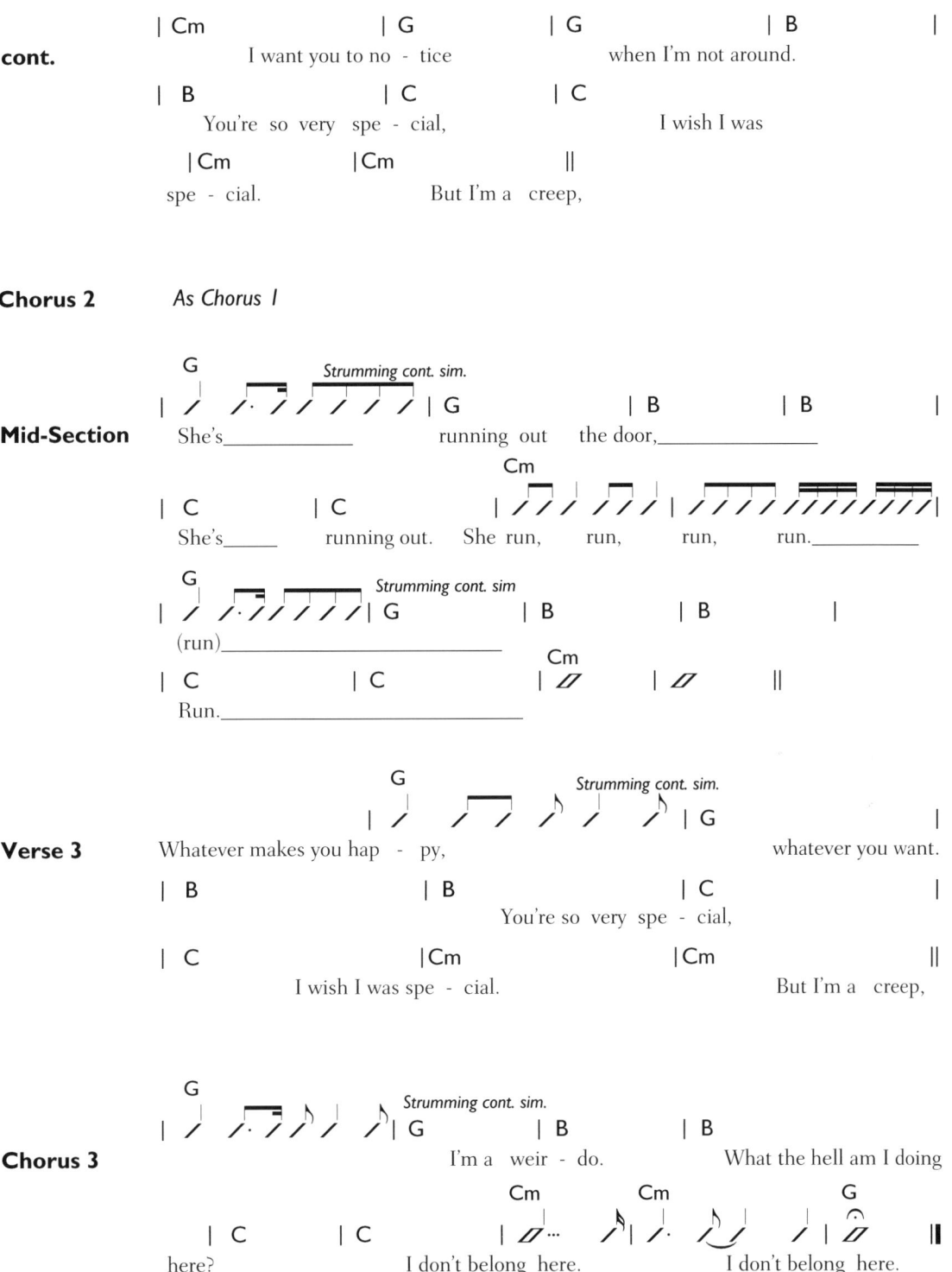

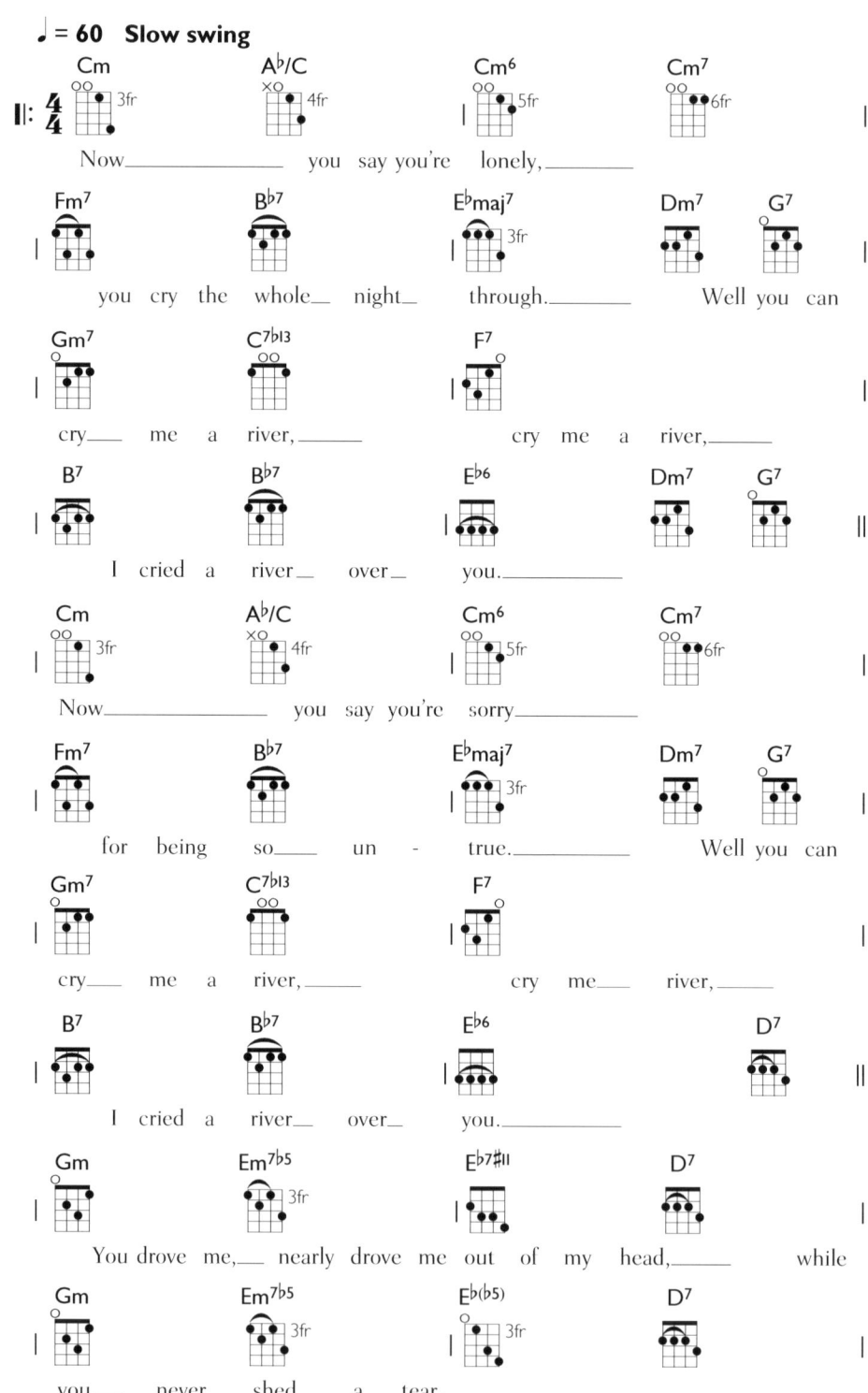

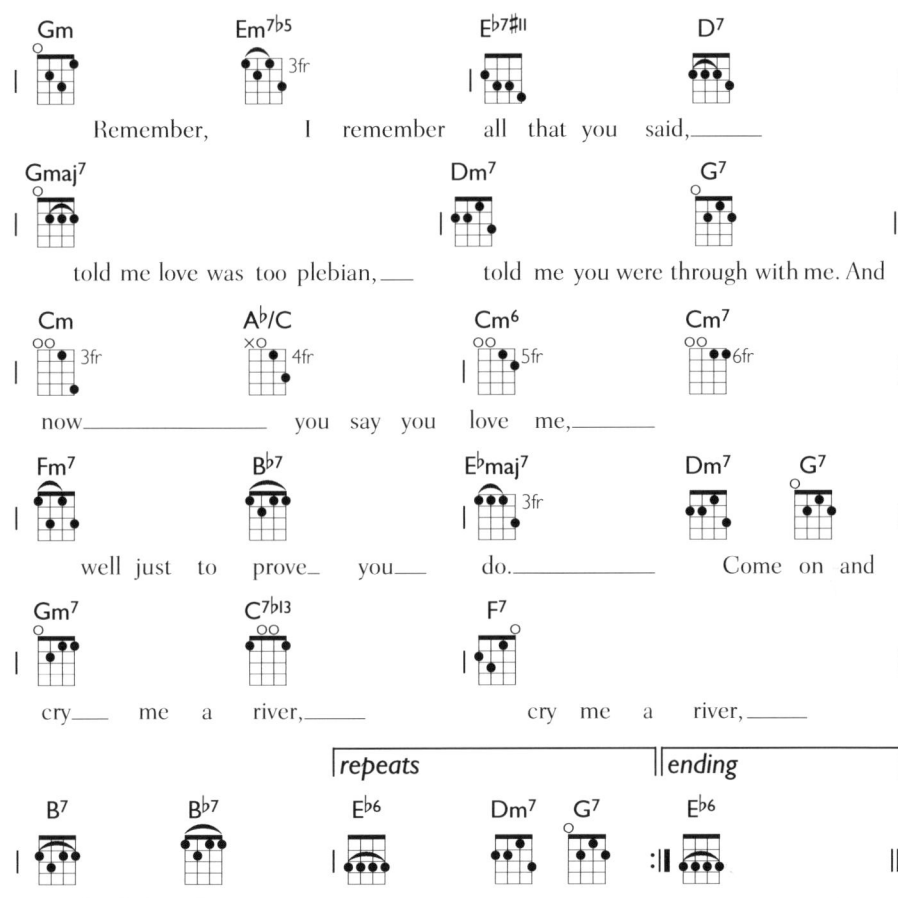

Chorus

F	F	B♭	F
Dai - sy,	Dai - sy,	give me your an - swer do.___	

C⁷	F	G⁷	C
I'm half cra - zy	all for the love__ of you.__		

C⁷	F	F	B♭	F
It won't be a stylish__	marriage,	I can't_	afford__ a	carriage.

F	C⁷	F	C⁷
But you'll__ look	sweet__	u - pon___	the seat of a

F	C⁷	F	
bicycle_____	made__	for two._____	:||

Dear Darlin'

Words and Music by Edward Drewett, James Eliot and Olly Murs

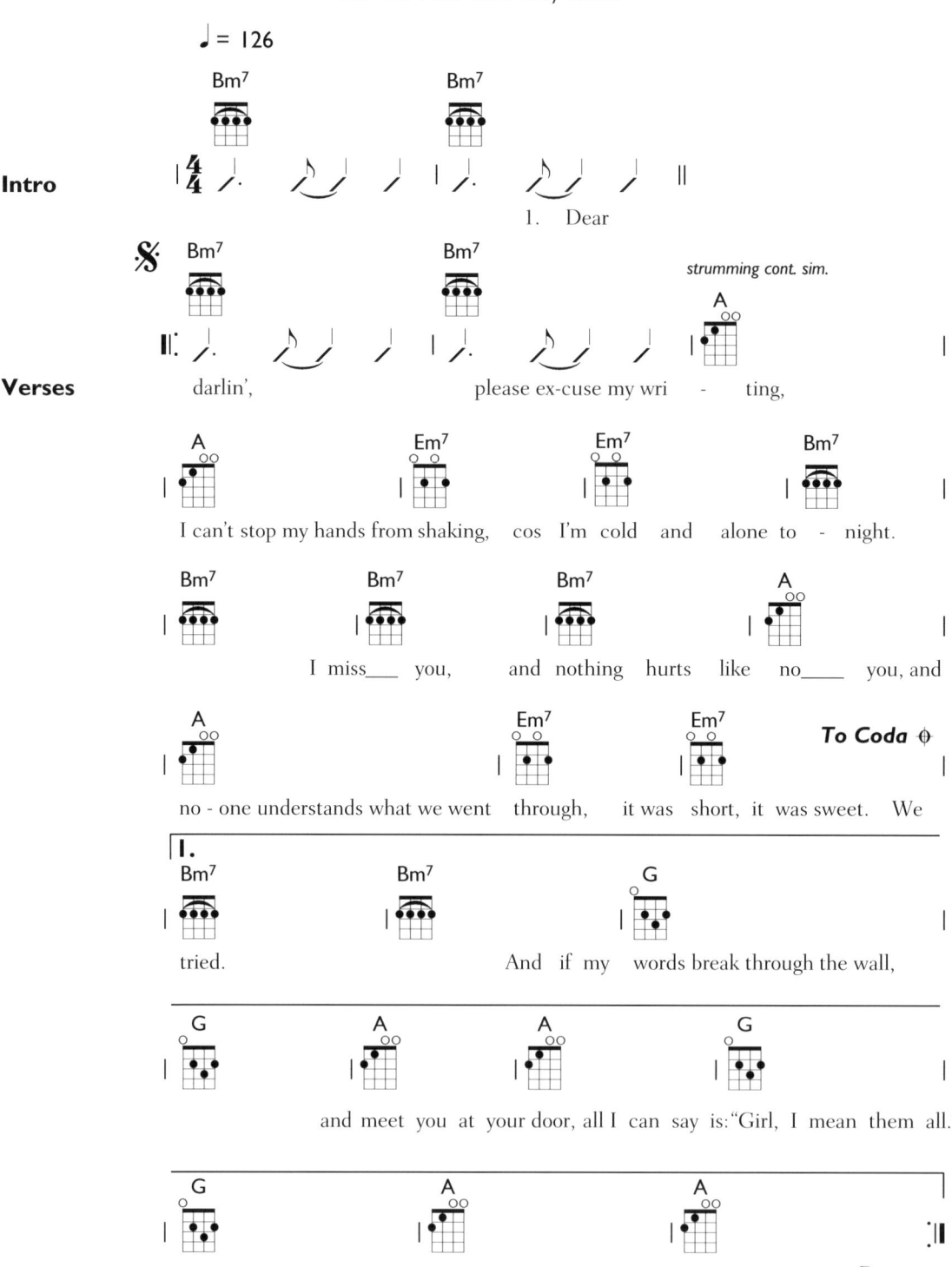

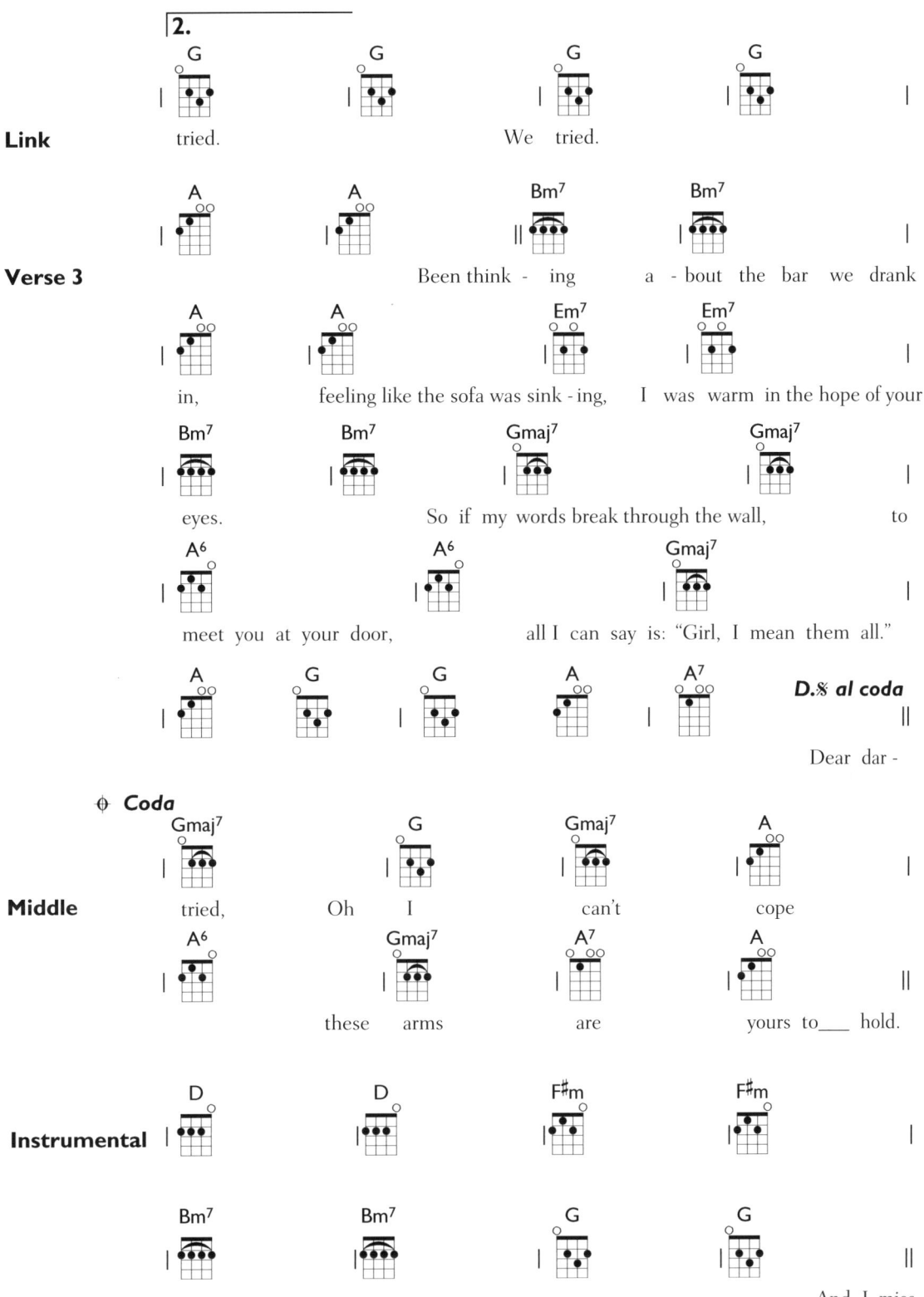

Outro

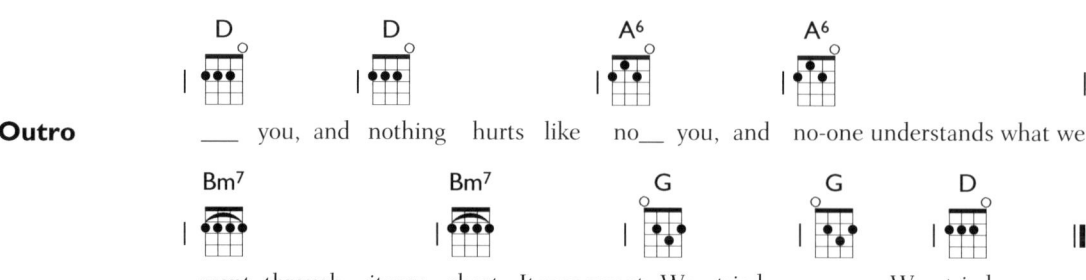

|D|D|A⁶|A⁶|
___ you, and nothing hurts like no__ you, and no-one understands what we went through, it was short. It was sweet. We tried. We tried.

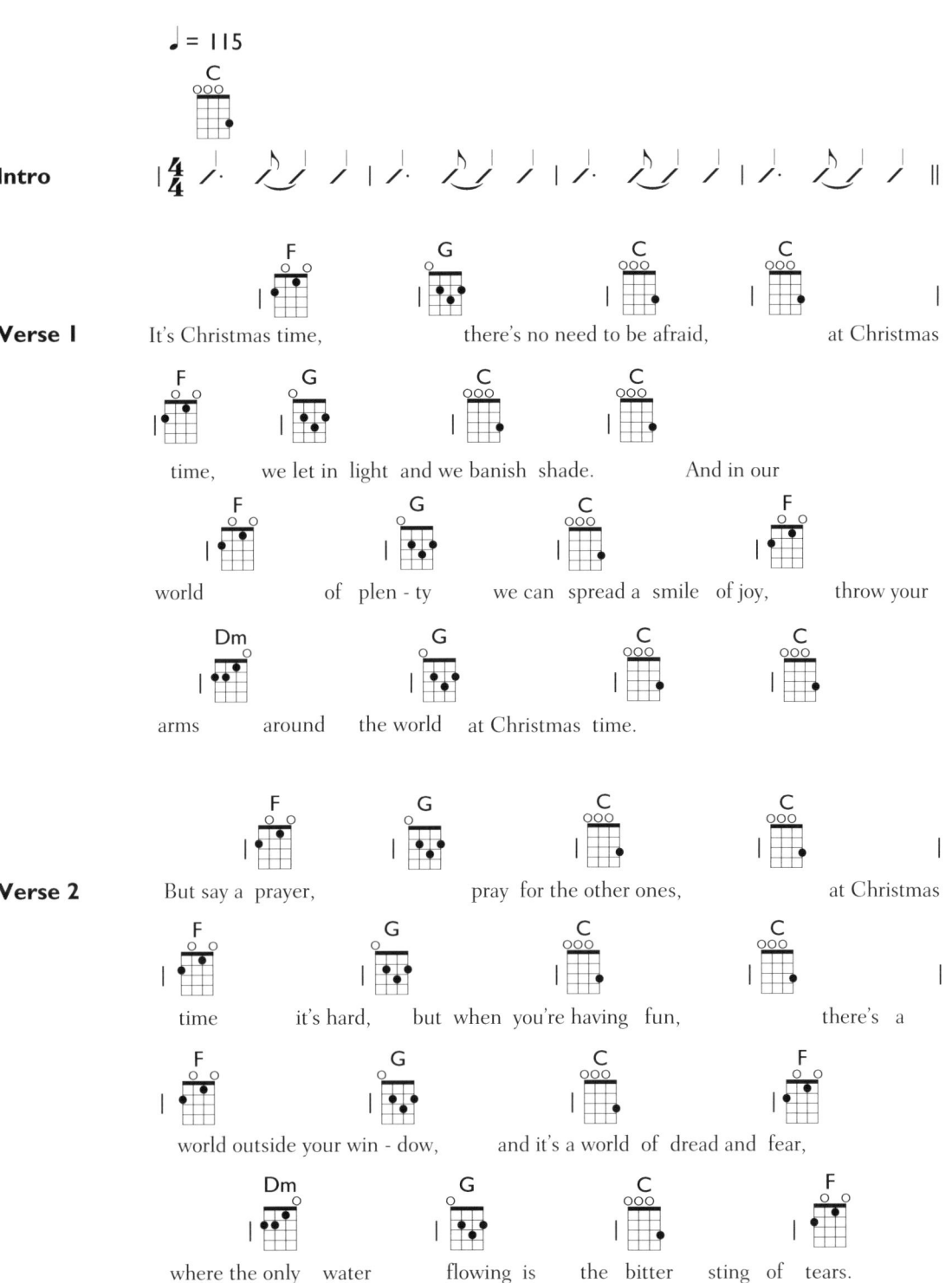

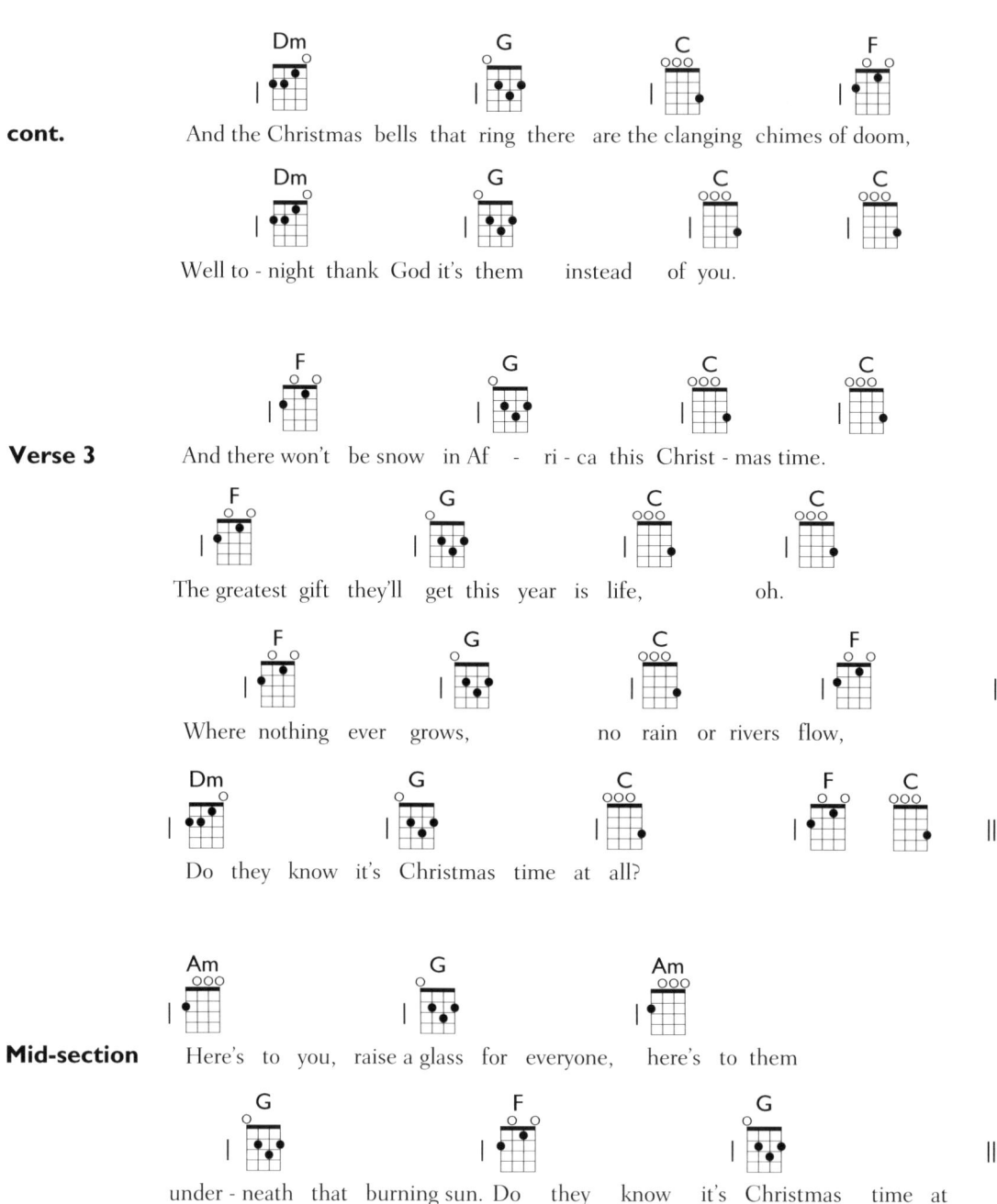

cont. And the Christmas bells that ring there are the clanging chimes of doom,
Well to-night thank God it's them instead of you.

Verse 3 And there won't be snow in Af - ri - ca this Christ - mas time.
The greatest gift they'll get this year is life, oh.
Where nothing ever grows, no rain or rivers flow,
Do they know it's Christmas time at all?

Mid-section Here's to you, raise a glass for everyone, here's to them
under-neath that burning sun. Do they know it's Christmas time at

Bridge

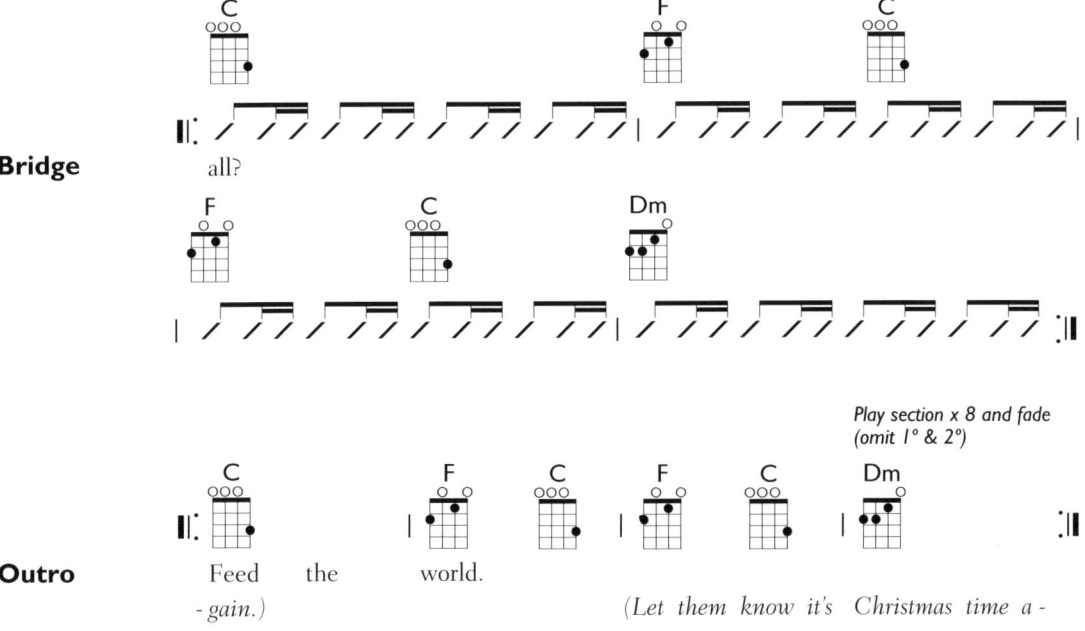

Outro

Lady Gaga

Edge Of Glory

Words and Music by Fernando Garibay,
Paul Blair and Stefani Germanotta

♩ = 130

Intro ‖: 4/4 / ≹ / ≹ | / ≹ / ≹ | / ≹ / ≹ | / ≹ / ≹ :‖

Verses

|: A   E

1. There ain't no reason you and me should be alone
2. Another shot before we kiss the other side

D   D

tonight, yeah baby tonight, yeah baby.
tonight, yeah baby tonight, yeah baby.

A   E

I got a reason that you're who should take me home
I'm on the edge of something final we call life

D   D

tonight.
tonight.

A   E

I need a man that thinks it's right when it's so wrong
Put on your shades 'cause I'll be dancing in the flames

D   D

tonight, yeah baby tonight, yeah baby.
tonight, yeah baby tonight, yeah baby.

A   E

Right on the limits where we know we both belong
It isn't hell if every - bo - dy knows my name

© 2011 Warner-Tamerlane Publishing Corp, Garibay Music Publishing, Sony/ATV Songs LLC,
Sony/ATV Music Publishing LLC, Sony/ATV Tunes LLC, House Of Gaga Publishing Inc and Universal Music Corp
Warner/Chappell North America Ltd, Universal/MCA Music Ltd and Sony/ATV Music Publishing (UK) Ltd
All Rights Reserved.

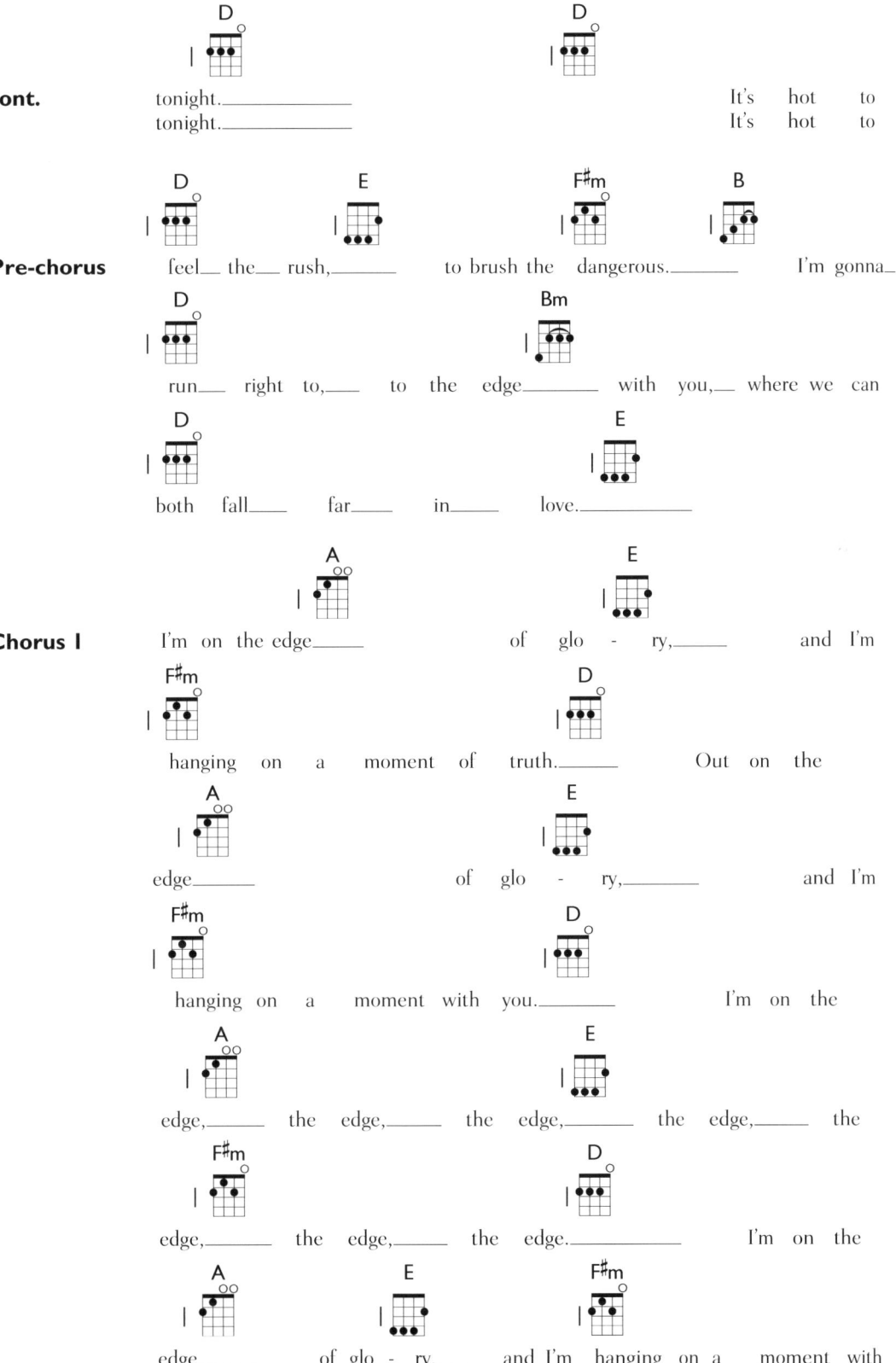

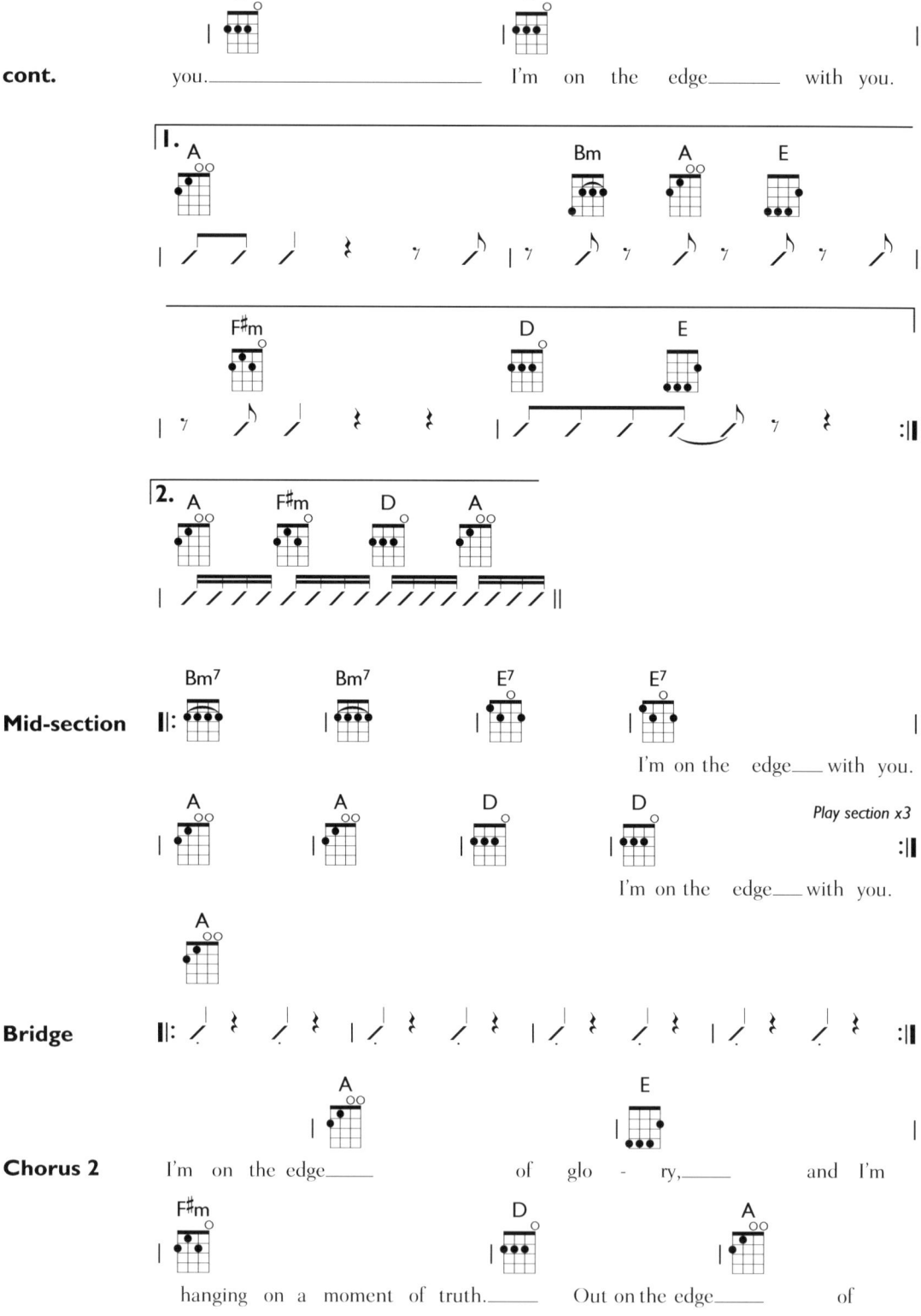

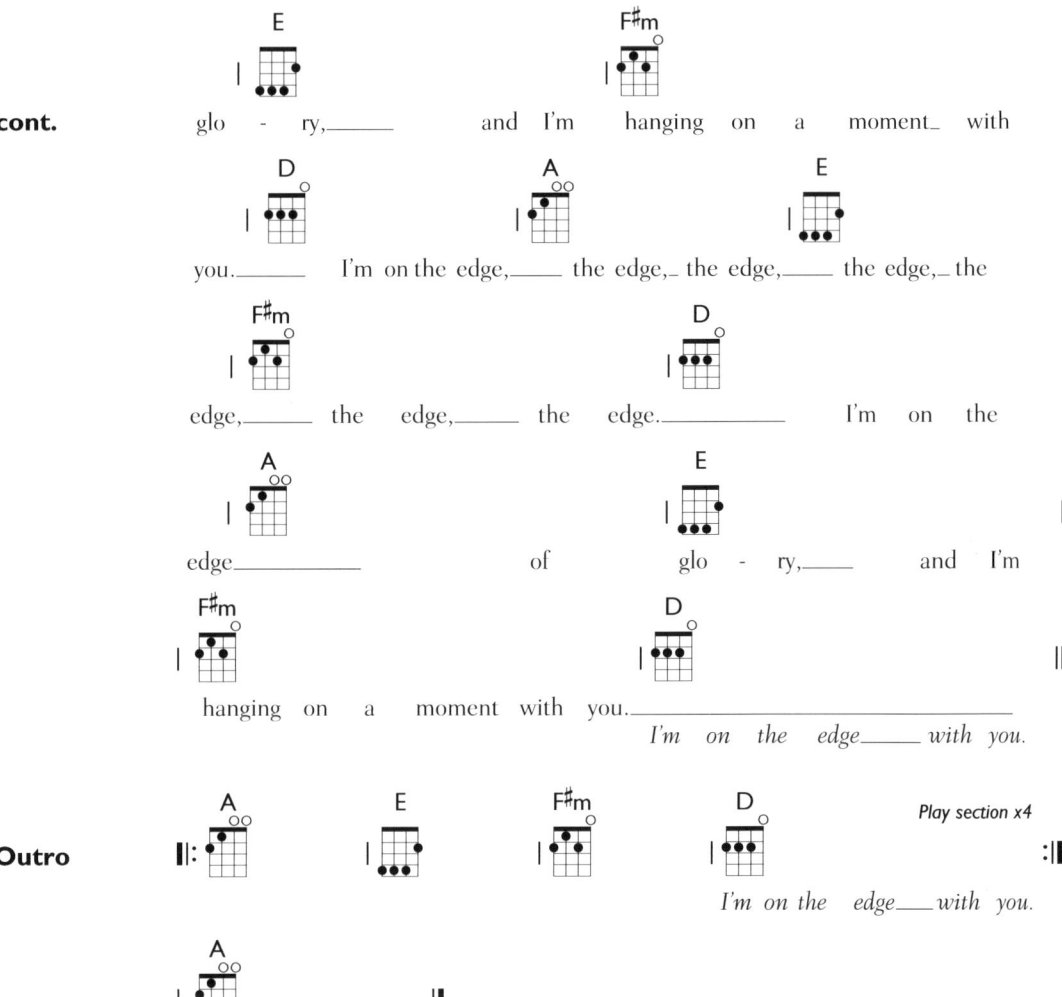

Traditional

Early One Morning
Words and Music Traditional

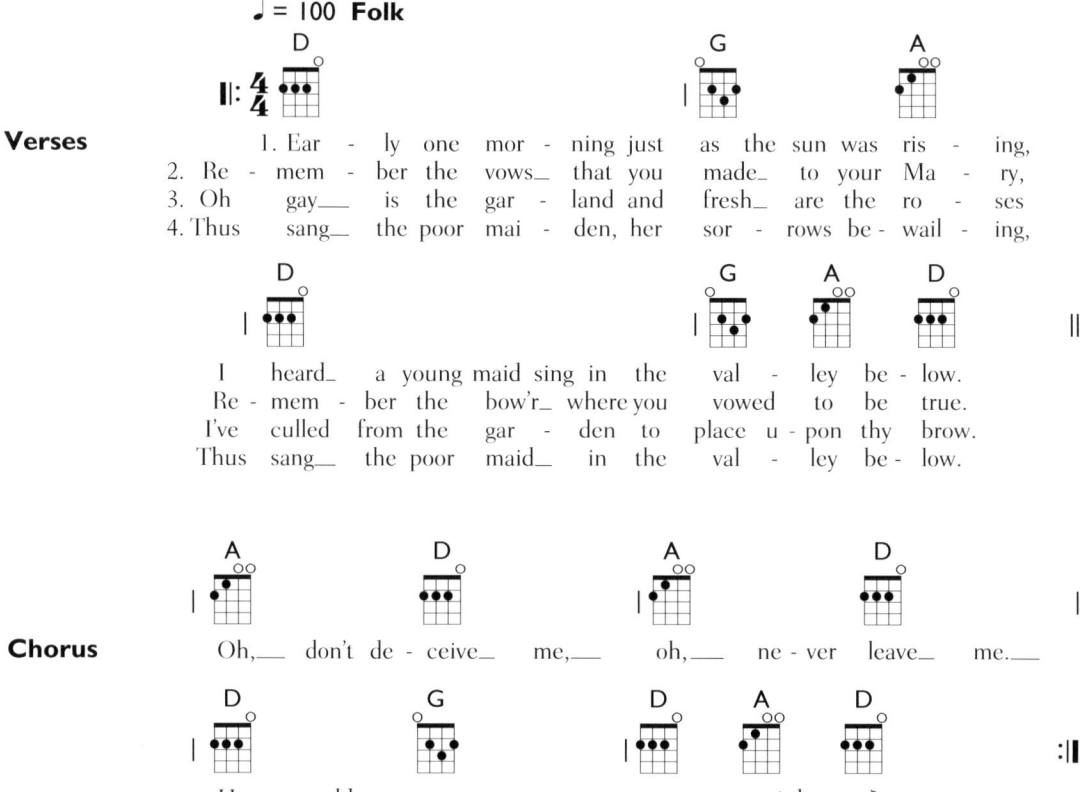

♩ = 100 **Folk**

Verses

1. Ear - ly one mor - ning just as the sun was ris - ing,
2. Re - mem - ber the vows that you made to your Ma - ry,
3. Oh gay is the gar - land and fresh are the ro - ses
4. Thus sang the poor mai - den, her sor - rows be - wail - ing,

I heard a young maid sing in the val - ley be - low.
Re - mem - ber the bow'r where you vowed to be true.
I've culled from the gar - den to place u - pon thy brow.
Thus sang the poor maid in the val - ley be - low.

Chorus

Oh, don't de - ceive me, oh, ne - ver leave me.
How could you use a poor mai - den so?

© 2014 Faber Music Ltd
All Rights Reserved.

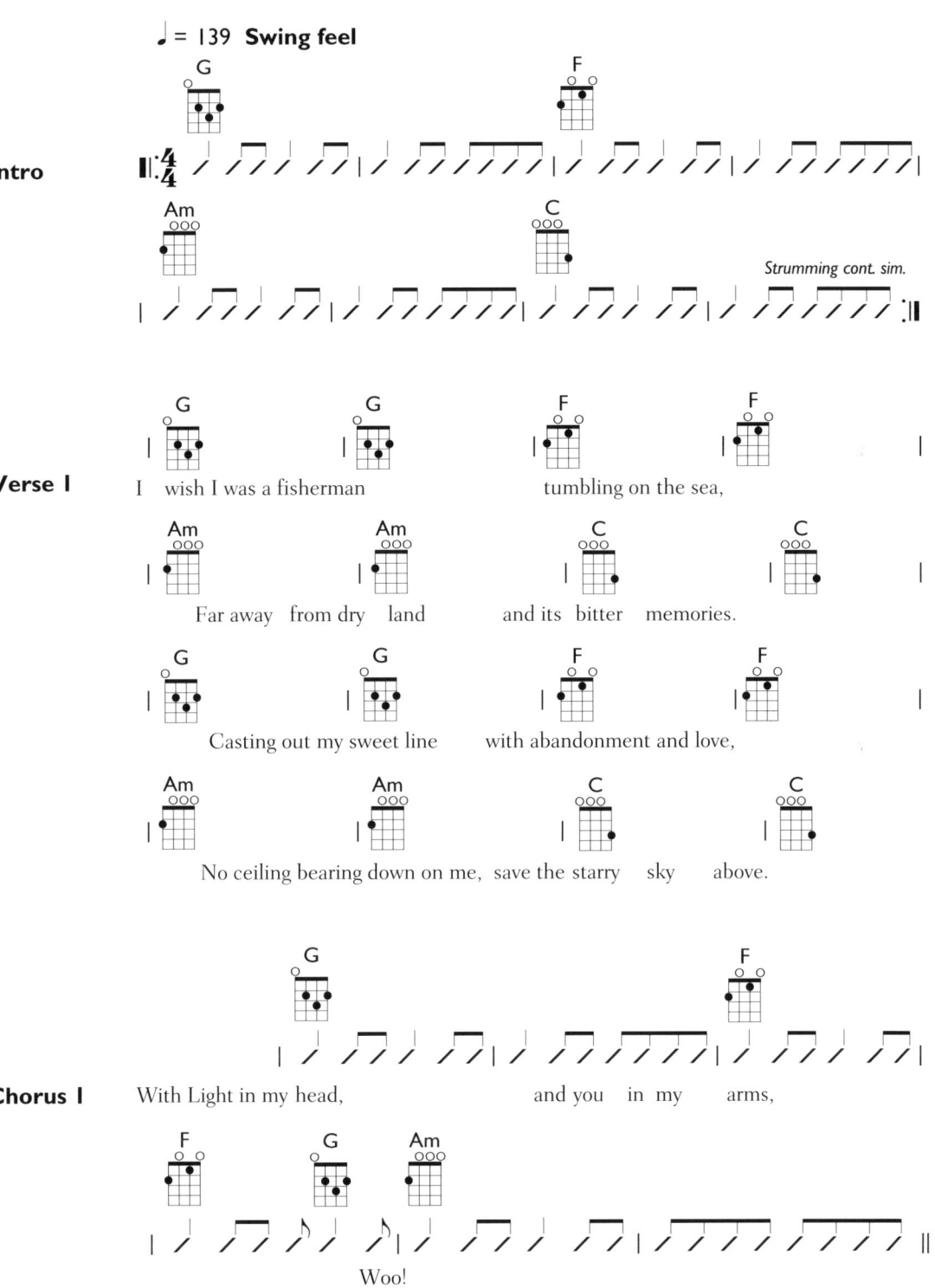

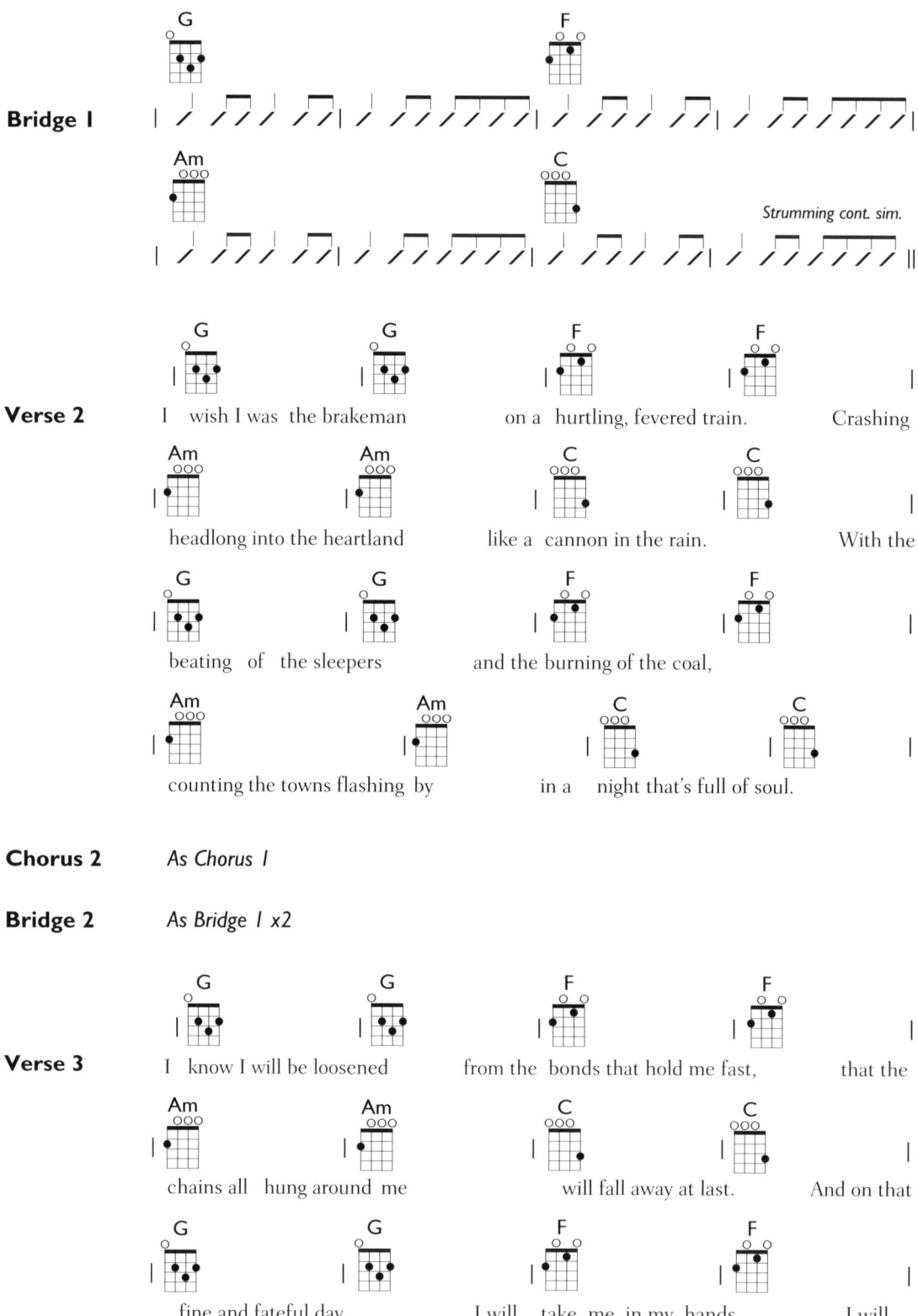

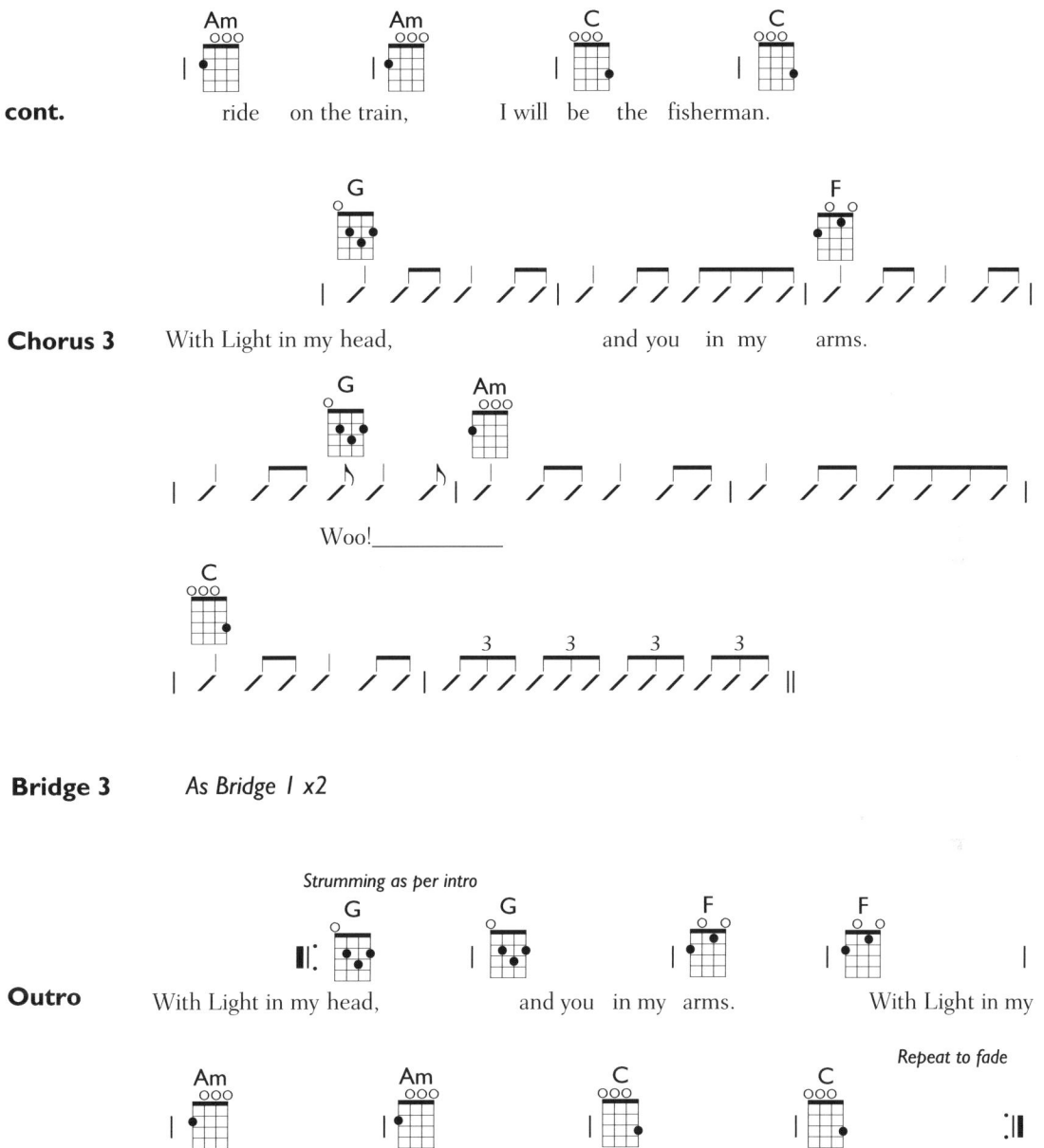

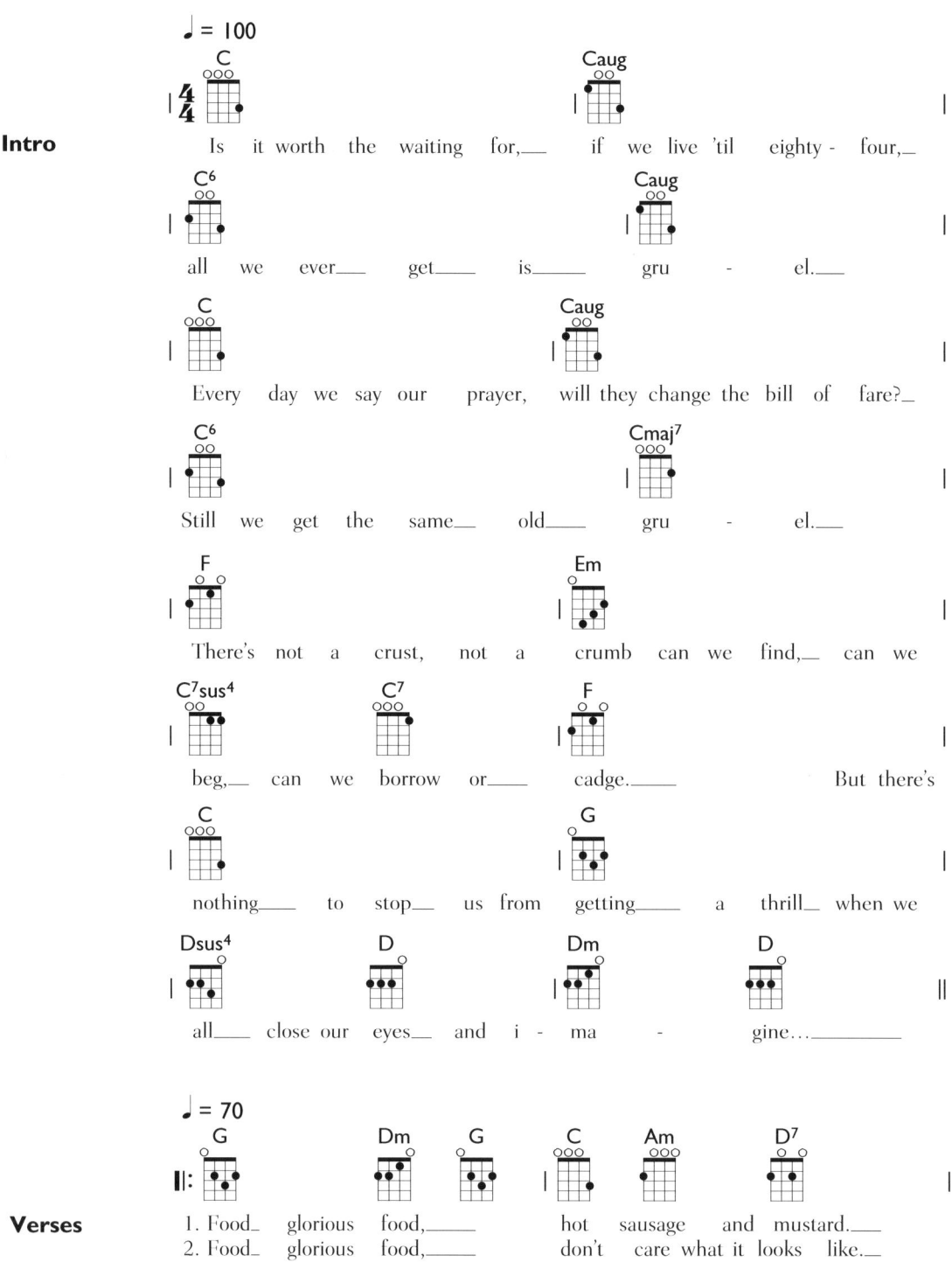

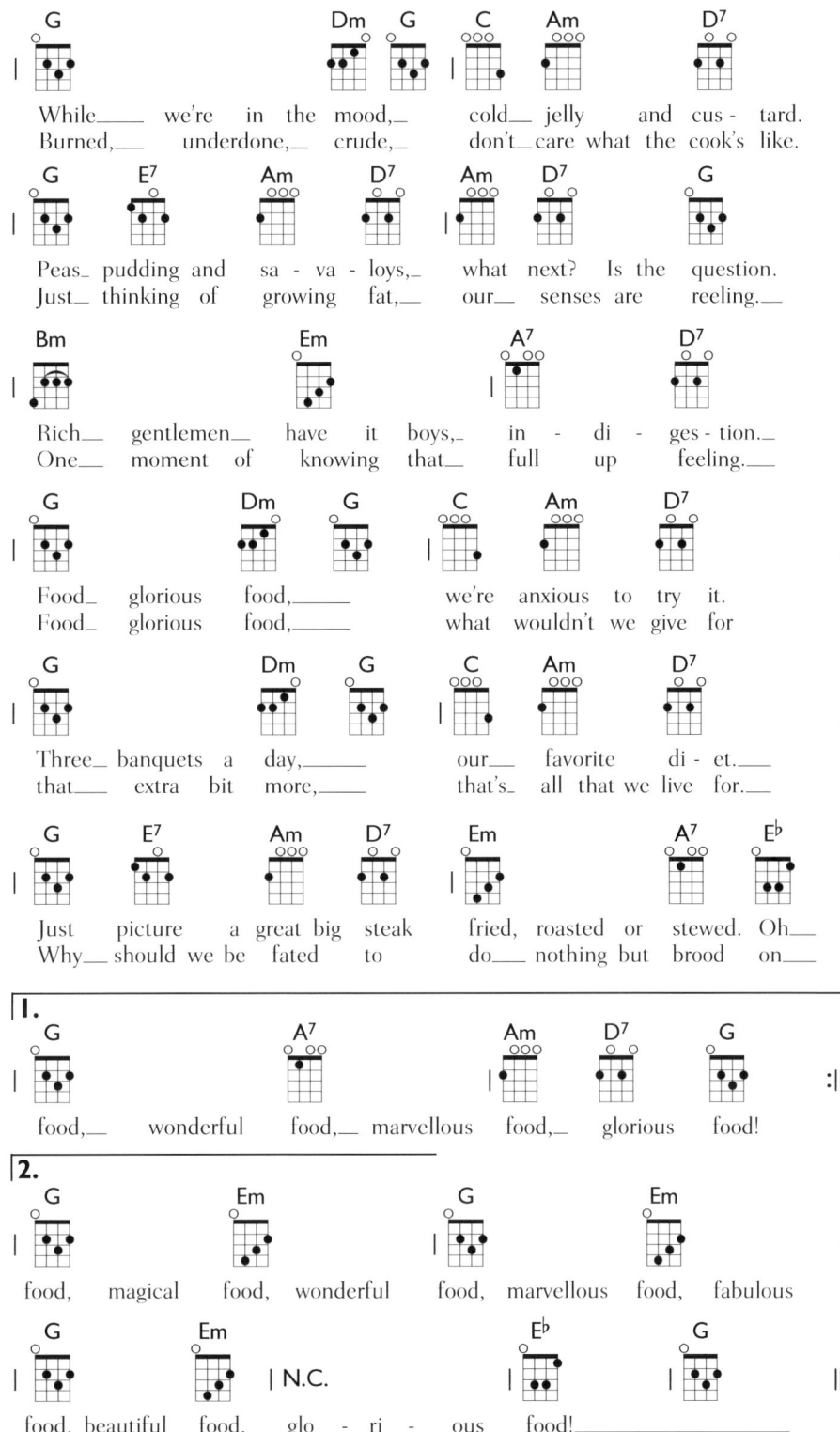

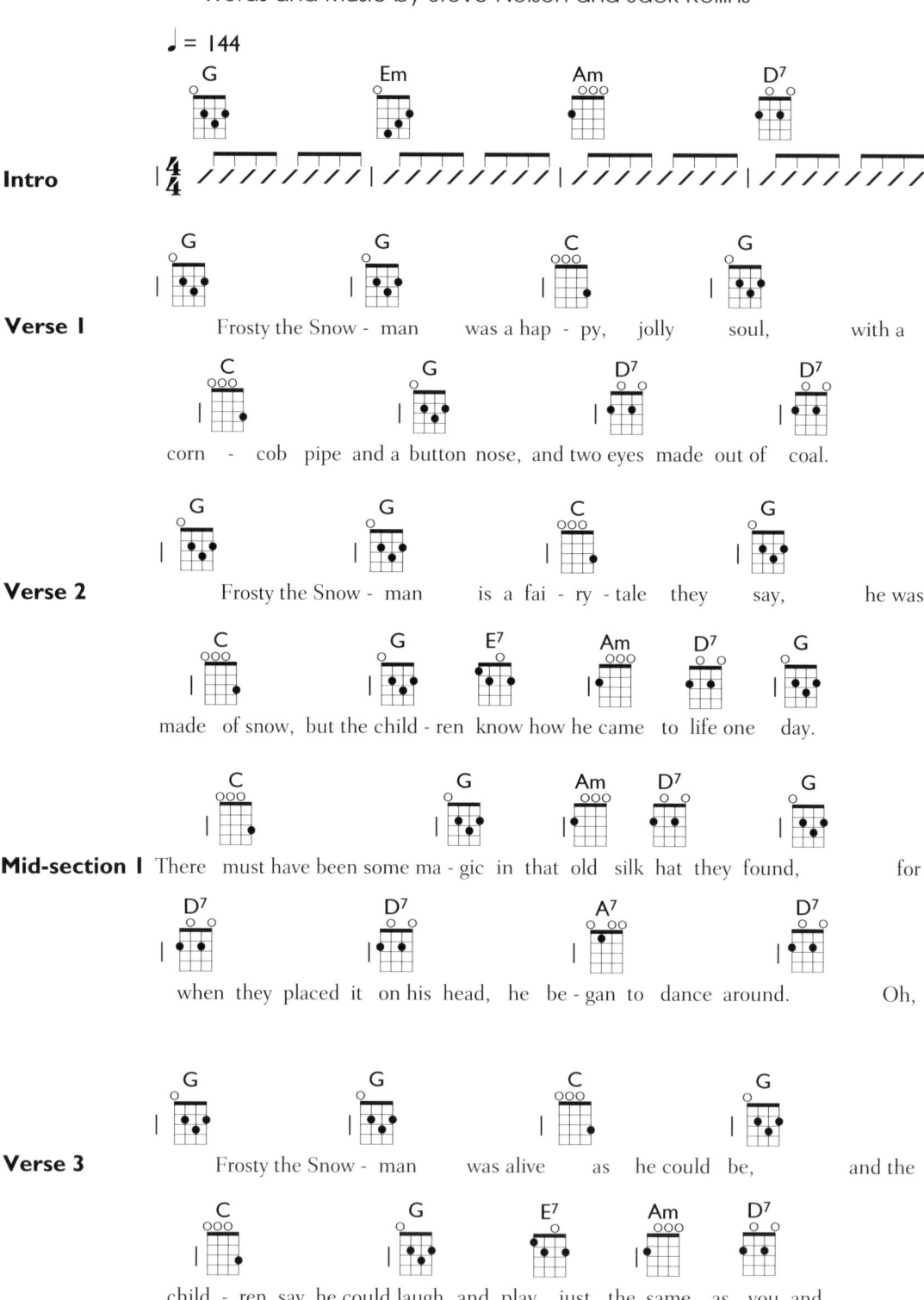

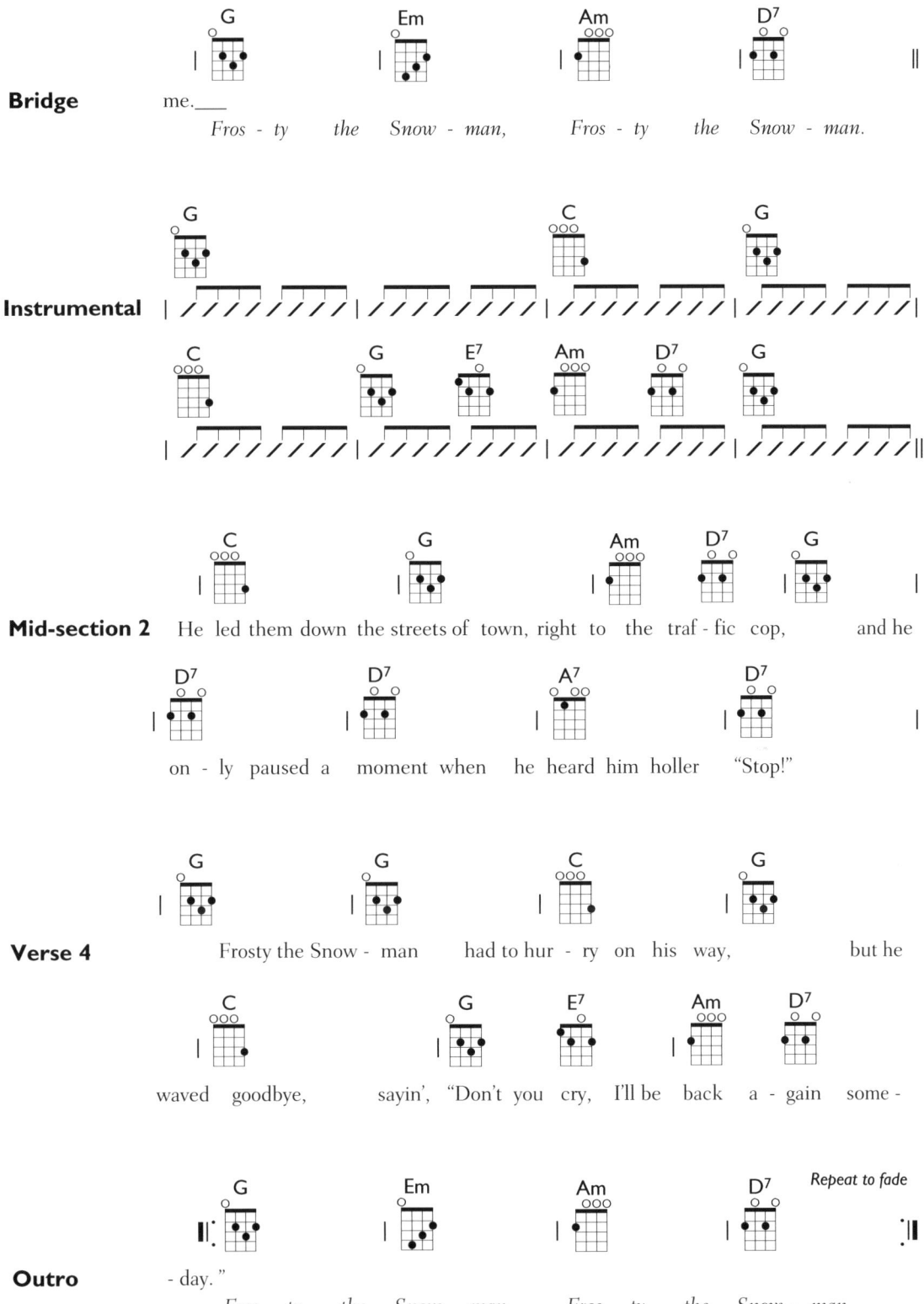

Grease

Words and Music by Barry Gibb

Frankie Valli

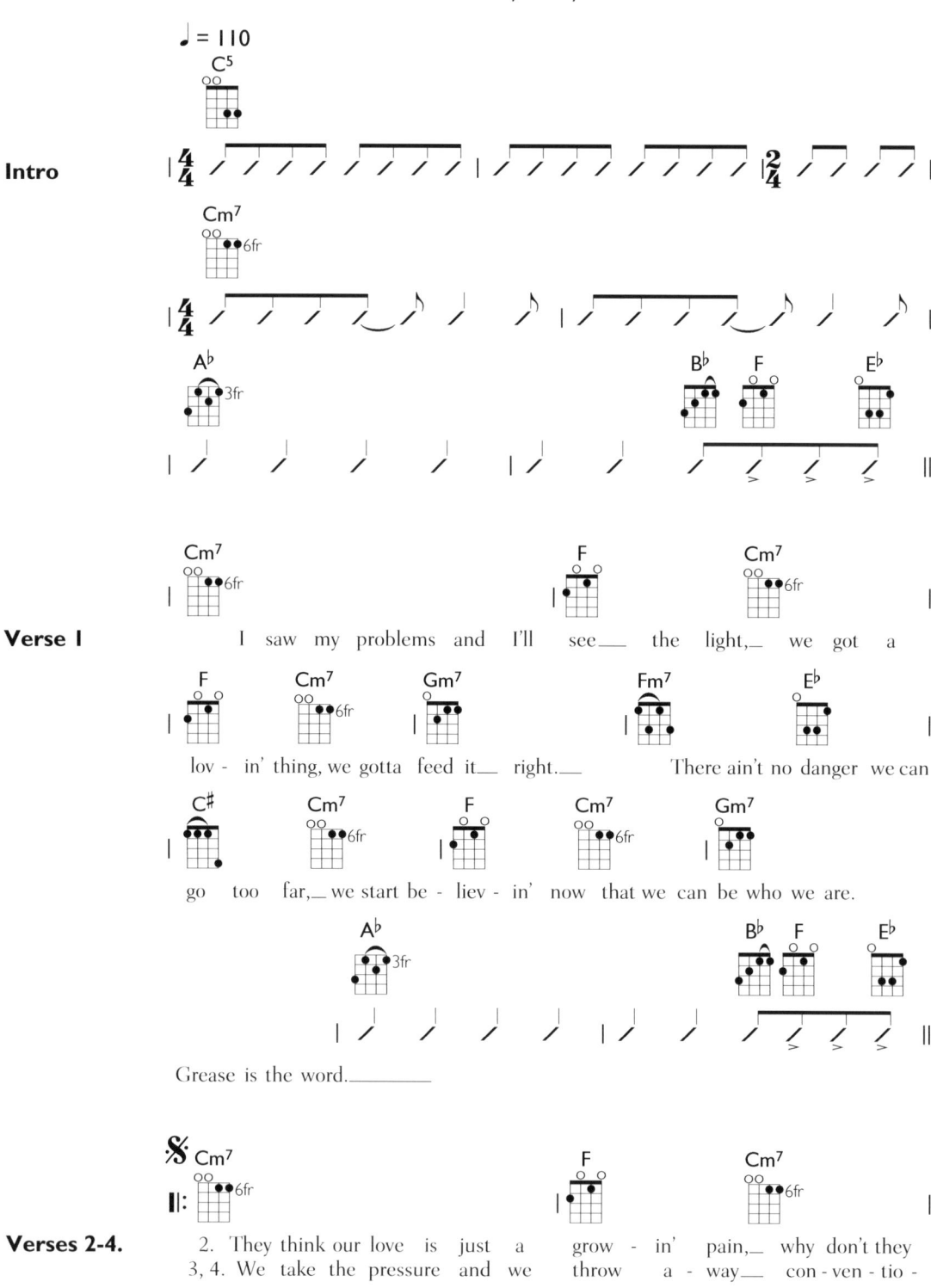

© 1978 Crompton Songs LLC
Warner/Chappell Music Ltd
All Rights Reserved.

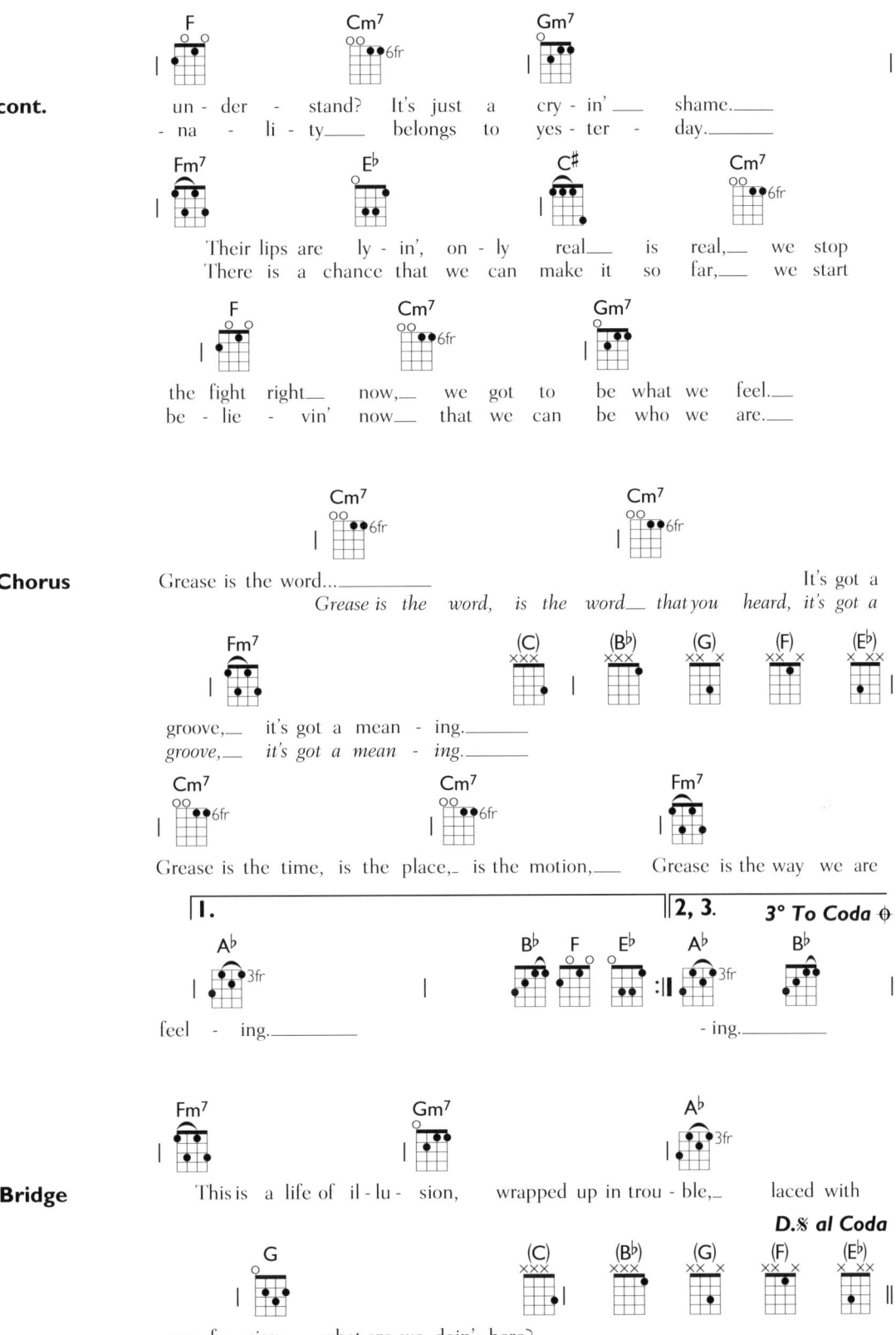

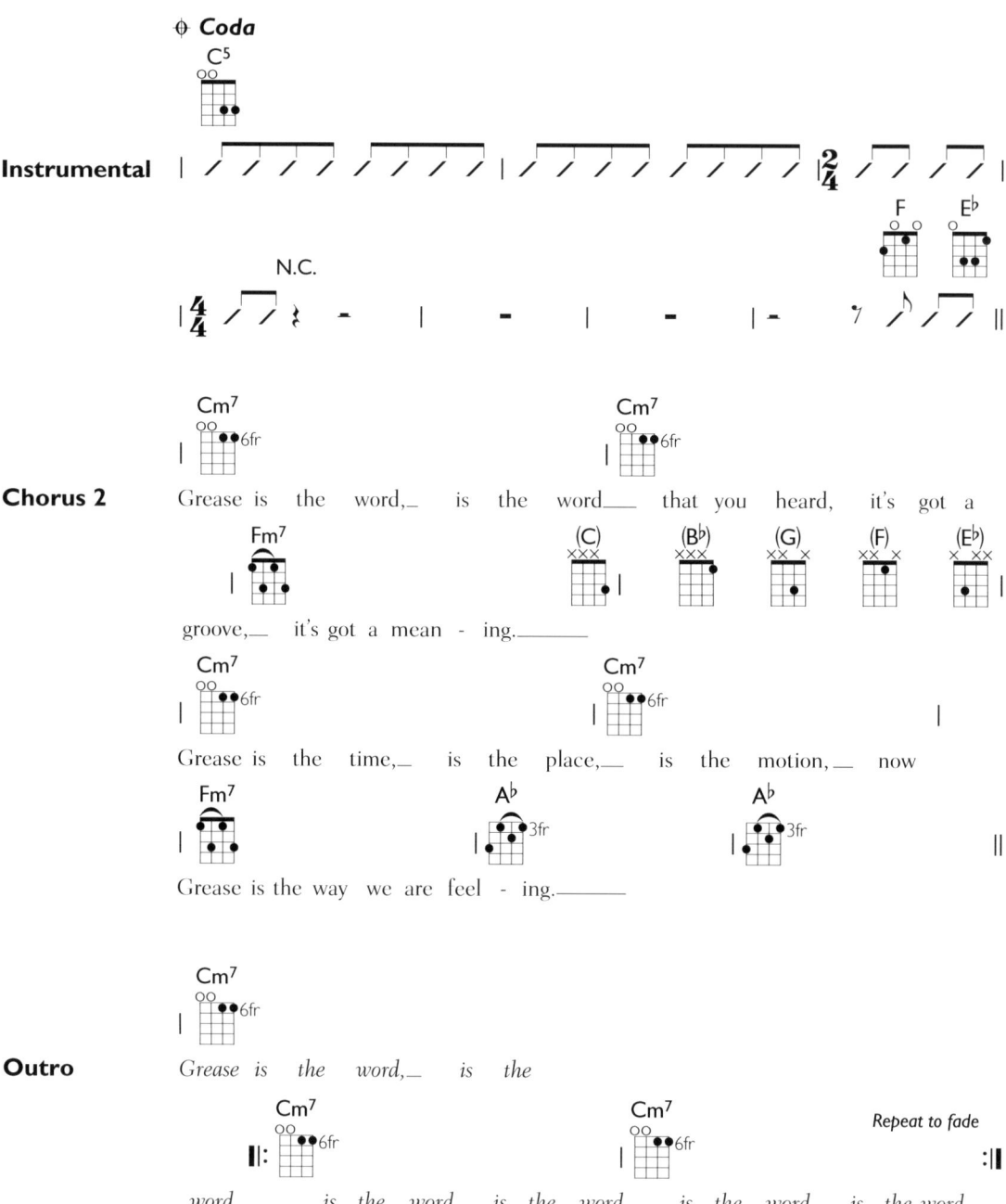

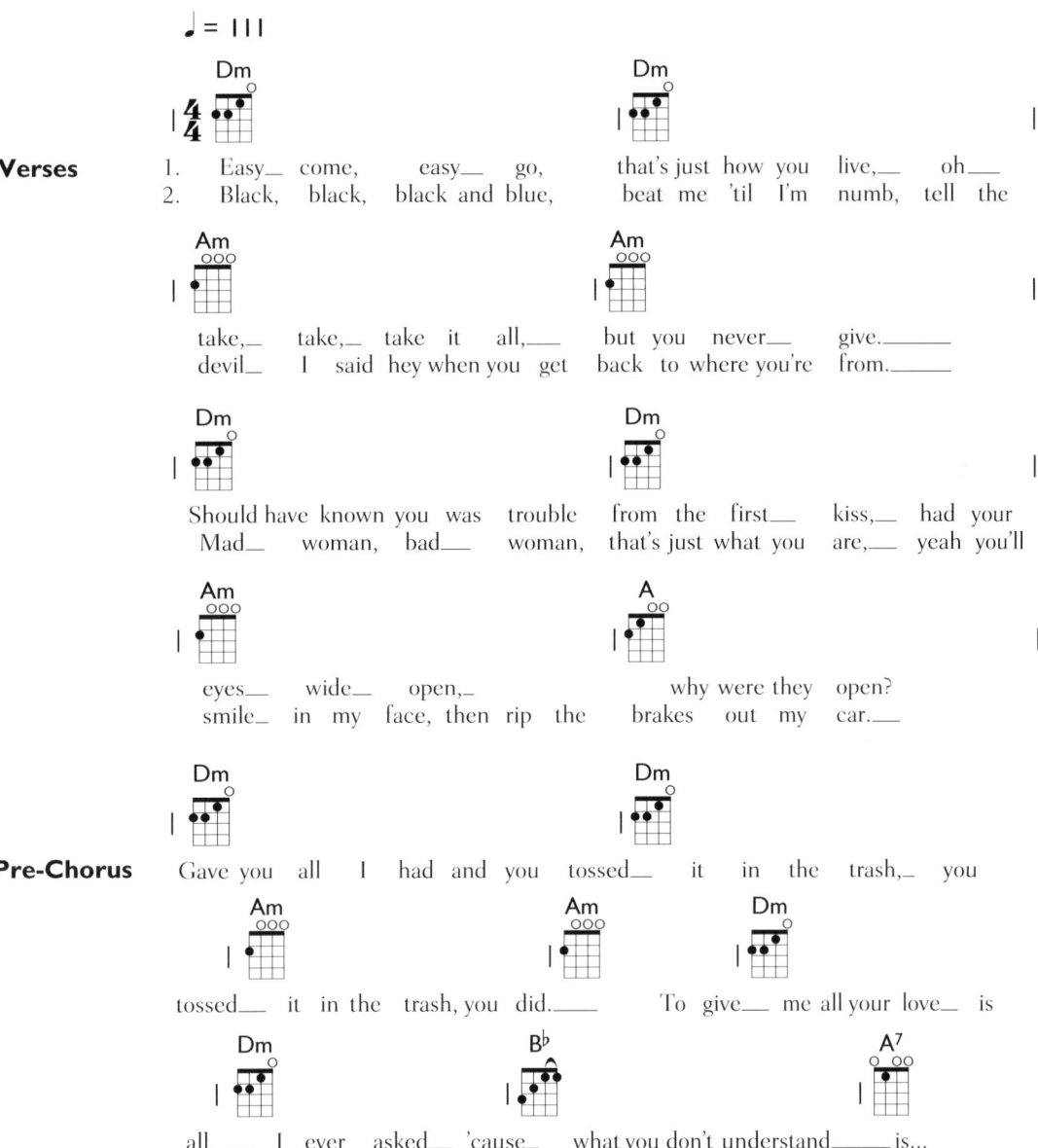

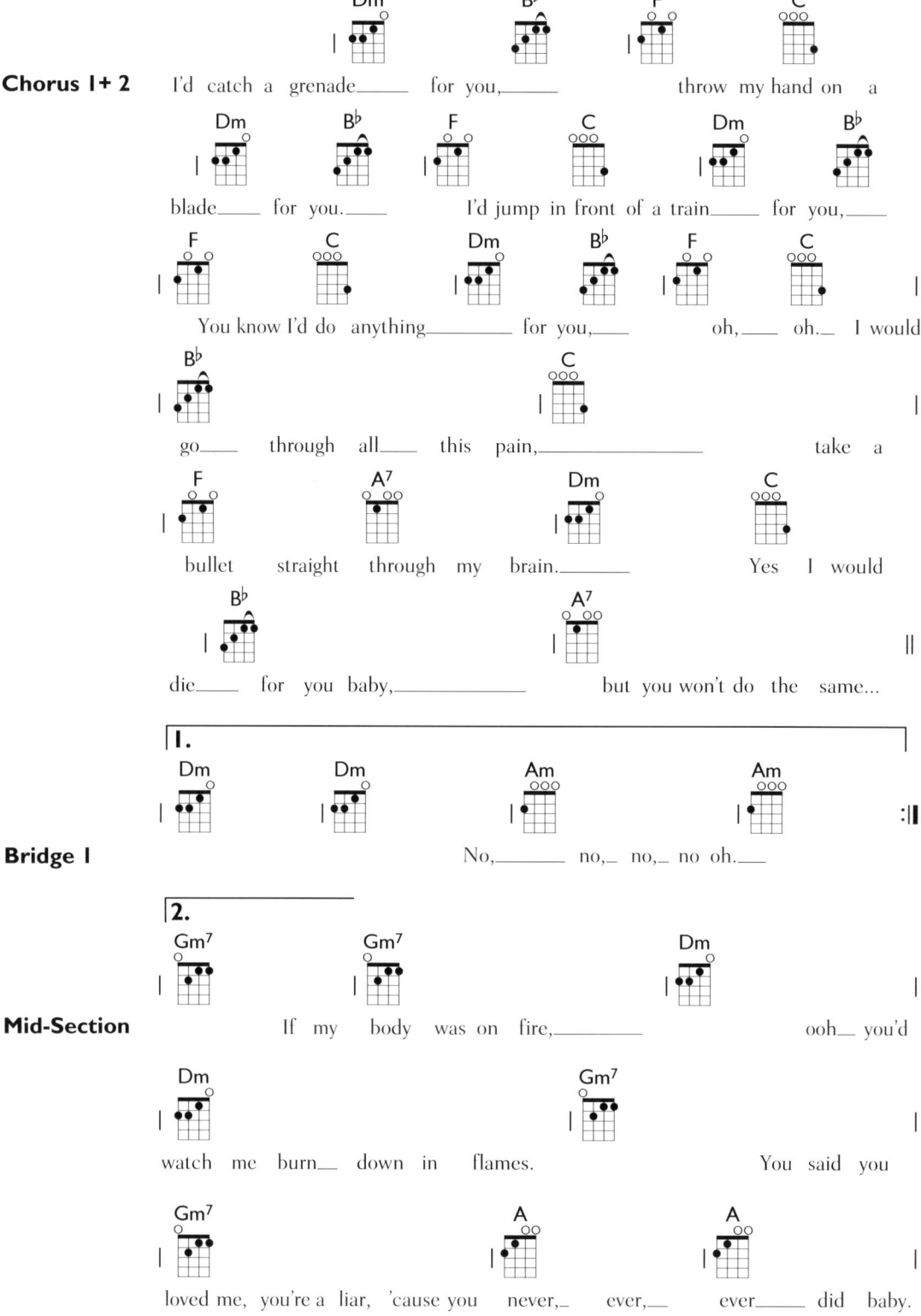

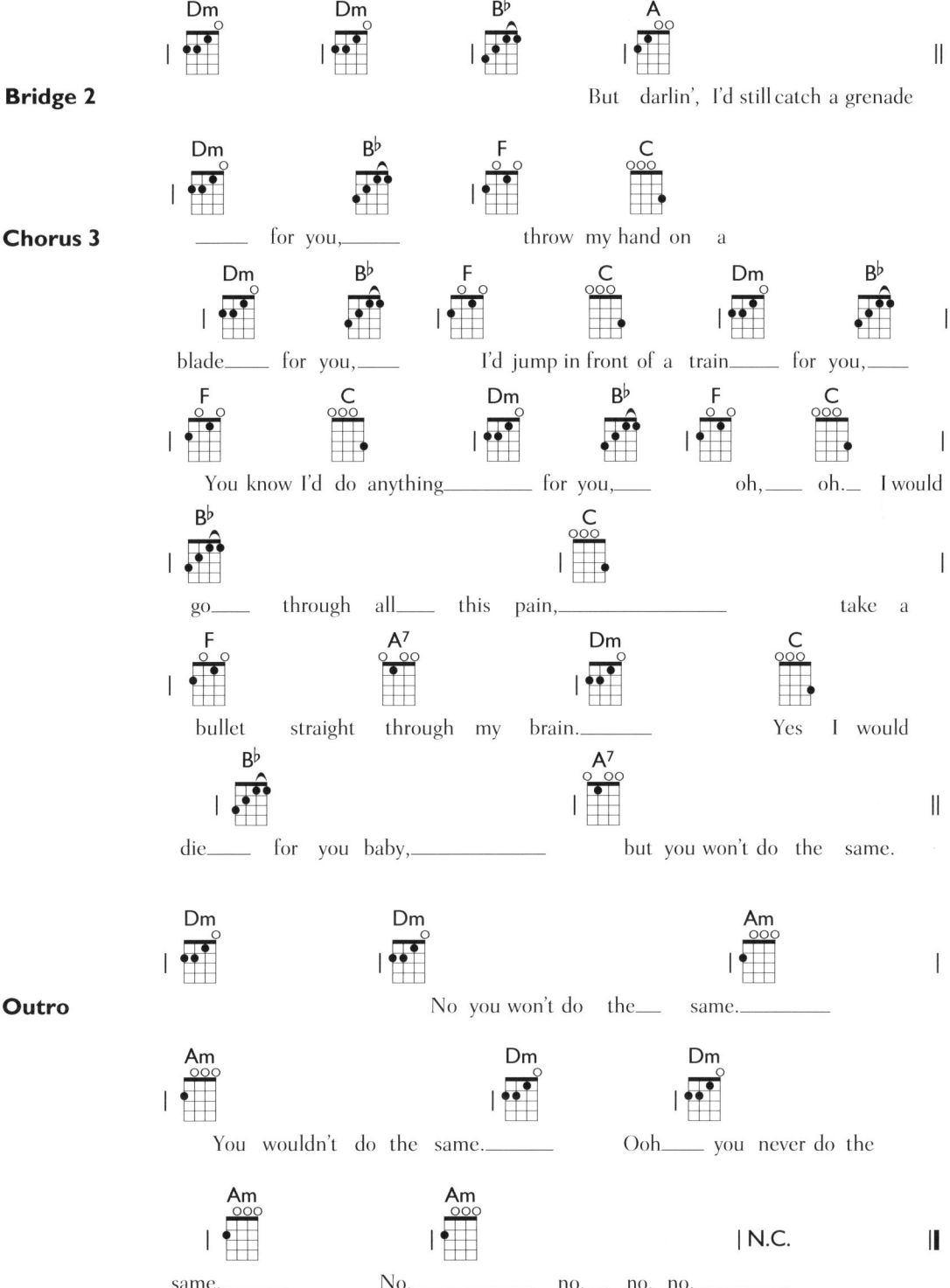

John Travolta

Greased Lightnin'

Words and Music by Jim Jacobs and Warren Casey

♩ = 150

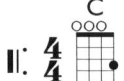

Verses   1. We'll get some   overhead   lifters   and four barrel quads, oh yeah.   Keep talkin',
     (2.) purple fringe tail-lights and thirty inch fins, oh yeah.

whoa   keep   talkin'.   Fuel injection cutoffs   and chrome   plated rods, oh yeah.
                         A   Palomino dashboard   and   duel muffler twins,   oh yeah.

We'll get it ready,   I'll kill to get it ready.   With a four-speed on the floor,   they'll be
                                With new pistons, plugs and shocks, I can

waitin' at the door.   You know that ain't no s***, we'll be gettin' lots of it in Greased
get off my rocks,   you   know that I ain't bragging, she's a real pussy wagon, Greased

Light - ning.   Light - ning,   go, go, go, go, go, go, go, go.

Chorus   Go Greased Lightning,   you're burning up the quarter   mile. *Greased   Lightning,*

Go   Greased Lightning. Go Greased Lightning, you're coastin' through the heat lap trial.

                                          You are su - preme,   the chicks'll
Greased Lightning,   go   Greased Lightning.   Uh!   Uh!

© 1975 Edwin H Morris & Co Inc
Chappell Morris Ltd
All Rights Reserved.

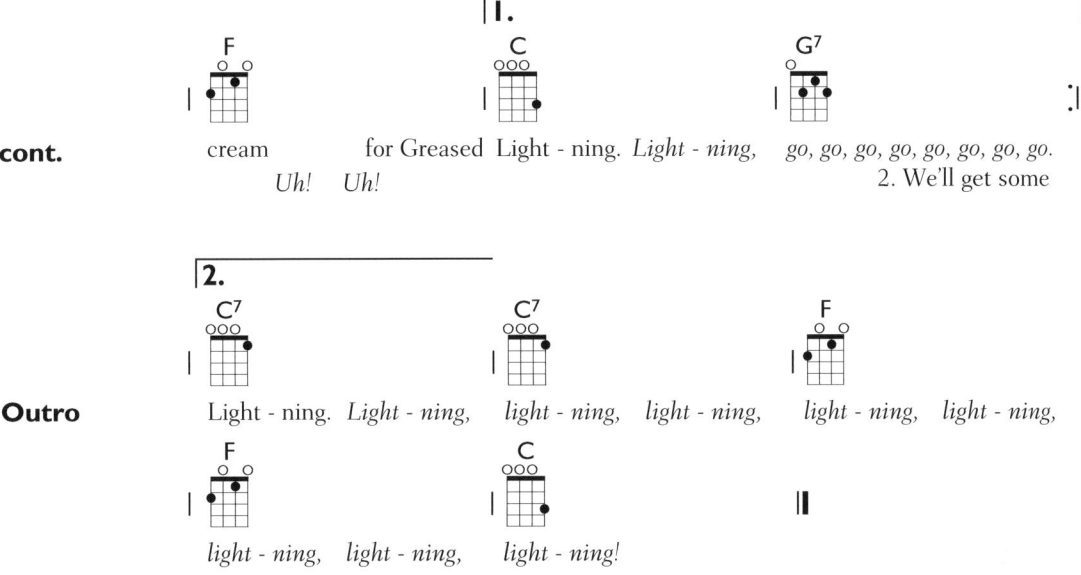

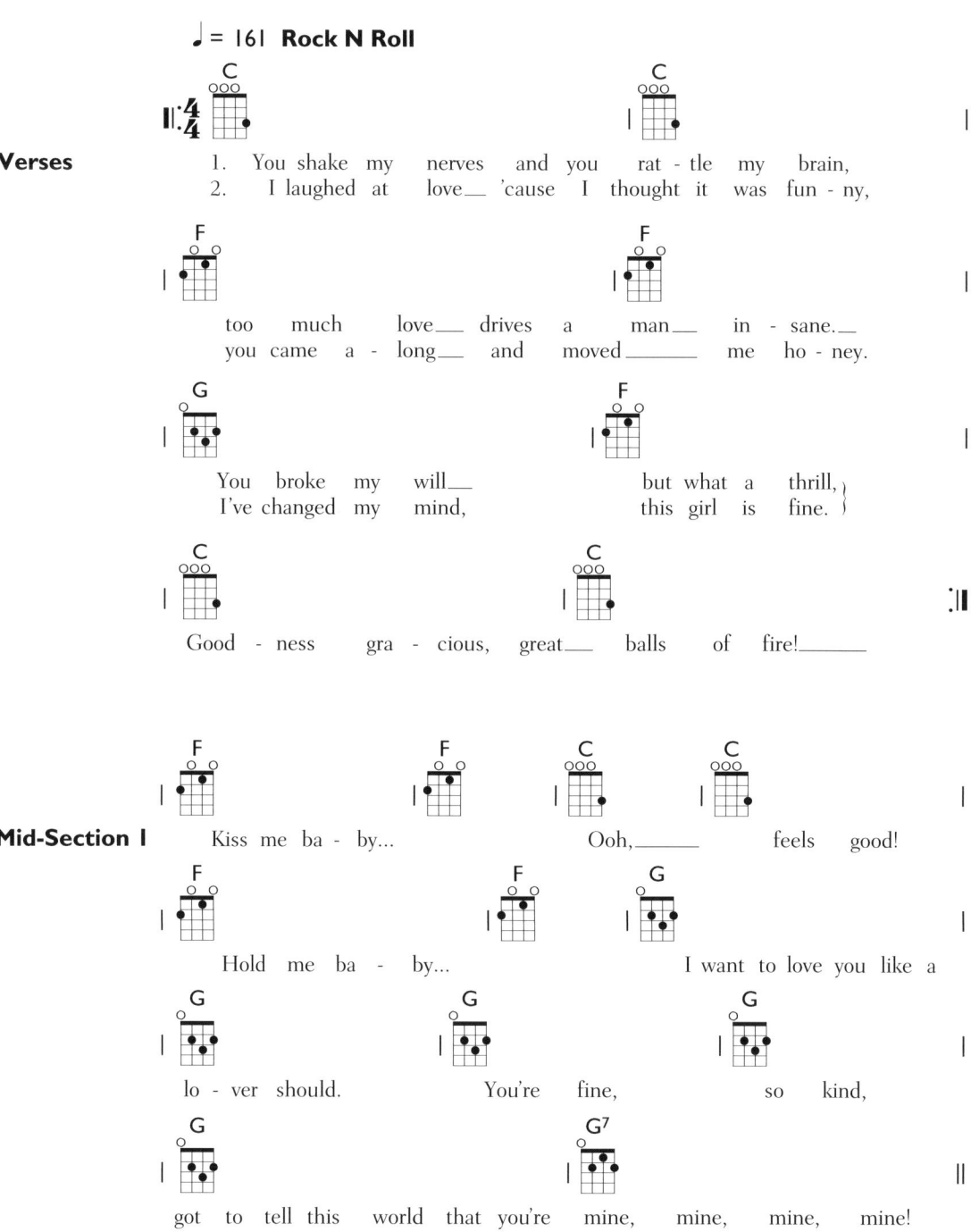

Verse 3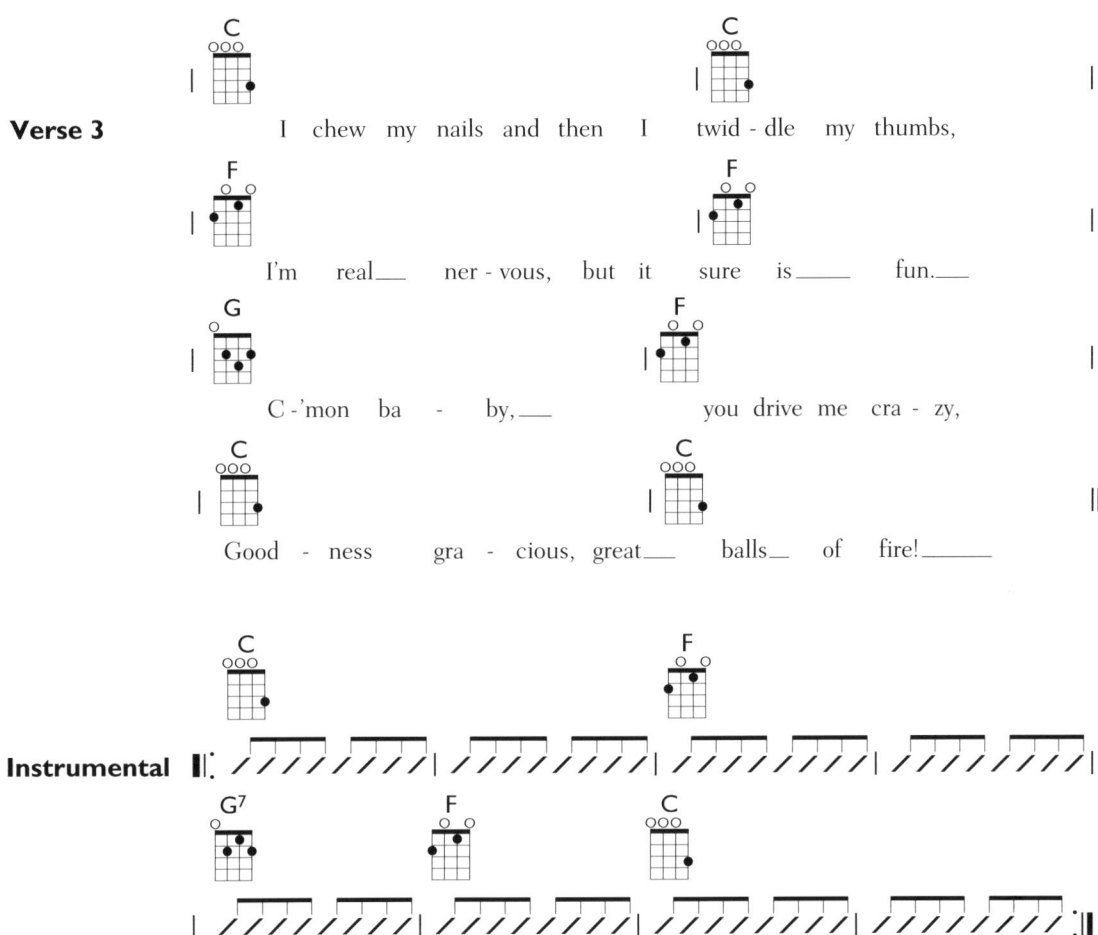

Mid-Section 2 As Mid-Section 1

Verse 4 As Verse 3

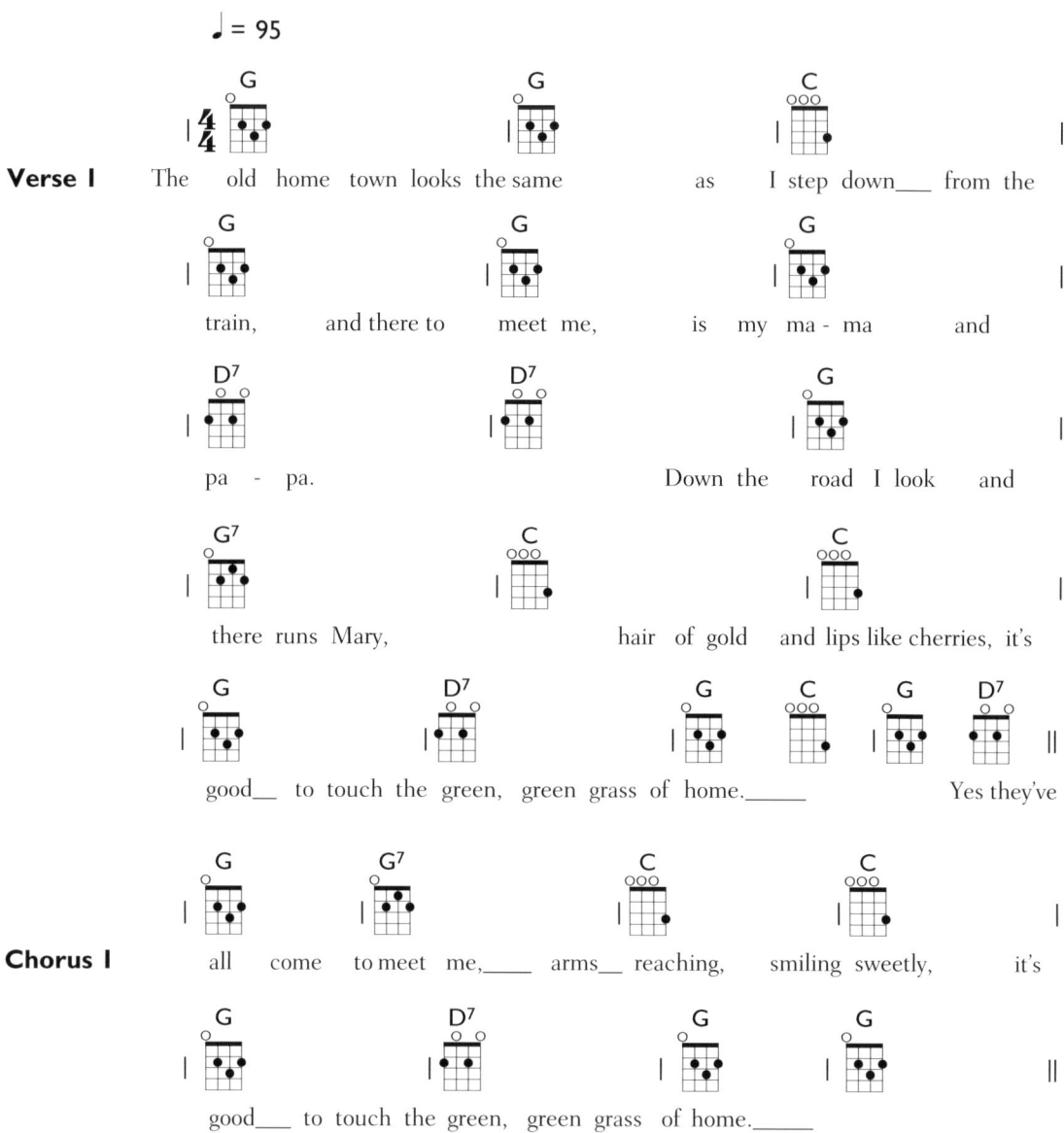

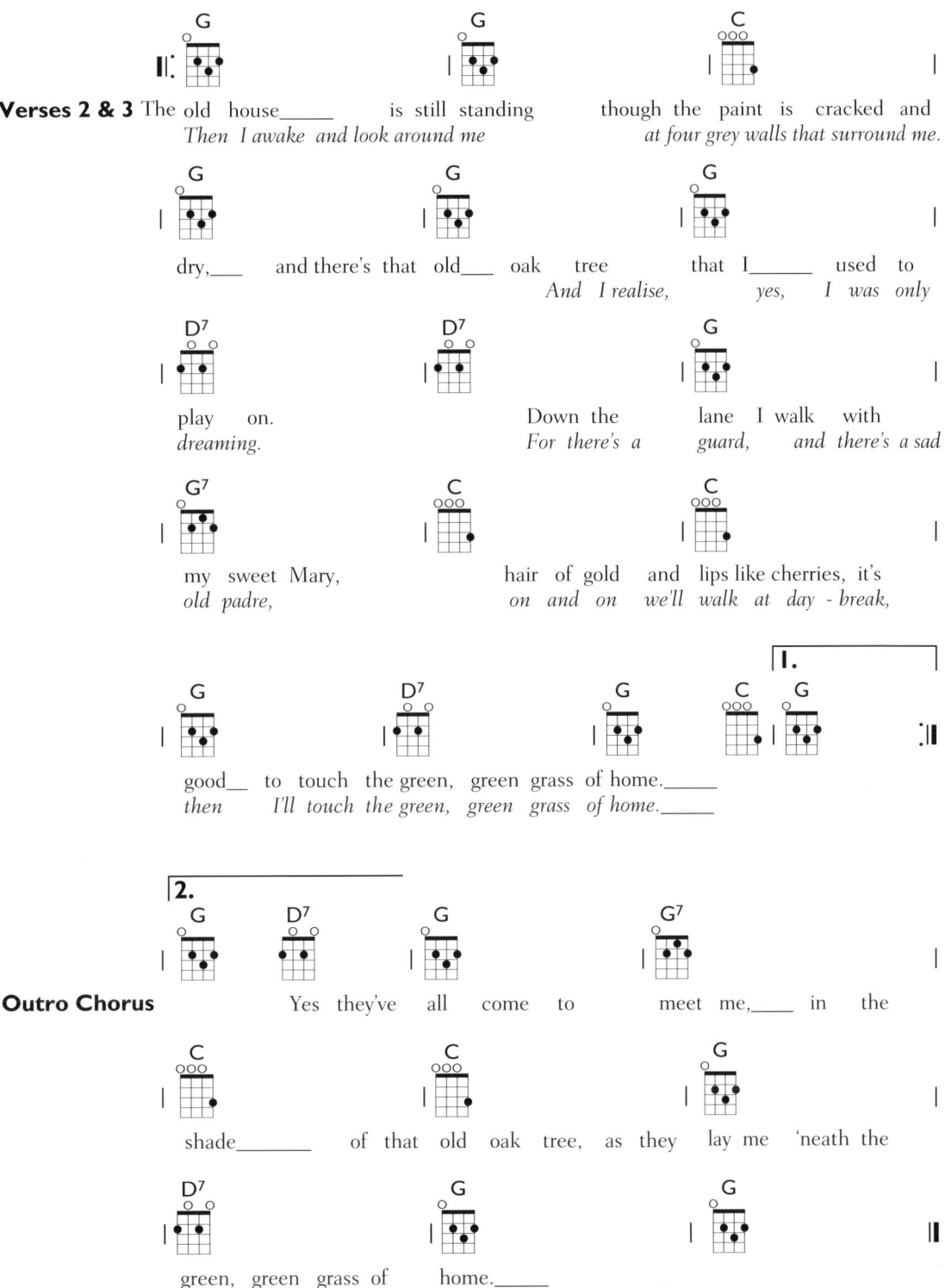

Have You Met Miss Jones?
(from "I'd Rather Be Right")

Words by Lorenz Hart
Music by Richard Rodgers

Robbie Williams

♩ = 127 **Swing feel**

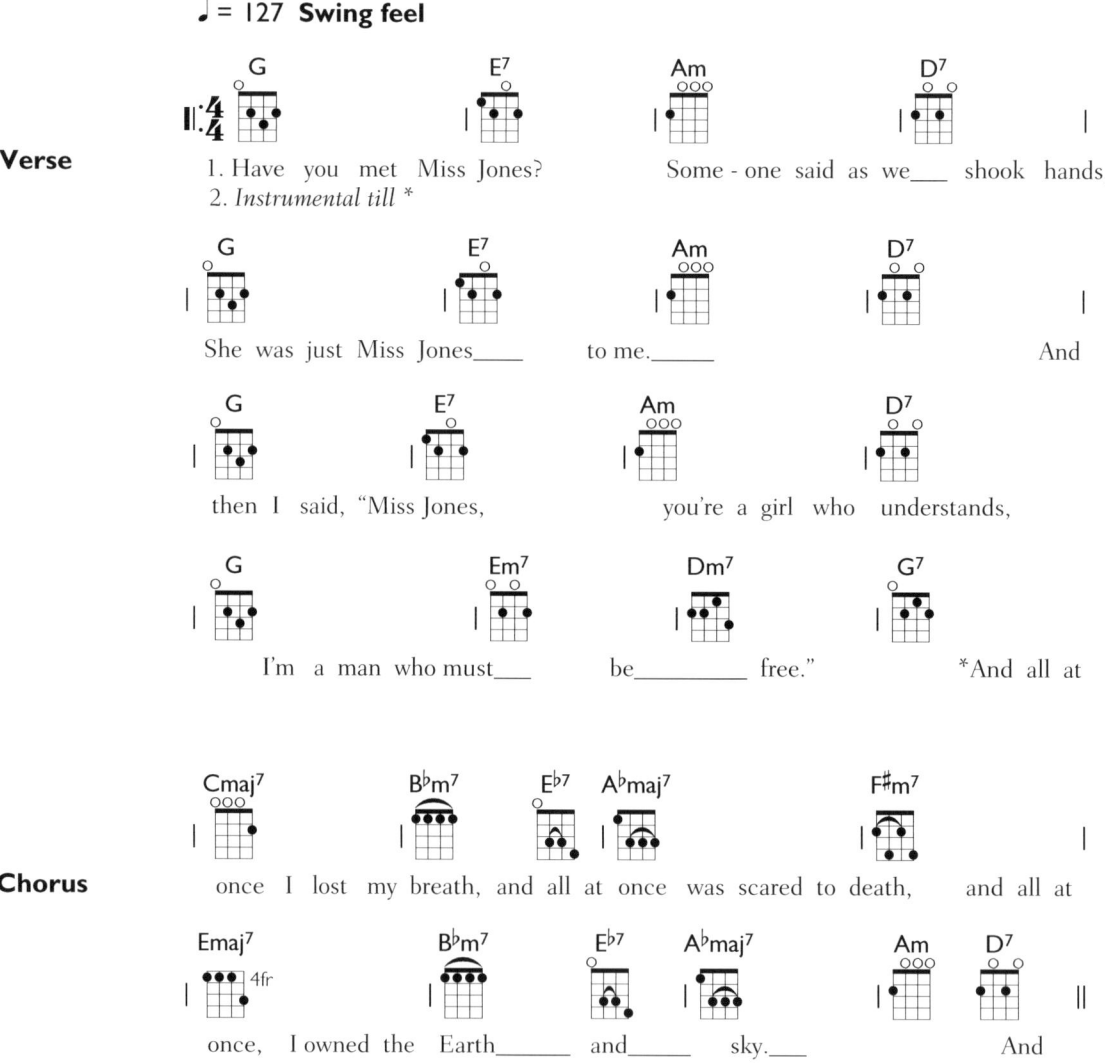

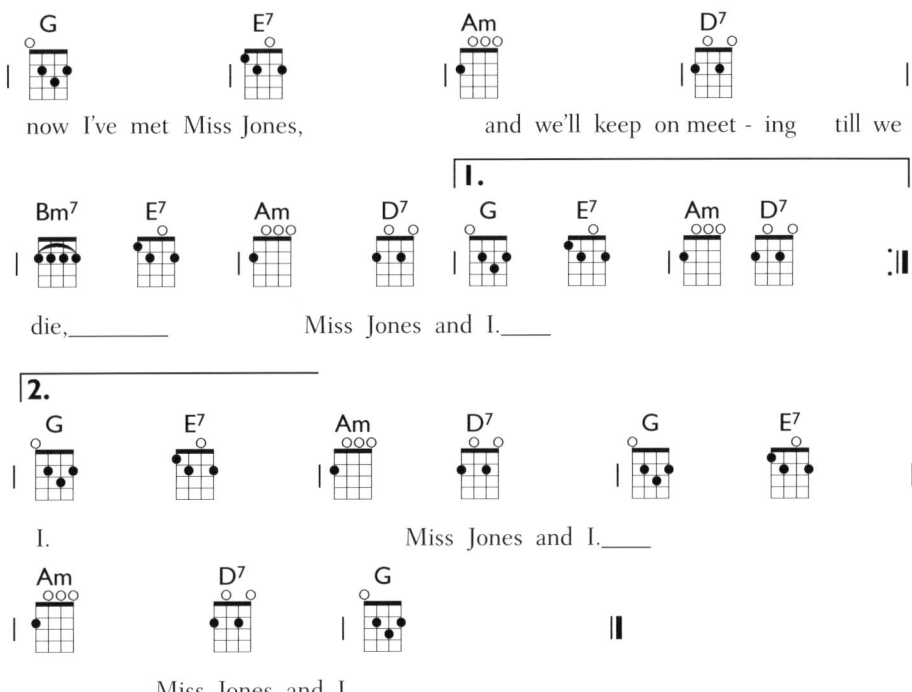

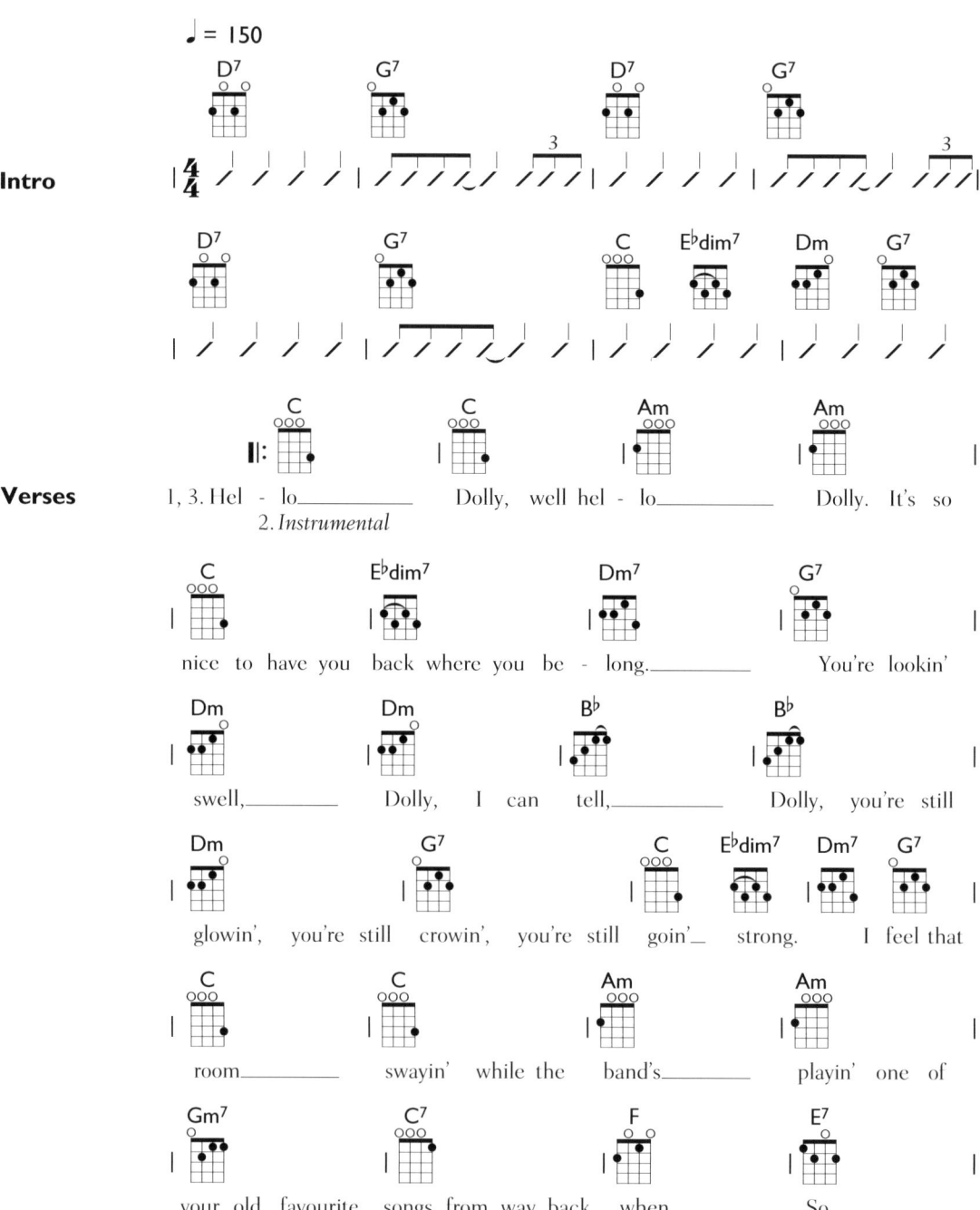

The Hippopotamus Song

Words by Michael Flanders
Music by Donald Swann

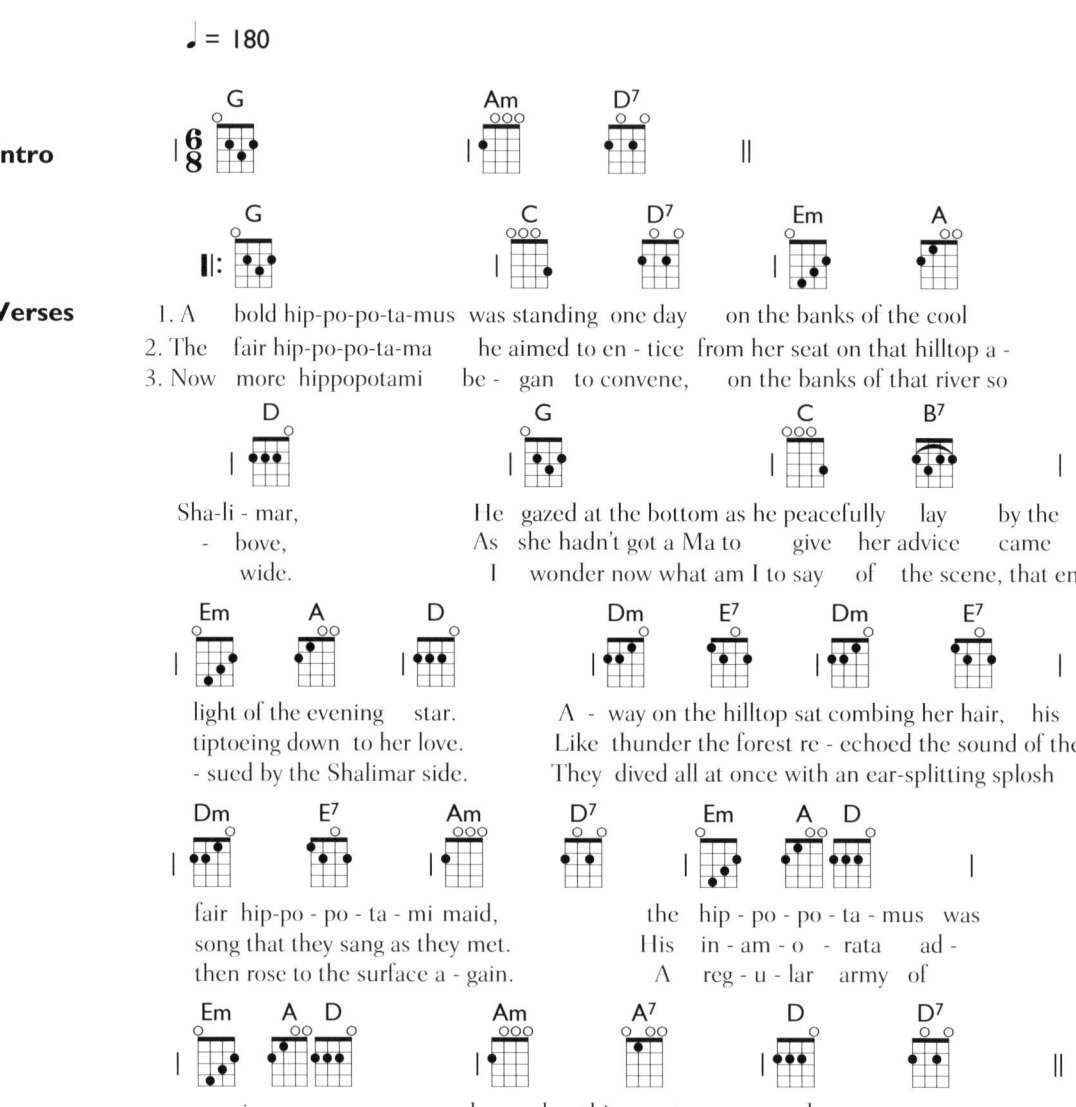

Flanders & Swann

Chorus Mud, mud, glorious mud, nothing quite like it for cooling the blood. So follow me follow, down to the hollow, and there let us wallow in glo - ri - ous mud! mud!

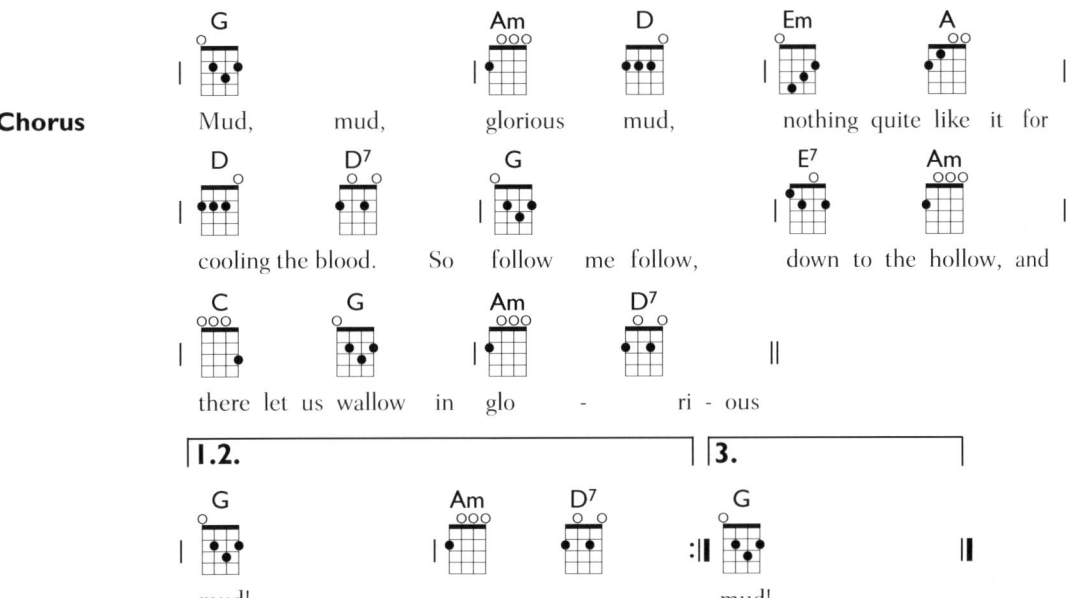

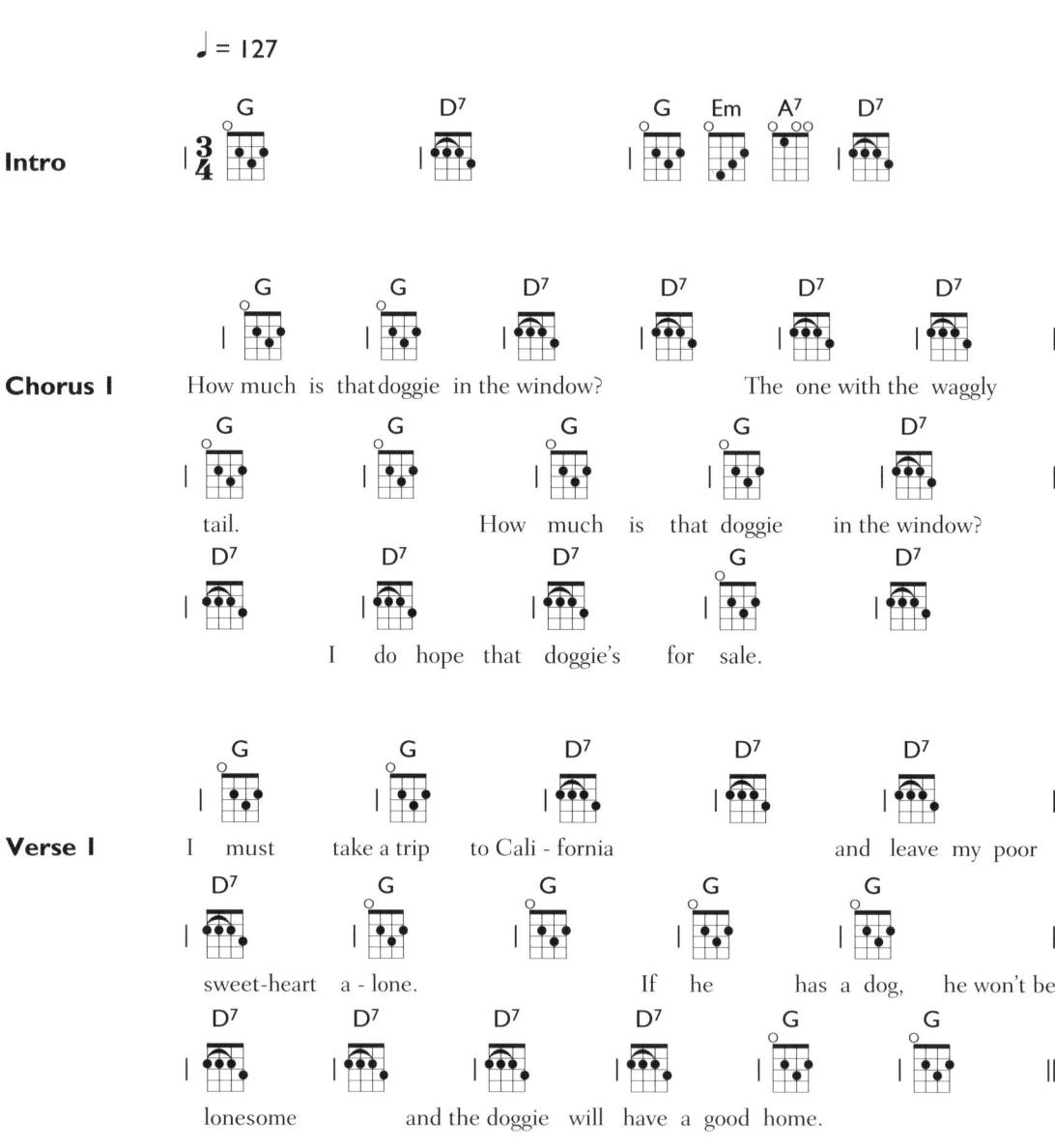

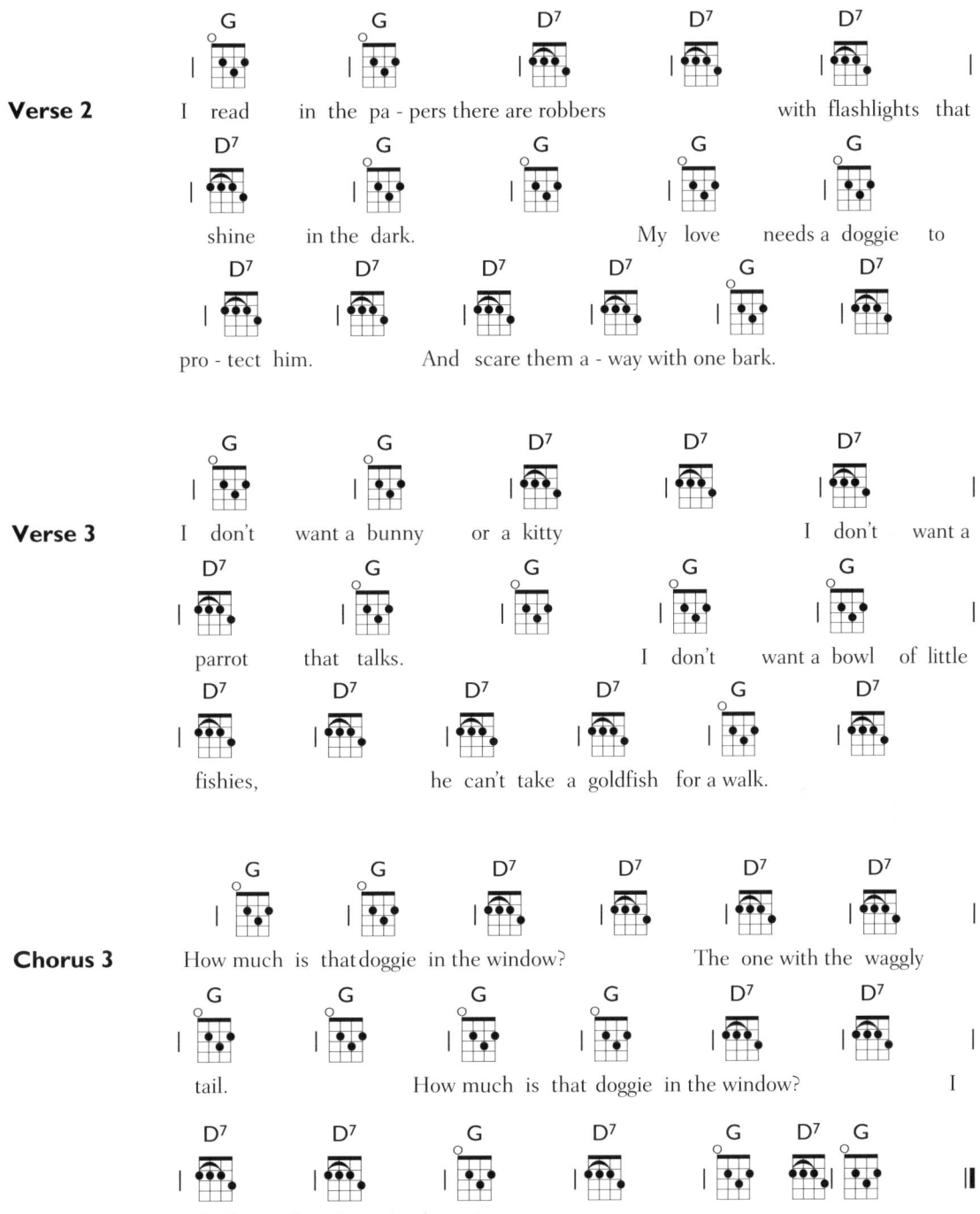

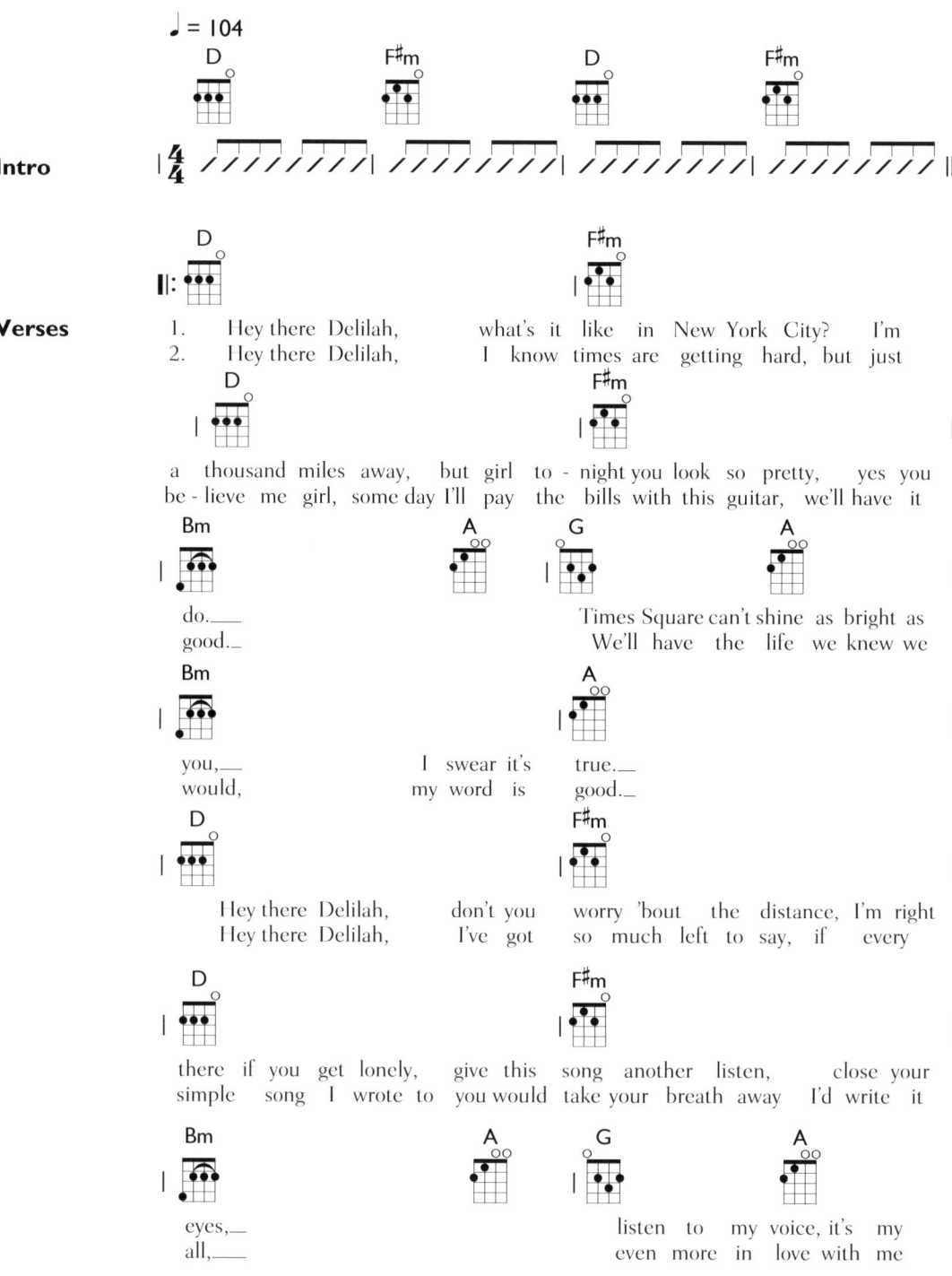

cont.

        Bm   **A**

dis - guise,   I'm by your side.
you'd fall,___   we'd have it all.___

Chorus 1+2

D   **Bm**   **D**

Oh___ it's what you do to me.___   Oh___ it's what you do to

Bm   **D**   **Bm**

me.___   Oh___ it's what you do to me.___

|**1.**

D   **Bm**

Oh___ it's what you do to me,___ what you do to

|**2.**

D   **Bm**

me.___   :|| me.___

Mid-Section

||: **G**   **A**   **A⁷**

1. A thousand miles seems pretty far, but they've got planes and trains and cars, I'd
2. Our friends would all make fun of us, and we'll just laugh along because we
3. De - lilah, I can promise you that by the time that we get through, the

|**1.2.**

D   **Bm**   **A**

walk to you if I had no other way.___
know that none of them have felt this way.___ :||

|**3.**

Bm   **Bm**

world will never, ever be the same___   and you're to

A   **A⁷**   **A**

blame.___

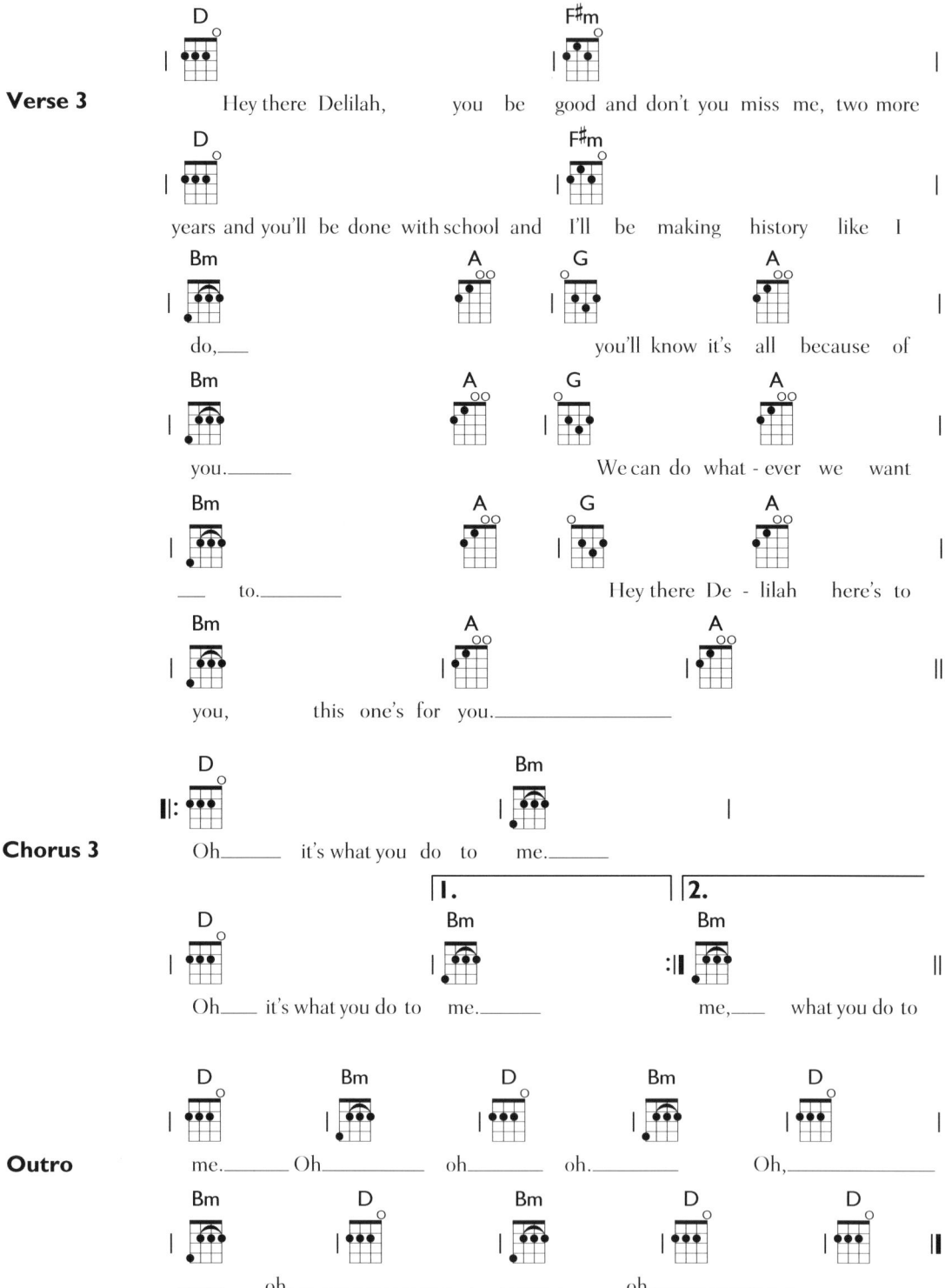

Sonny & Cher

I Got You Babe
Words and Music by Sonny Bono

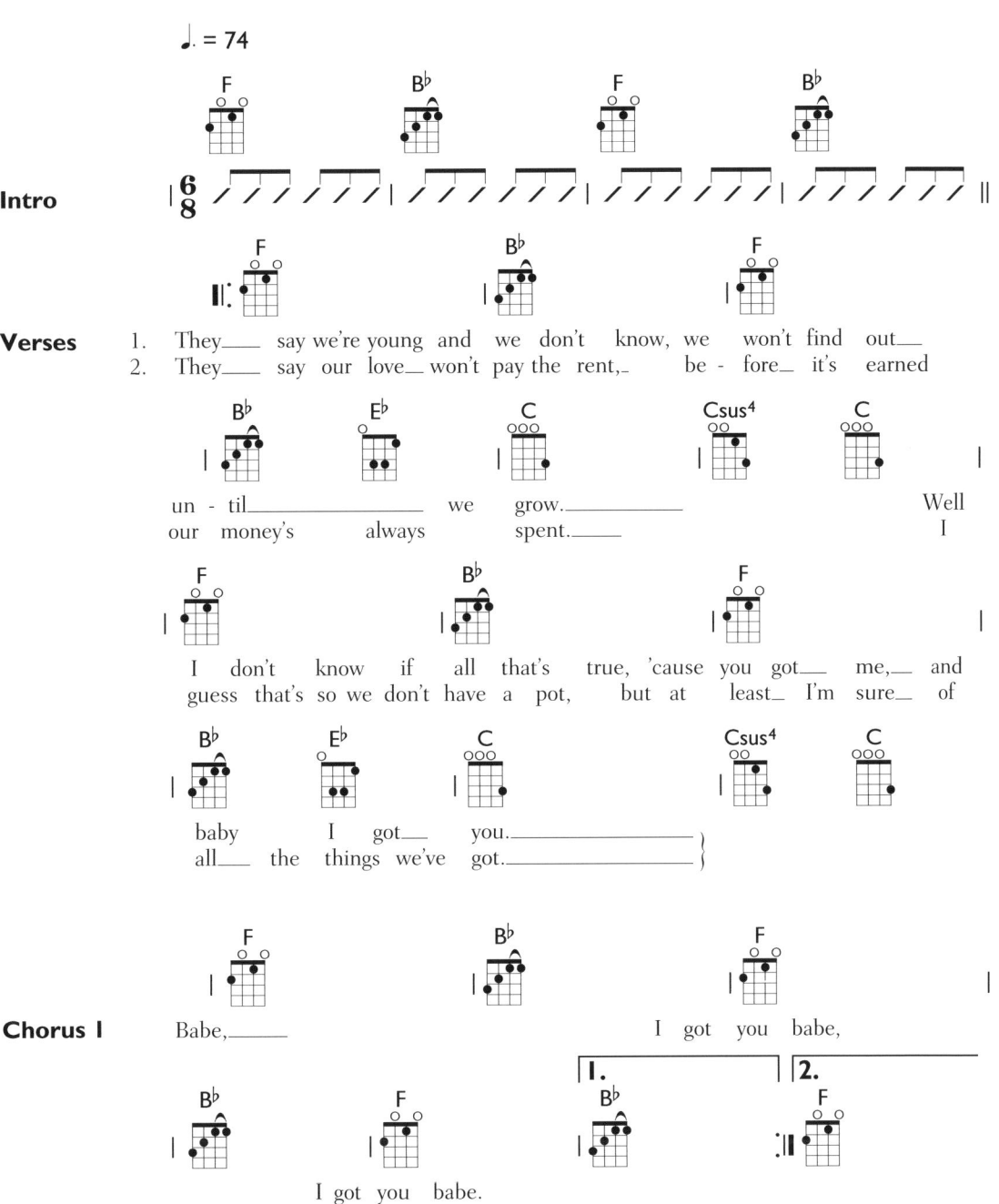

© 1965 (renewed) Cotillion Music Inc and Chris Marc Music
Warner/Chappell North America Ltd
All Rights Reserved.

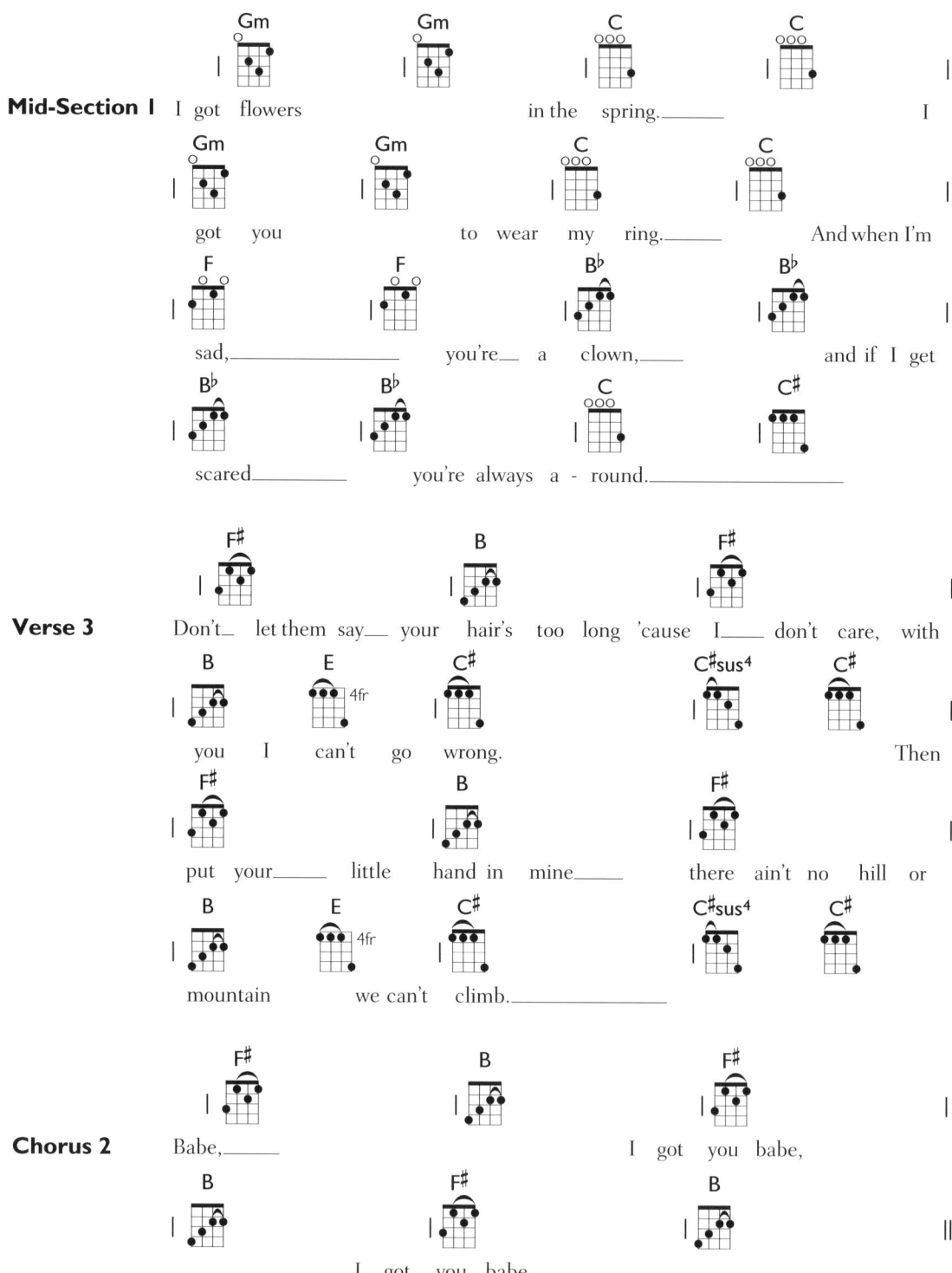

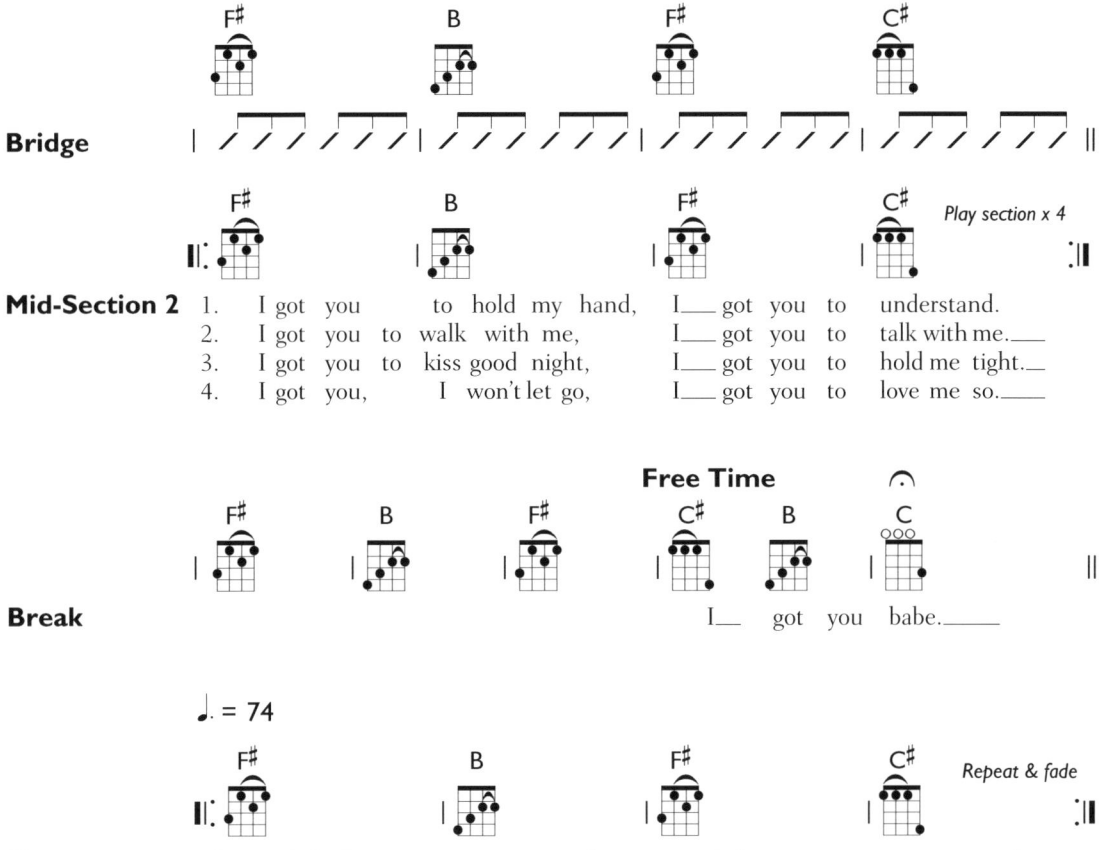

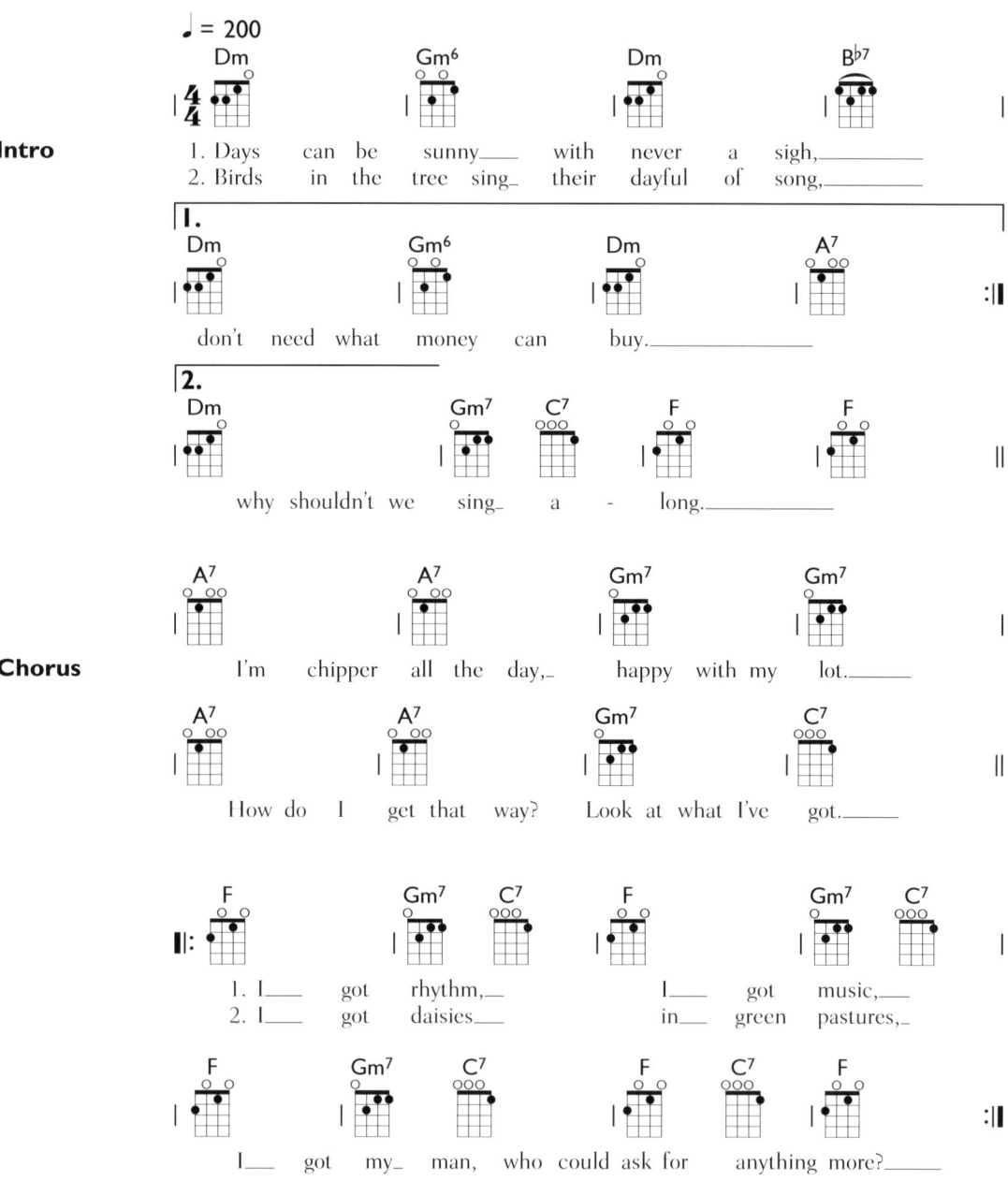

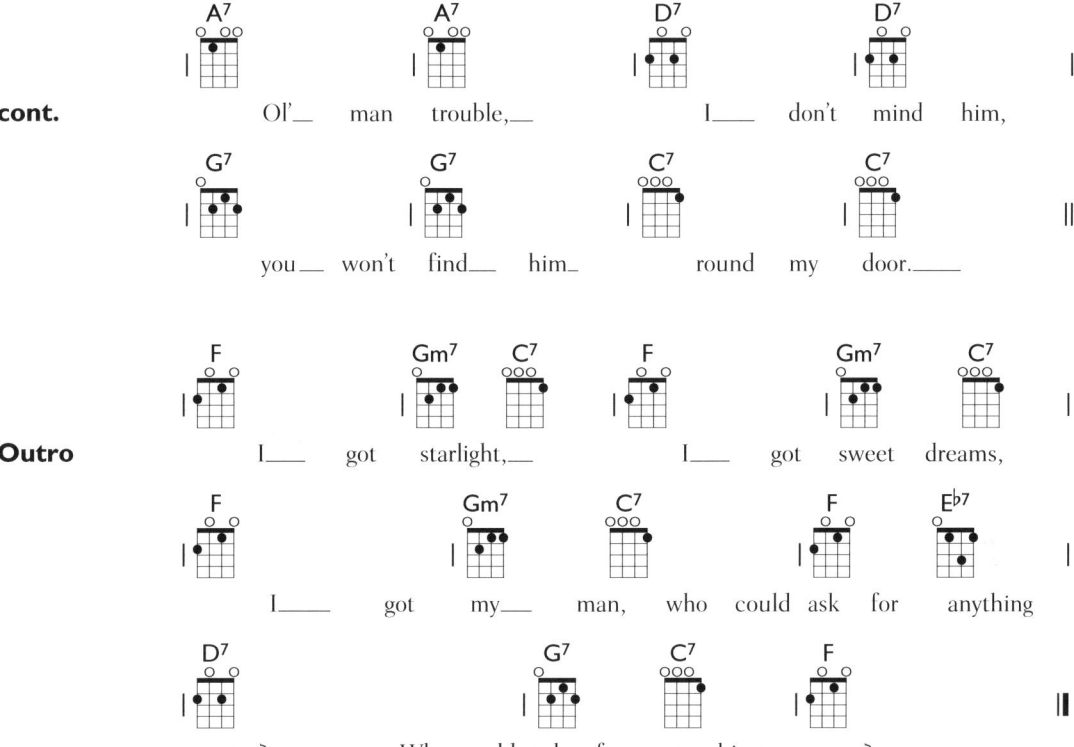

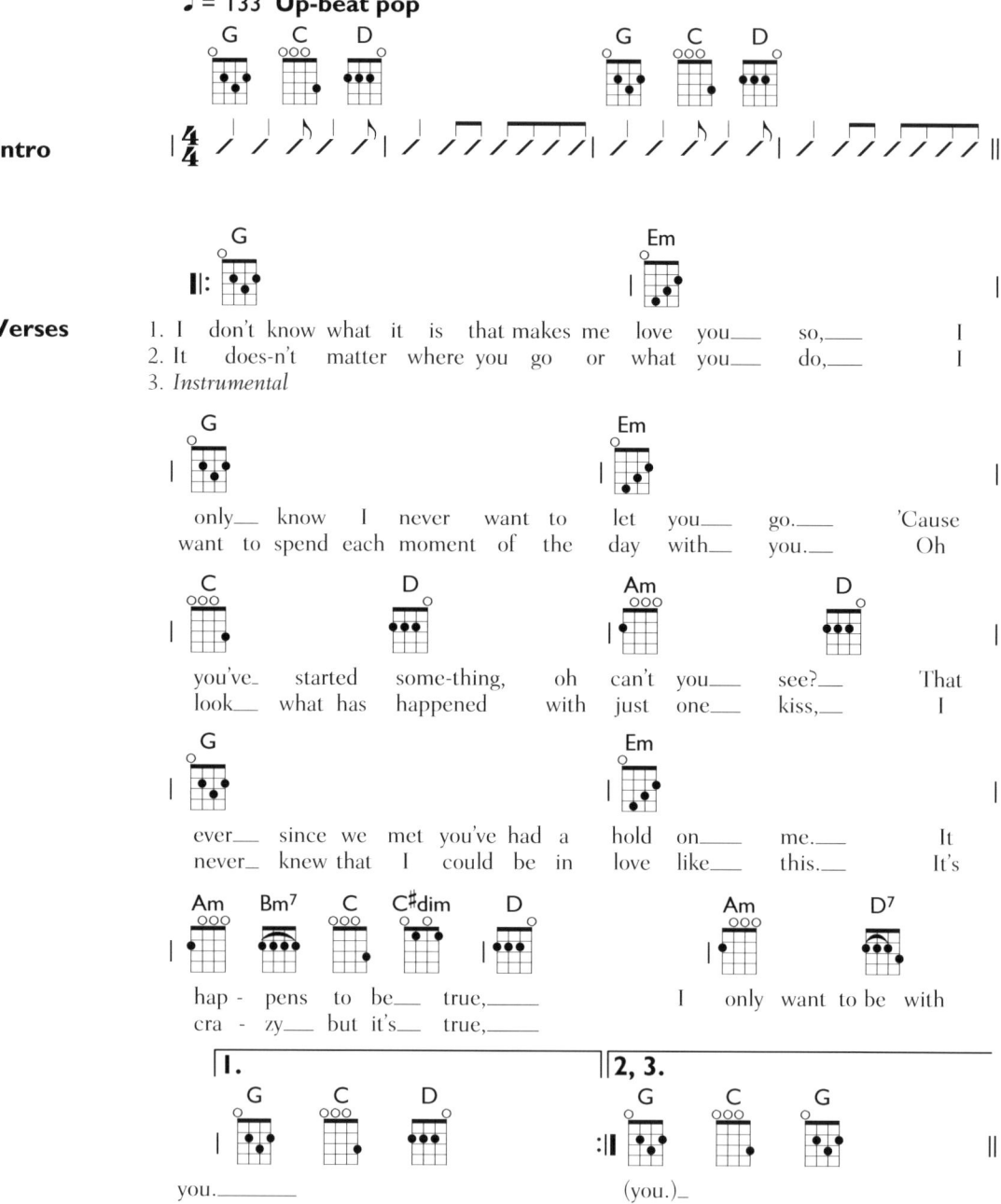

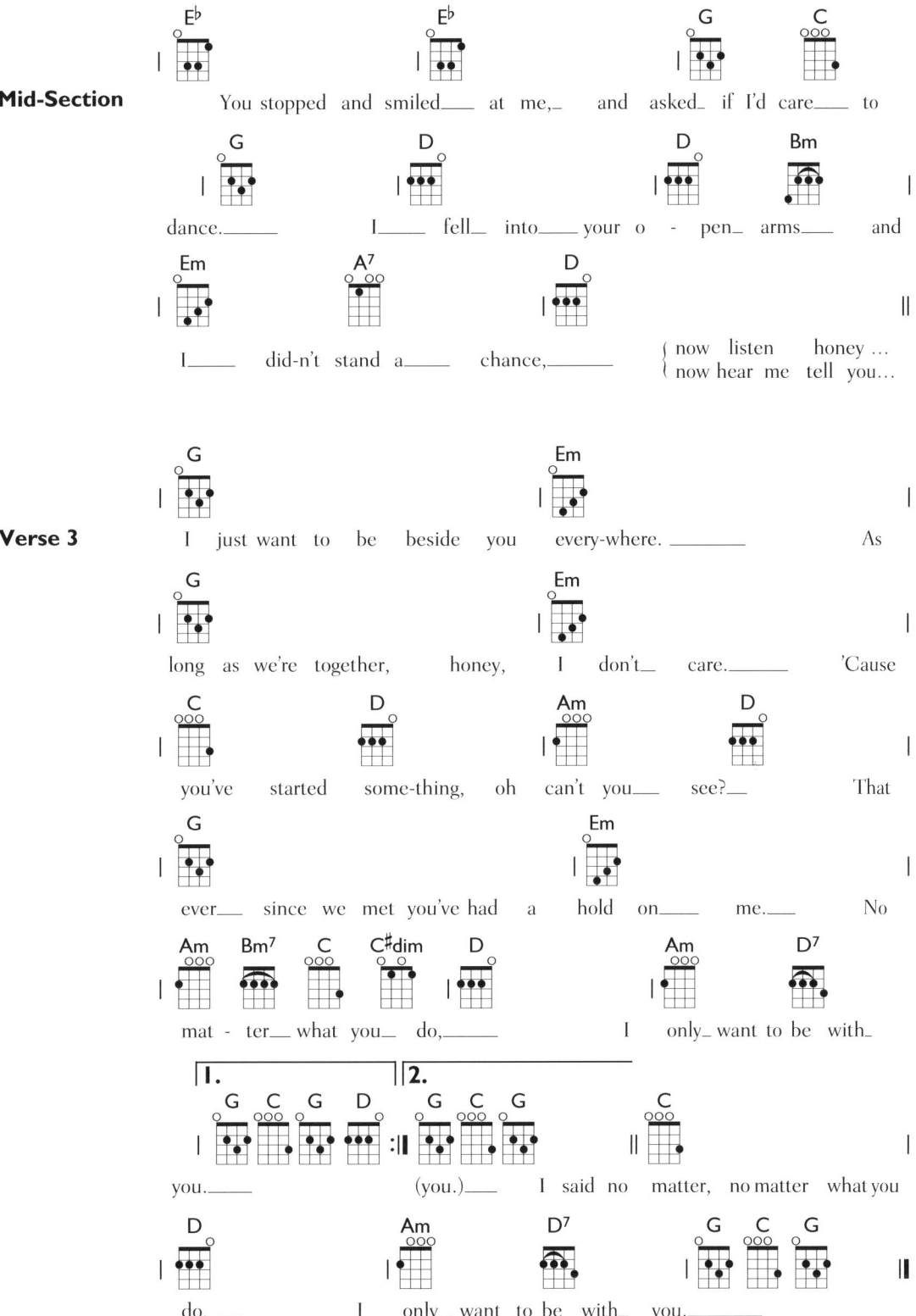

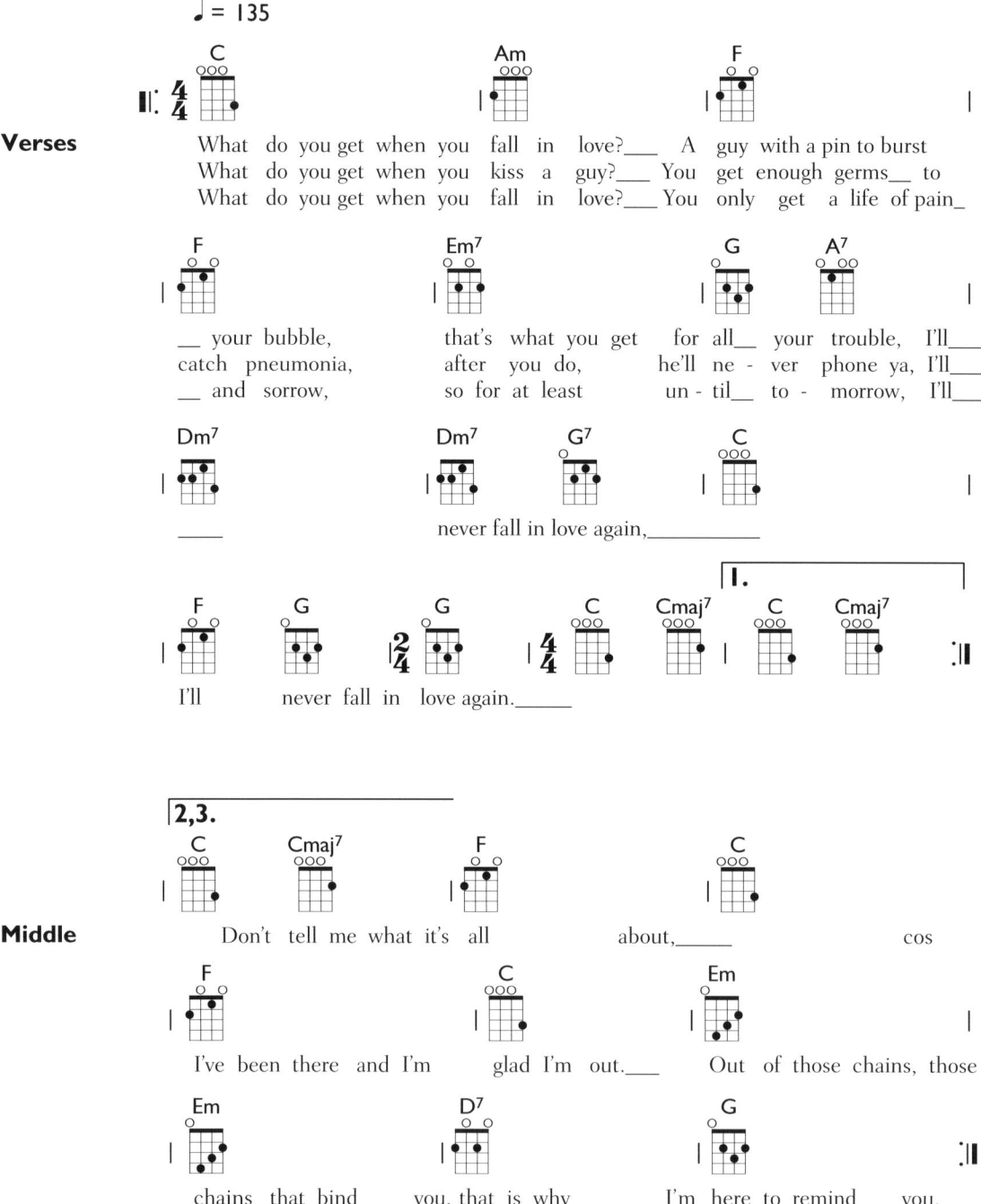

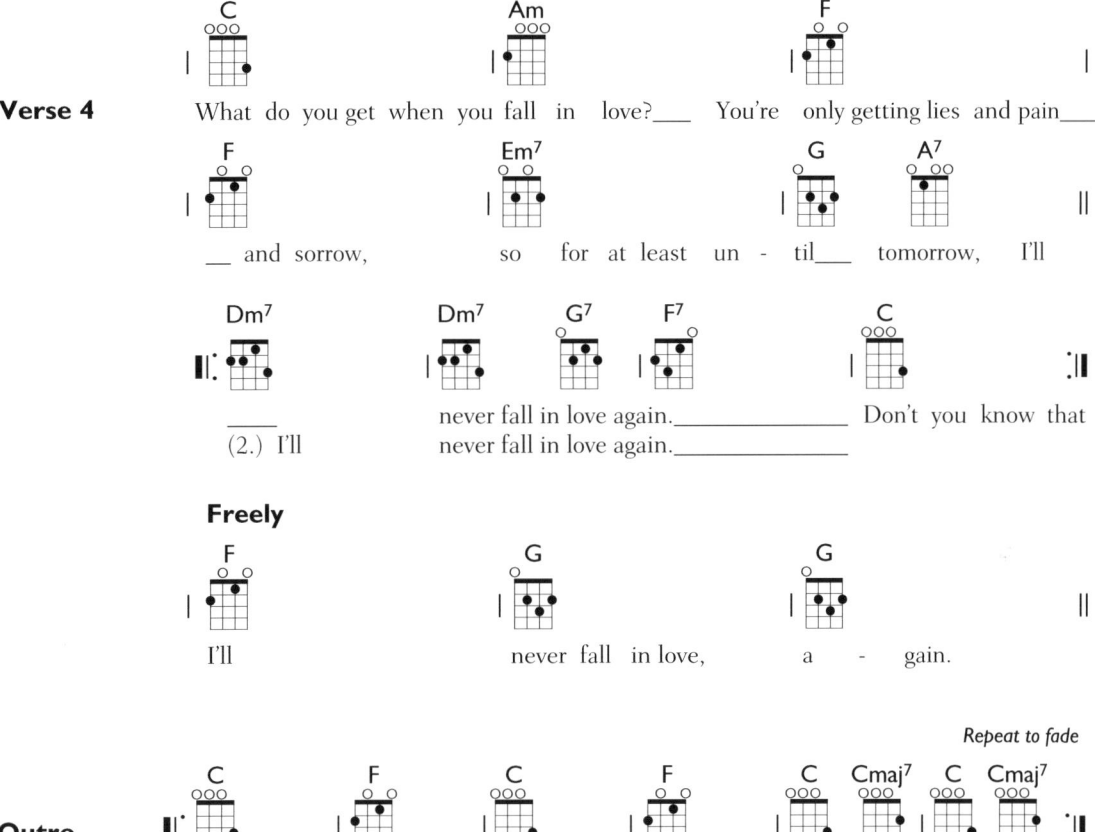

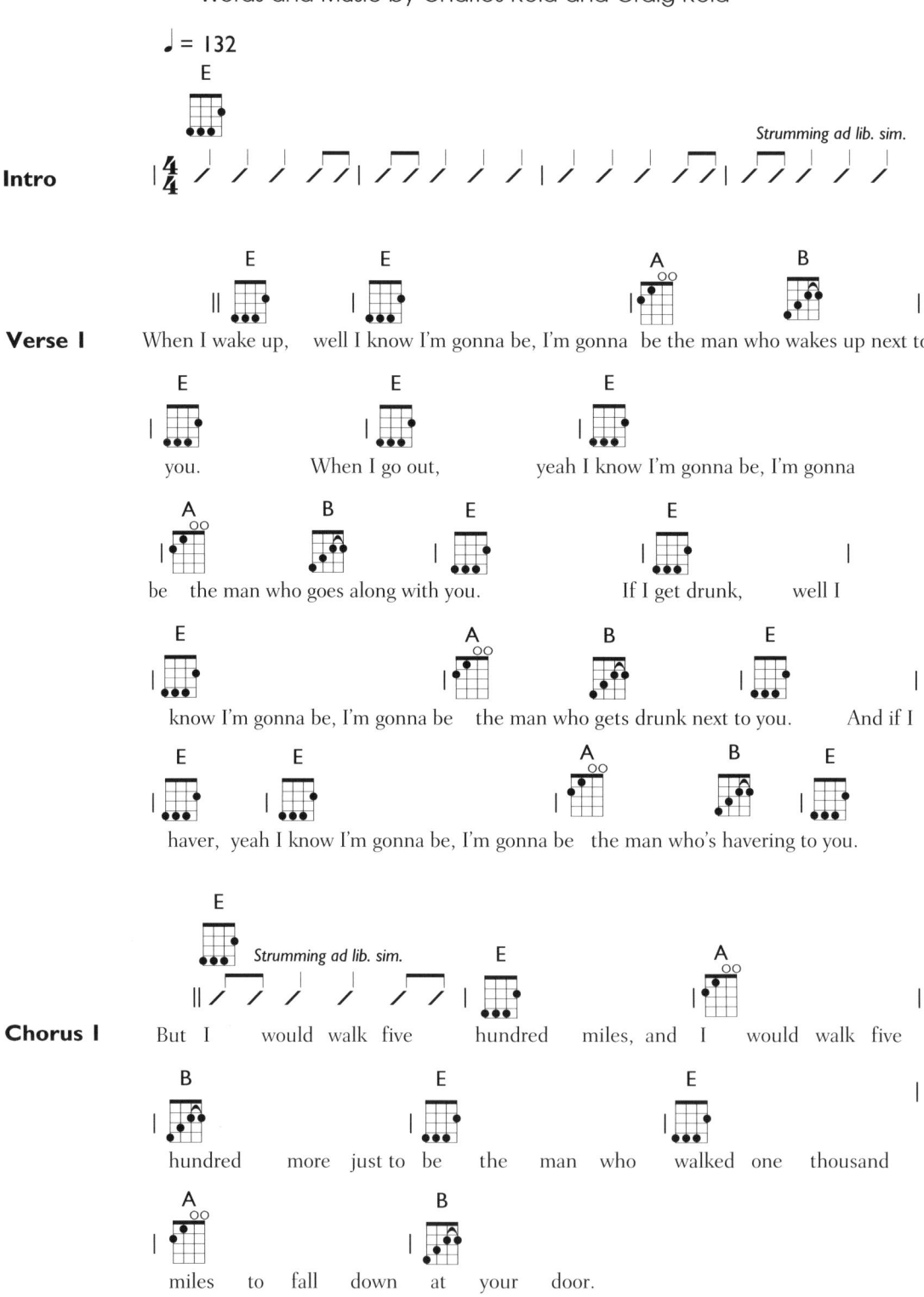

Verse 2

Strumming as per verse 1

When I'm working, [E] yes I know I'm gonna be, [E] I'm gonna be [A] the man who's working [B] hard for [E] you. And when the money [E] comes in for the work I do, [E] I'll pass almost [A] every penny [B] on to [E] you. When I come home, [E] *when I come home,* [E] oh I know I'm gonna be, I'm gonna be [A] the man who comes [B] back home to [E] you. And if I grow old, [E] well I know I'm gonna be, [E] I'm gonna be [A] the man who's [B] growing old with [E] you.

Chorus 2   *As Chorus 1*

Mid-Section 1

Strumming ad lib. sim.

[E] Da da lat da, *da da lat da,* [E] da da lat da, *da da lat da,* da da [A] la da da la, [B] da da la, [E] da da la da da. [E] Da da lat da, *da da lat da,* da da lat [E] da, *da da lat da,* [A] da da la [B] da da la, da da la, [E] da da la da da.

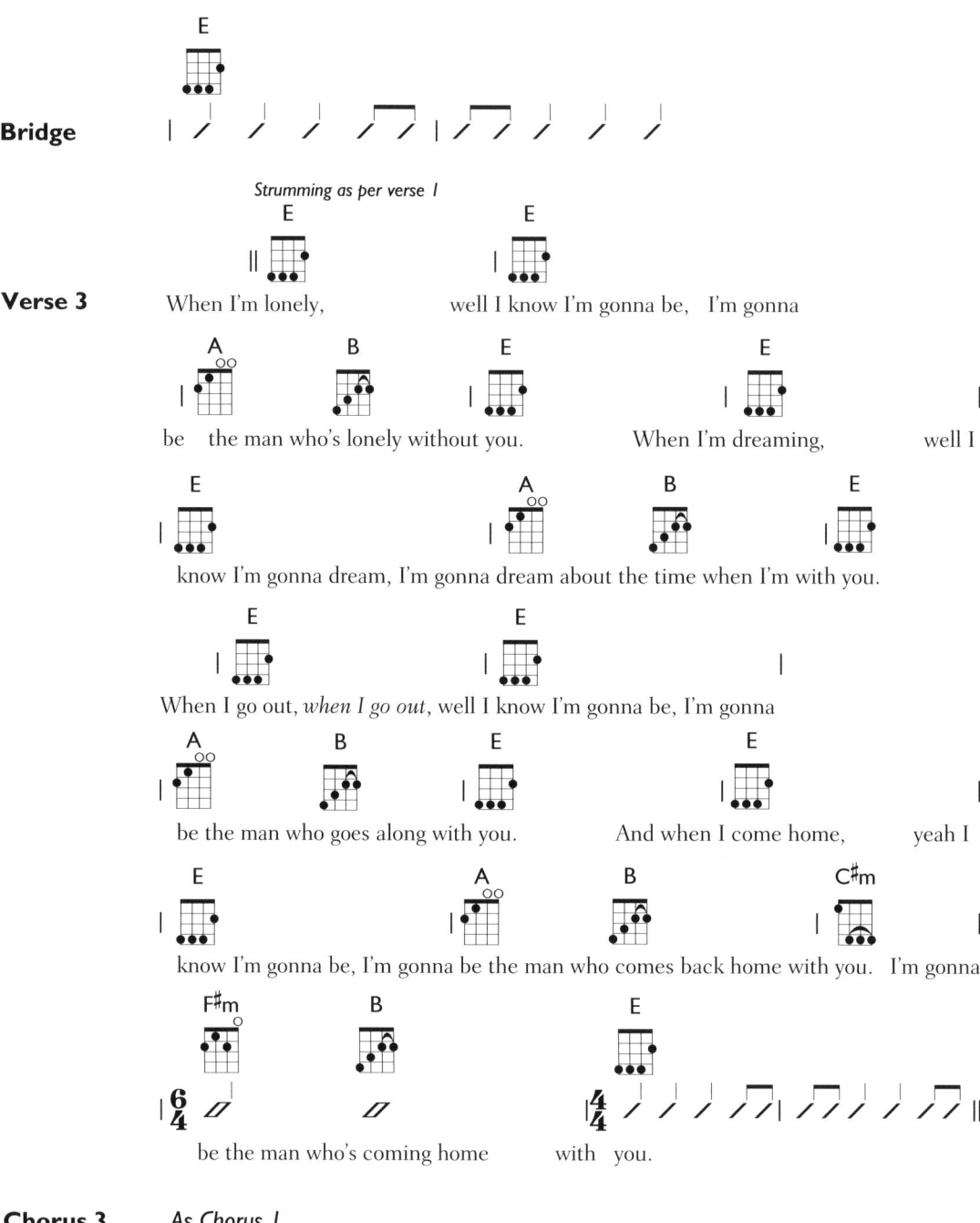

Judy Garland

It's A Long Way To Tipperary
Words and Music by Jack Judge and Harry Williams

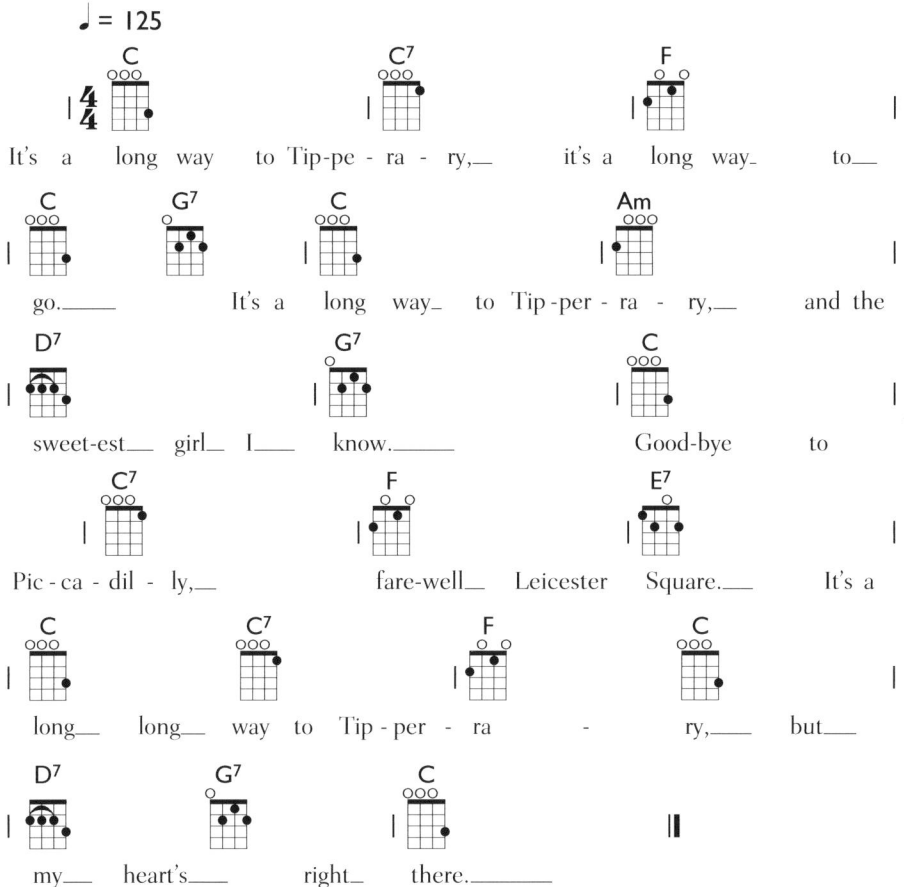

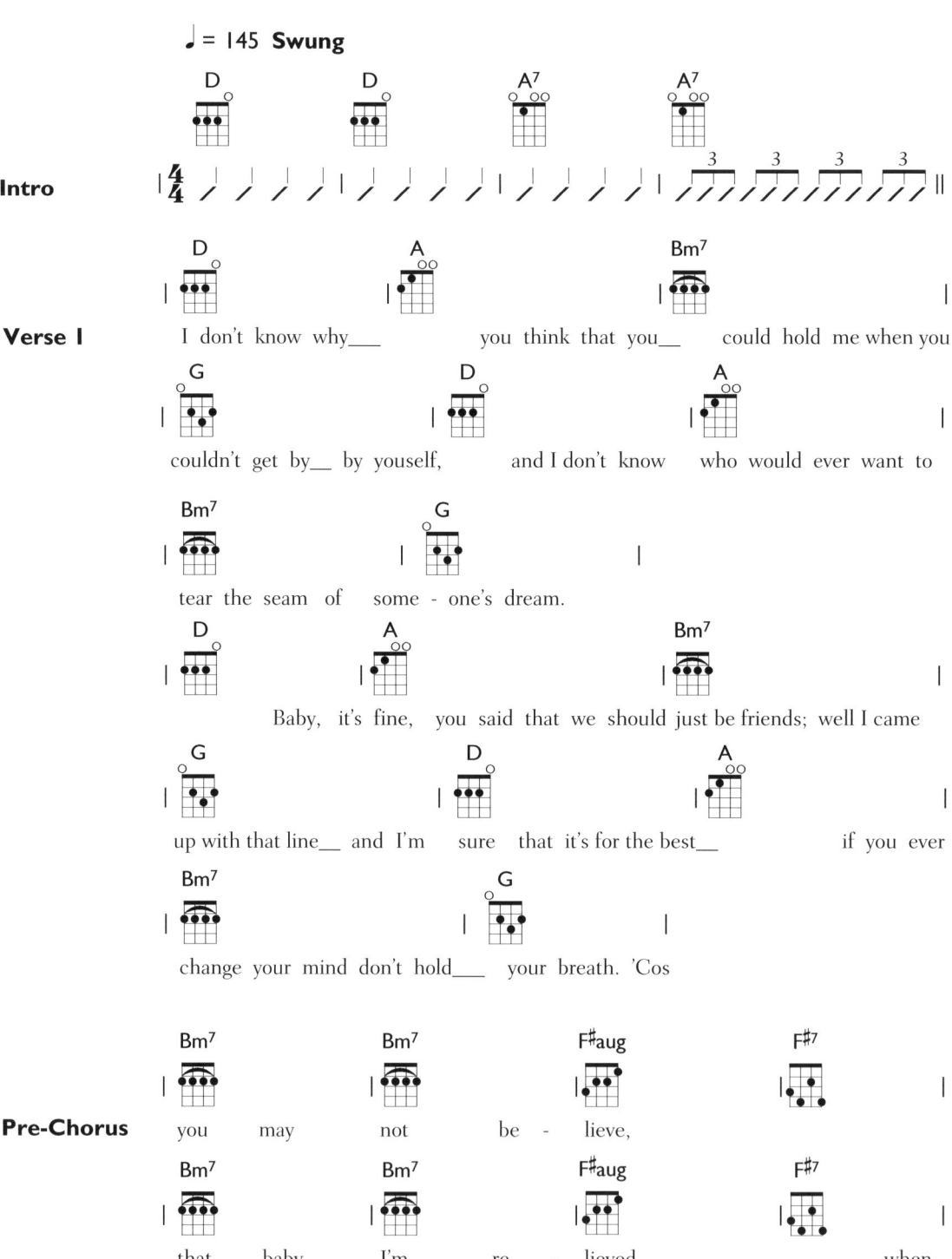

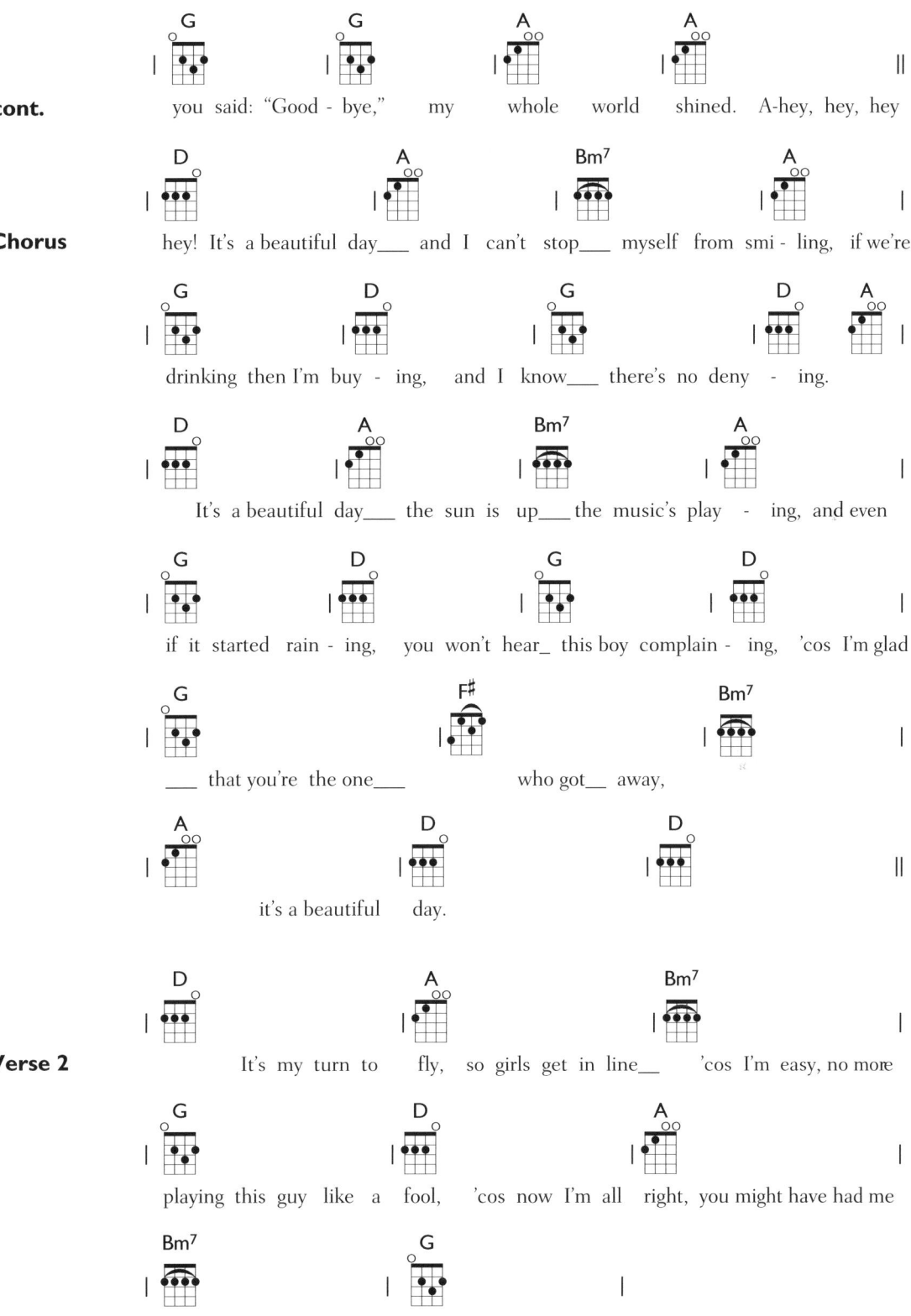

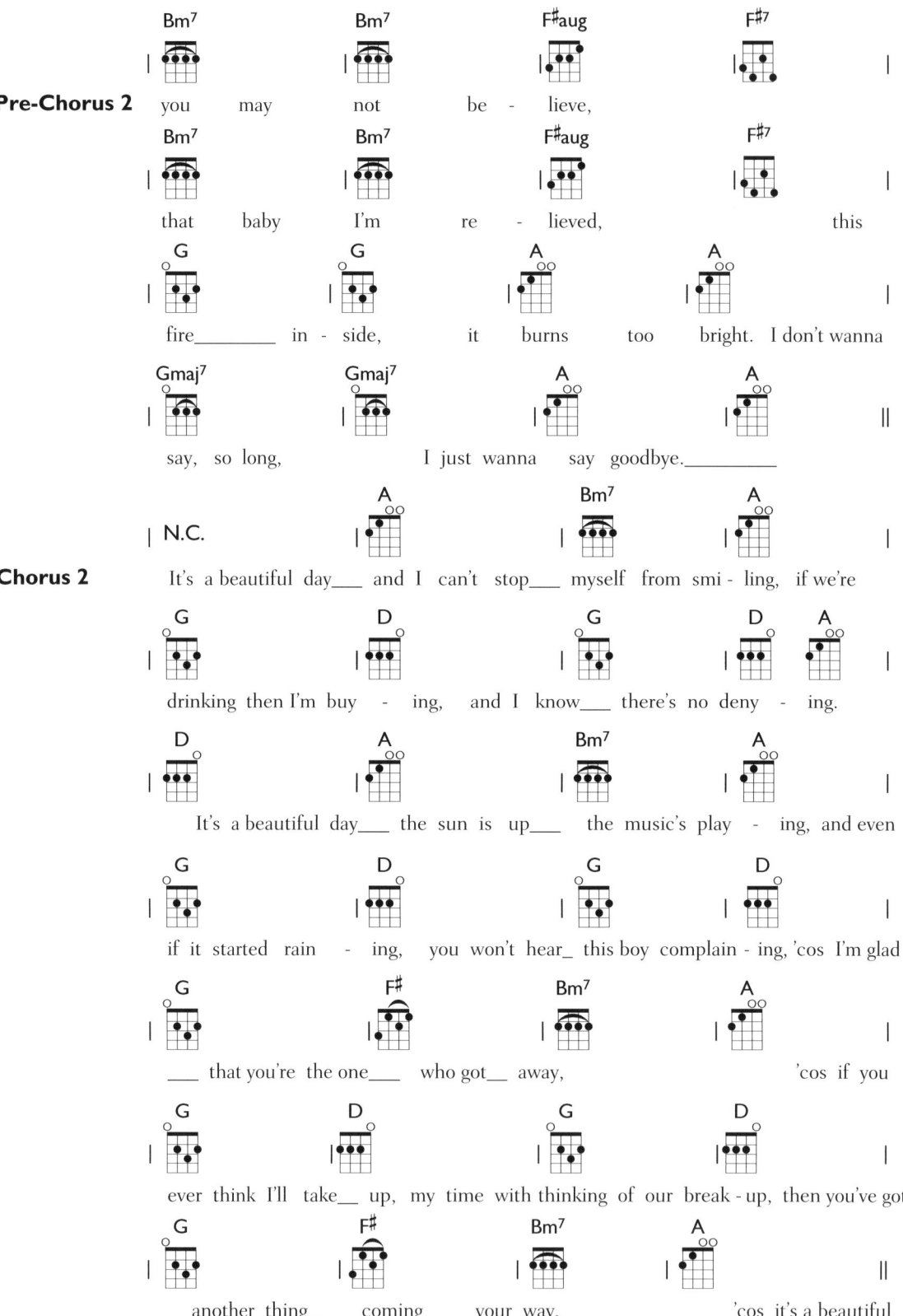

Outro

D	A	Bm7	G	
day.			Beautiful	

D	A	Bm7	
day.	Oh baby any day that you're	gone away,	

G Em7 A7	D	
it's a beau - ti - ful	day.	

Jingle bells

Words and Music by James Pierpont

Traditional

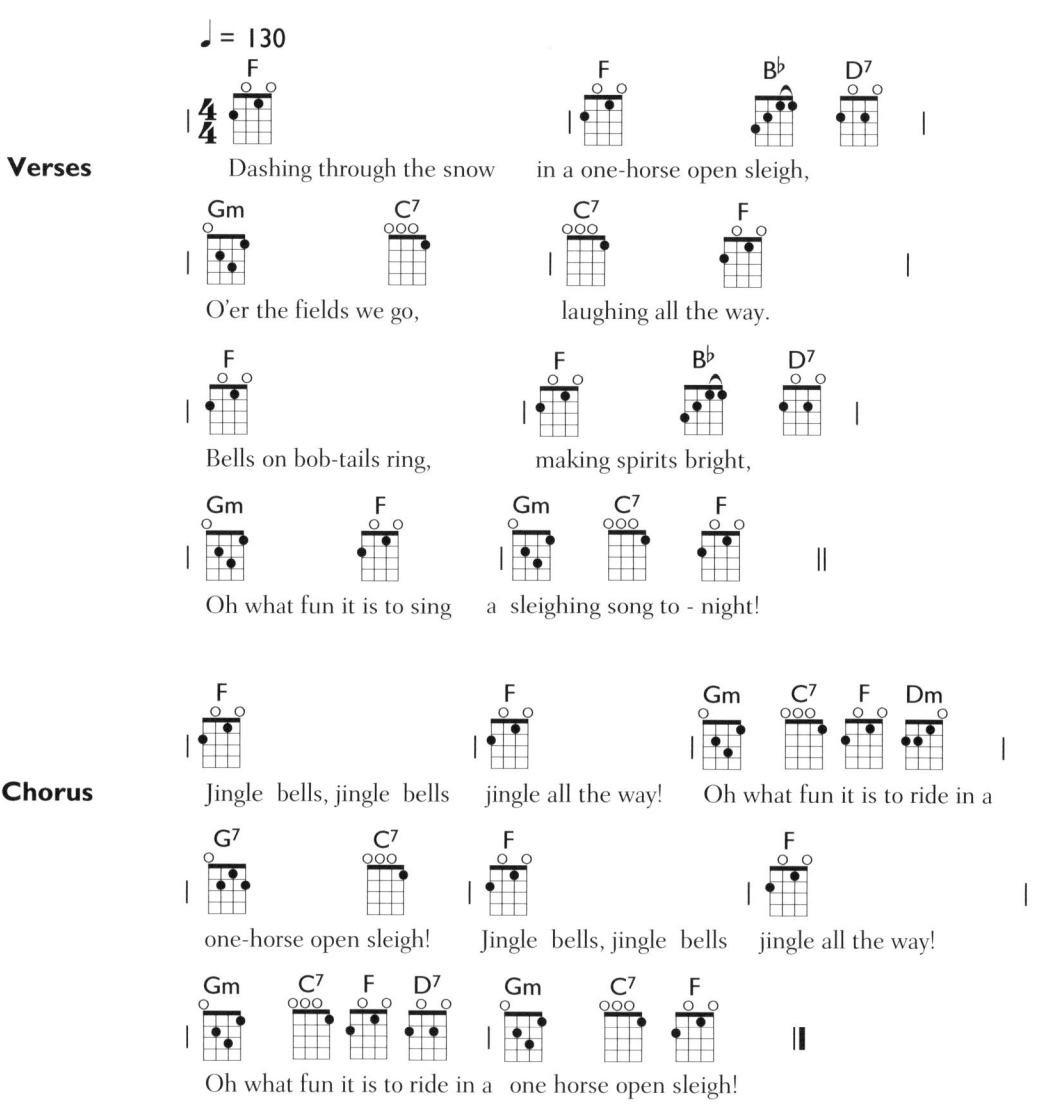

Verse 2

A day or two ago
I thought I'd take a ride
And soon, Miss Fanny Bride
Was seated by my side.
The horse was lean and lank
Misfortune seemed his lot
He got into a drifted bank
And then we got up sot!

Verse 3

A day or two ago,
The story I must tell
I went out on the snow
And on my back I fell
A gent was riding by
In a one-horse open sleigh
He laughed as there I sprawling lie,
But quickly drove away

Verse 4

Now the ground is white
Go it while you're young
Take the girls tonight
And sing this sleighing song
Just get a bob-tailed nag
Two forty as his speed
Hitch him to an open sleigh
And crack! You'll take the lead, oh...

© 2014 Faber Music Ltd
All Rights Reserved.

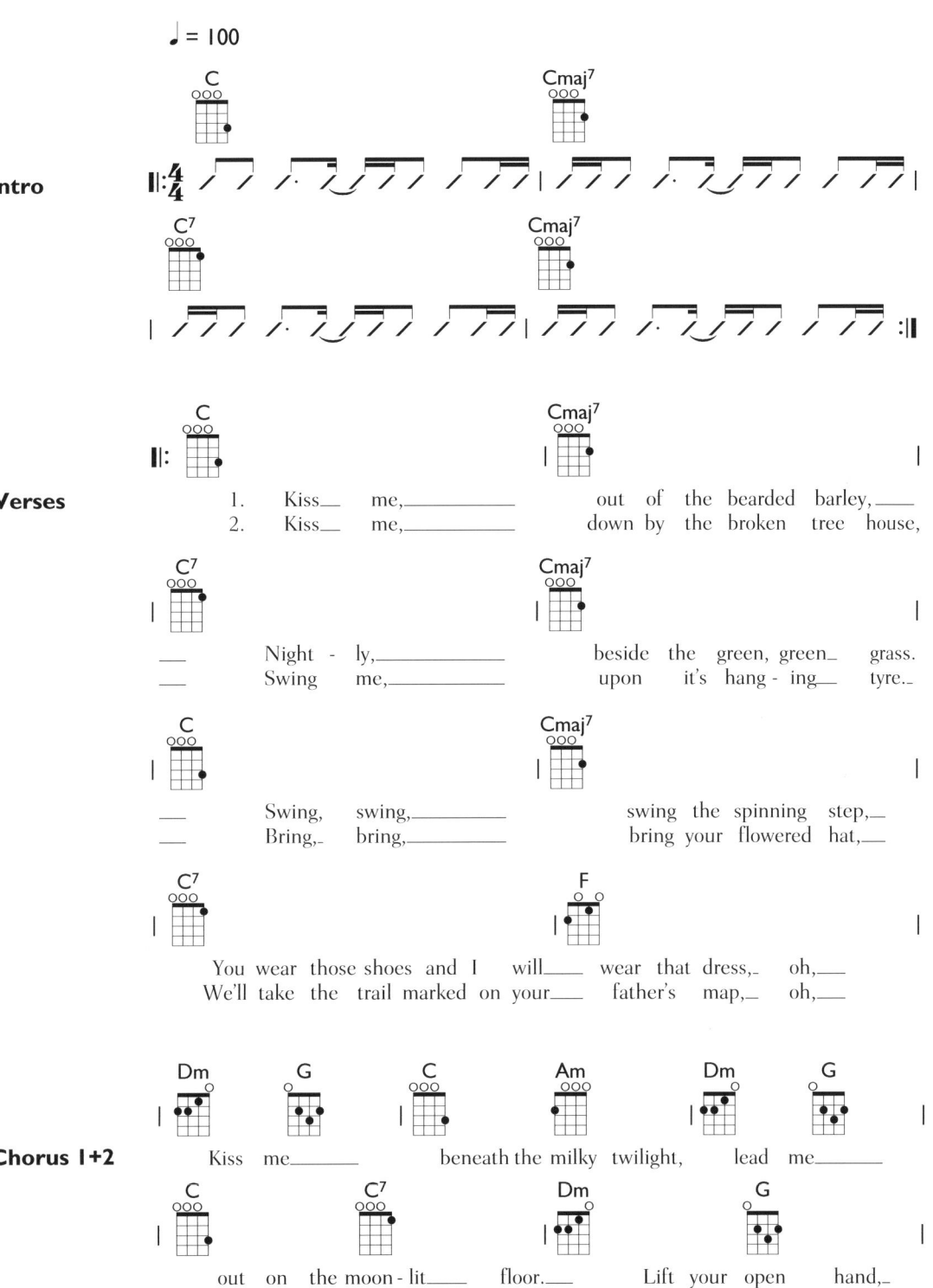

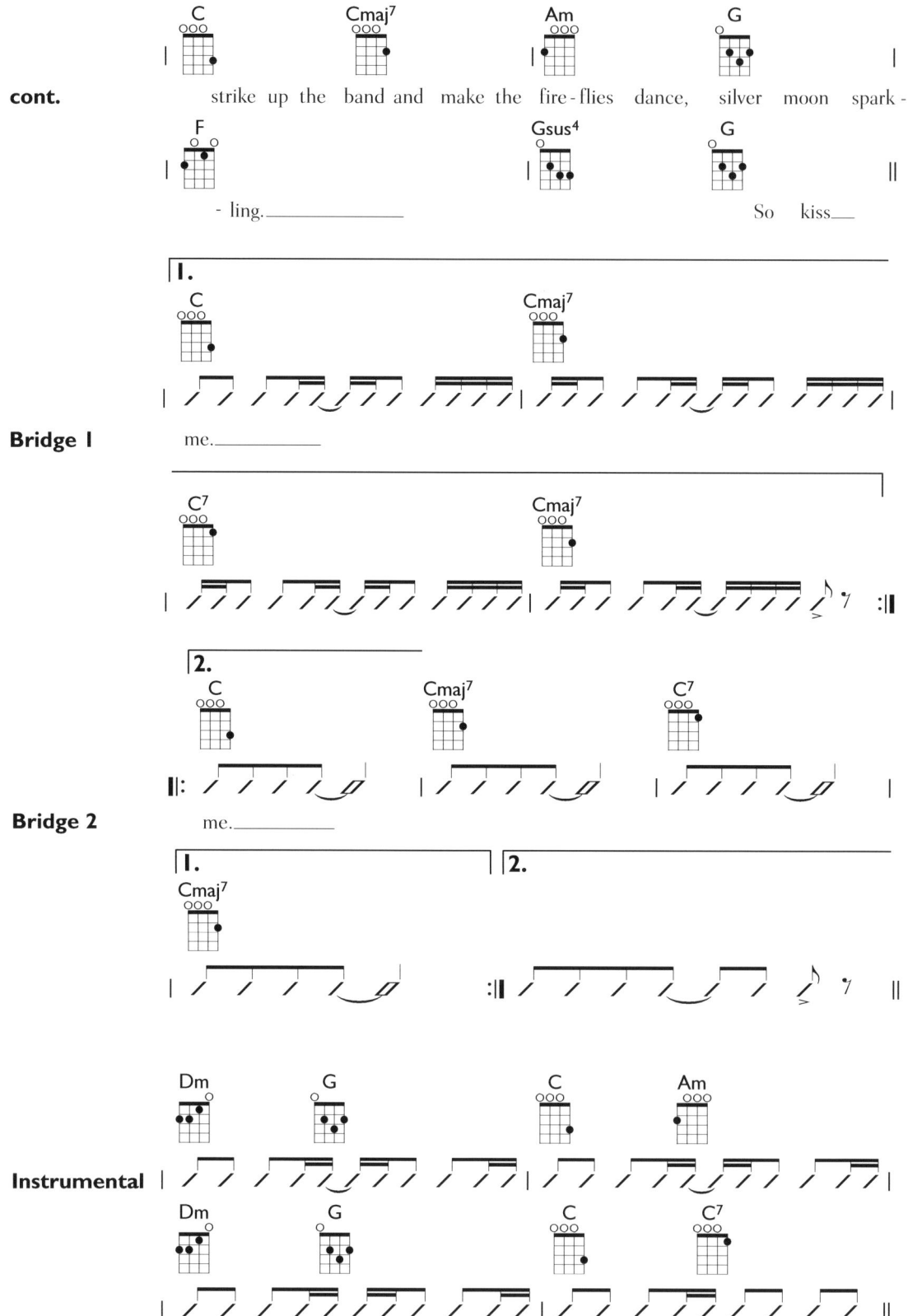

Kum Ba Yah

Words and Music Spiritual

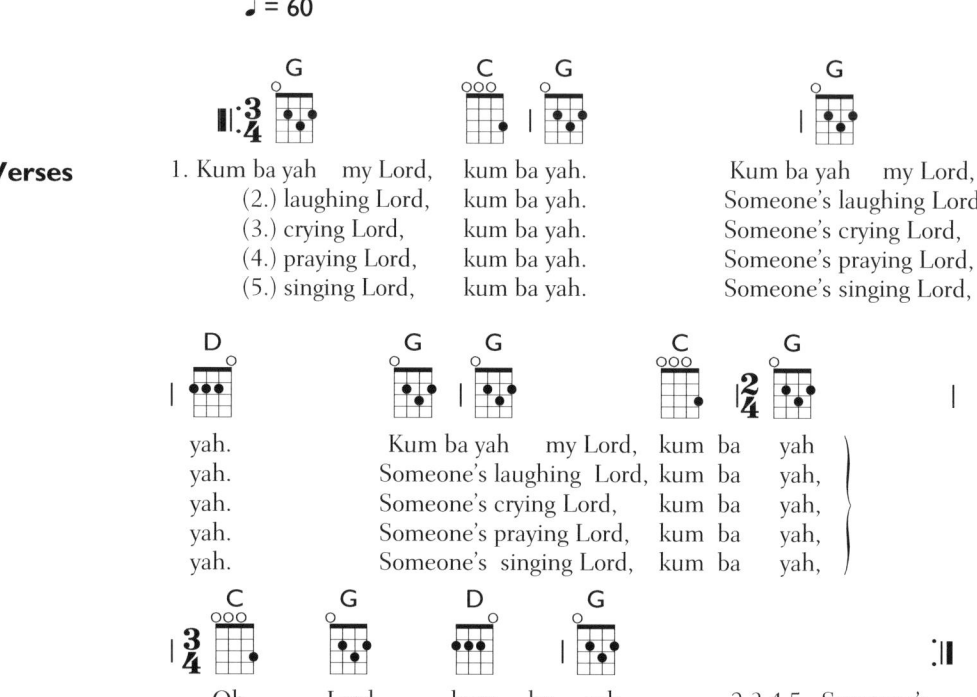

Spiritual

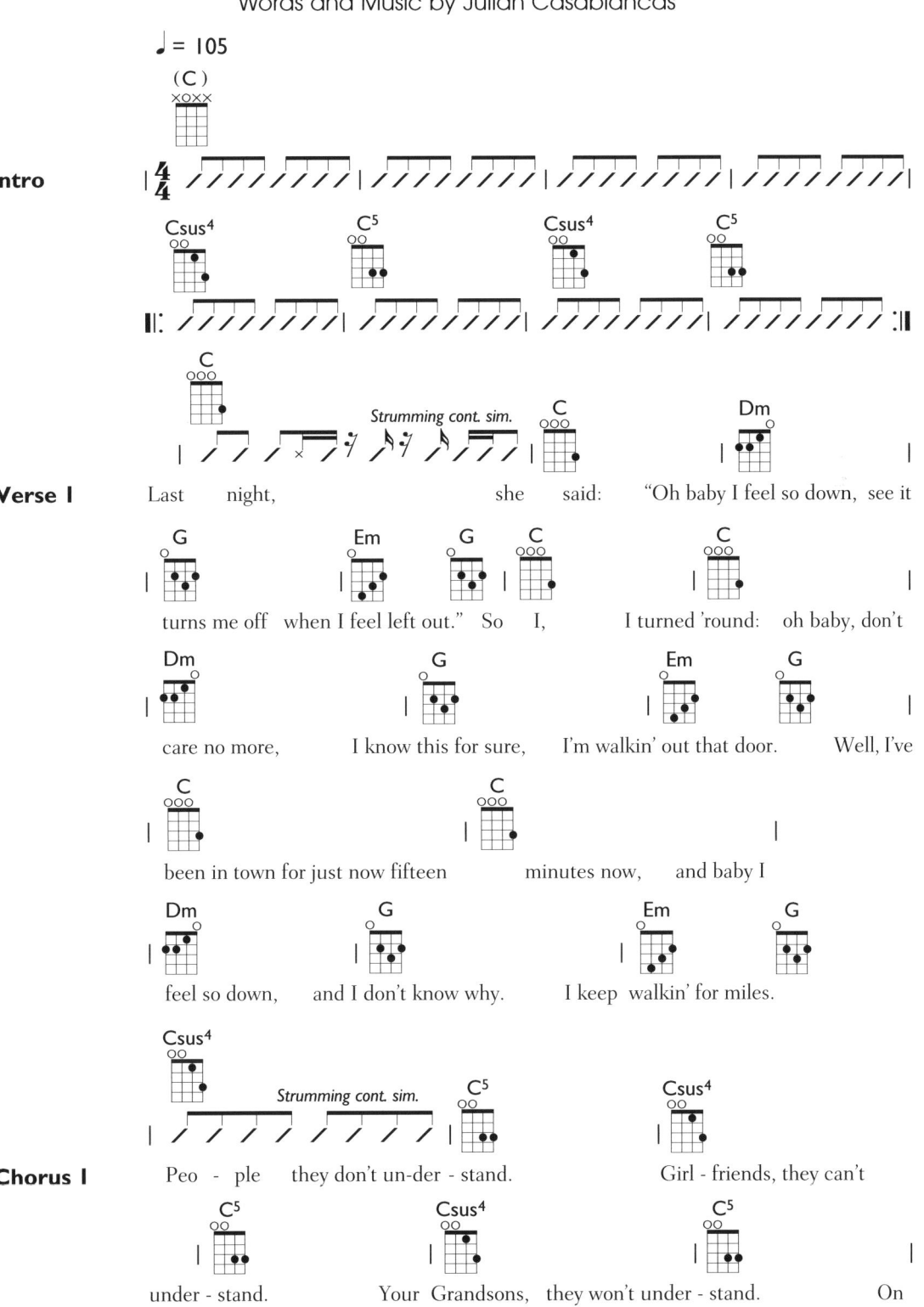

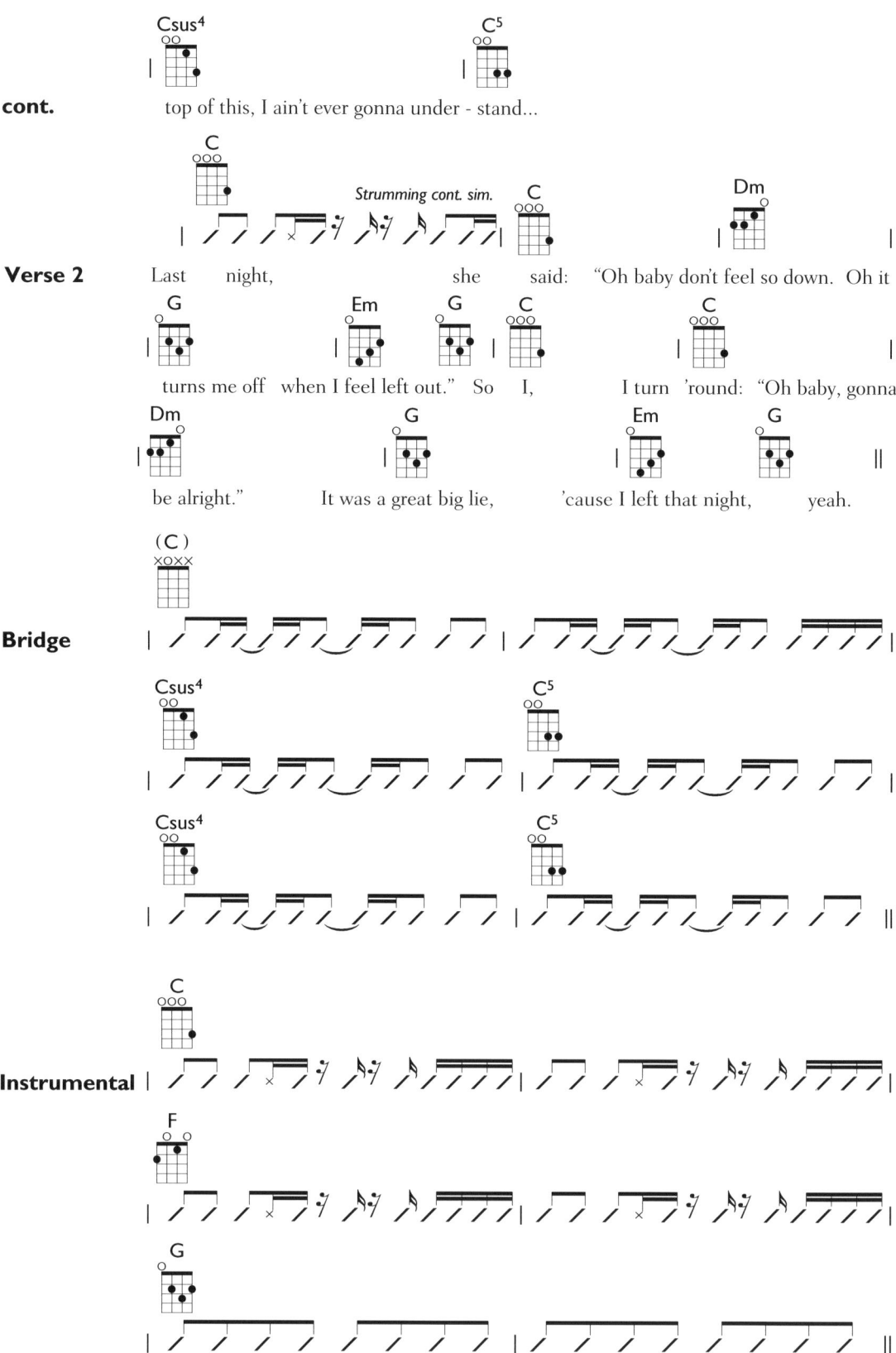

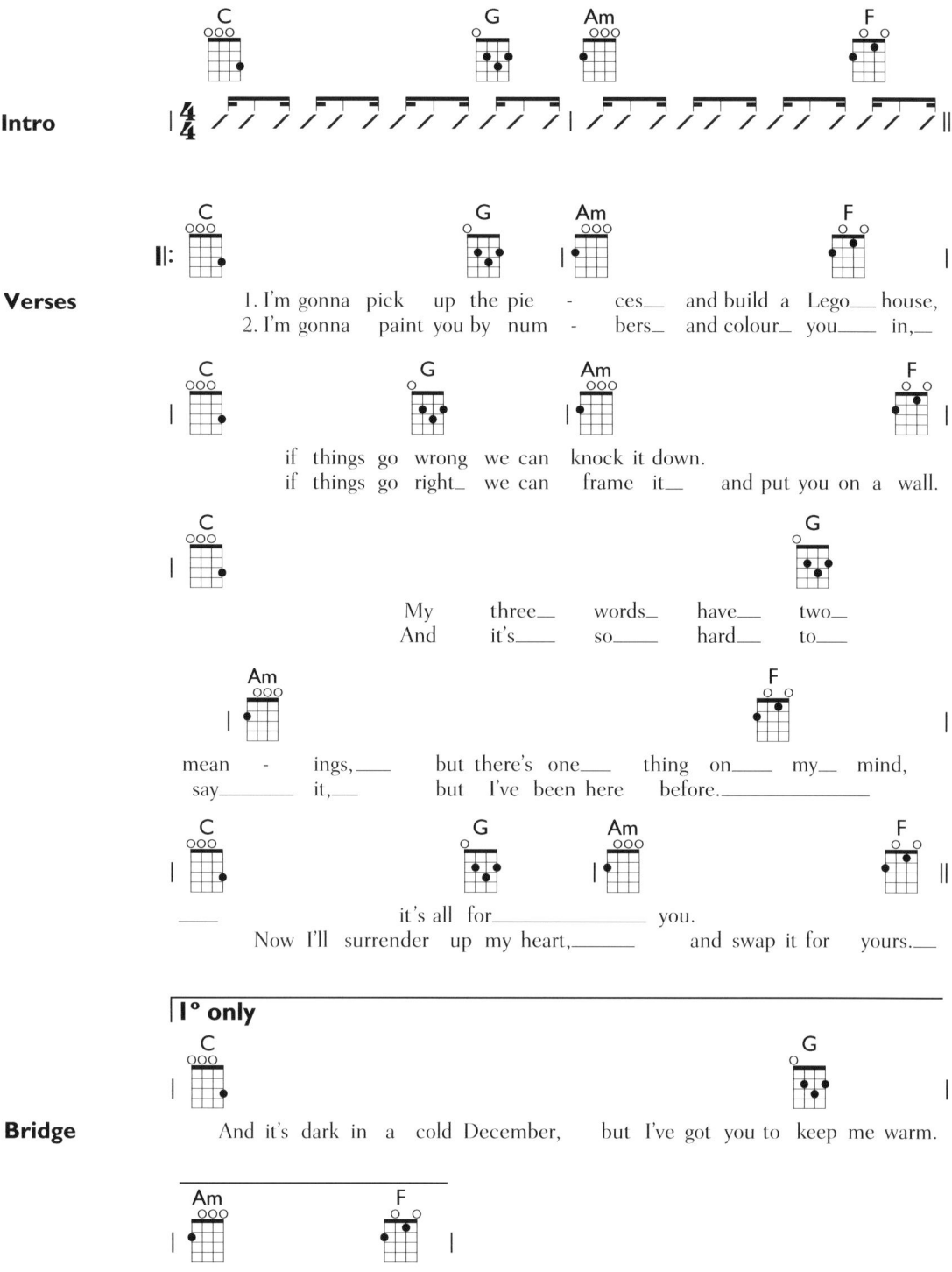

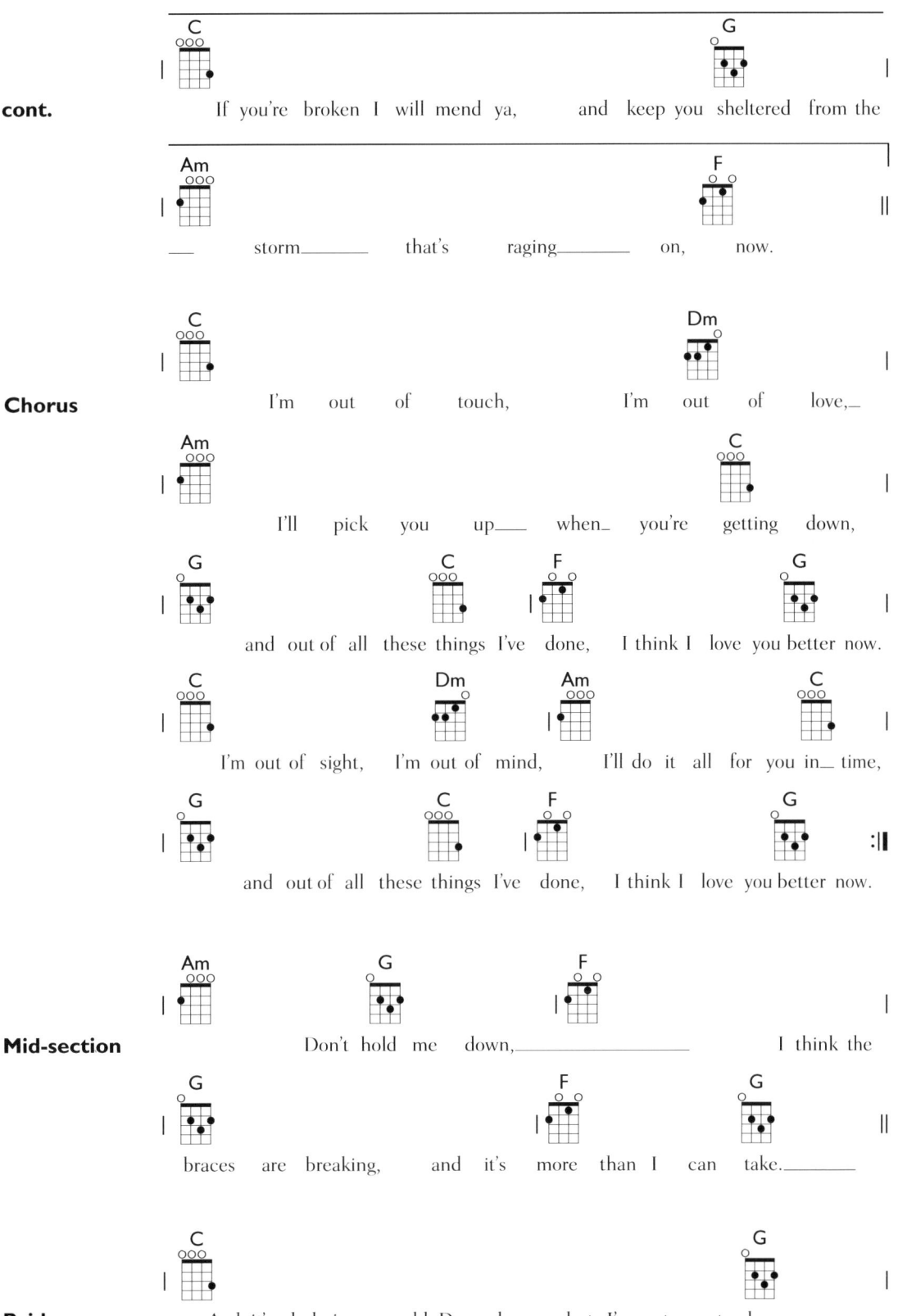

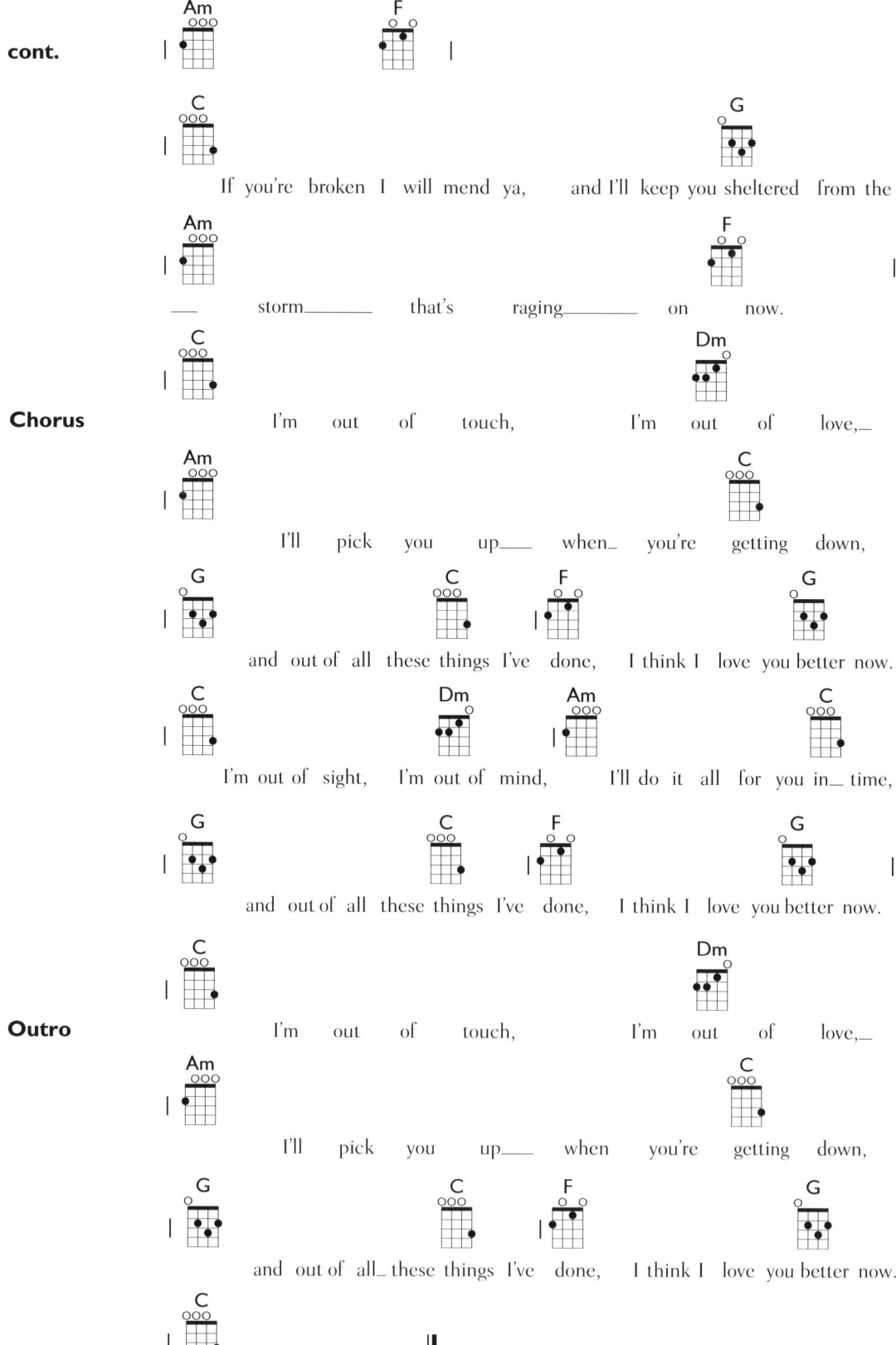

David Bowie

Life On Mars?
Words and Music by David Bowie

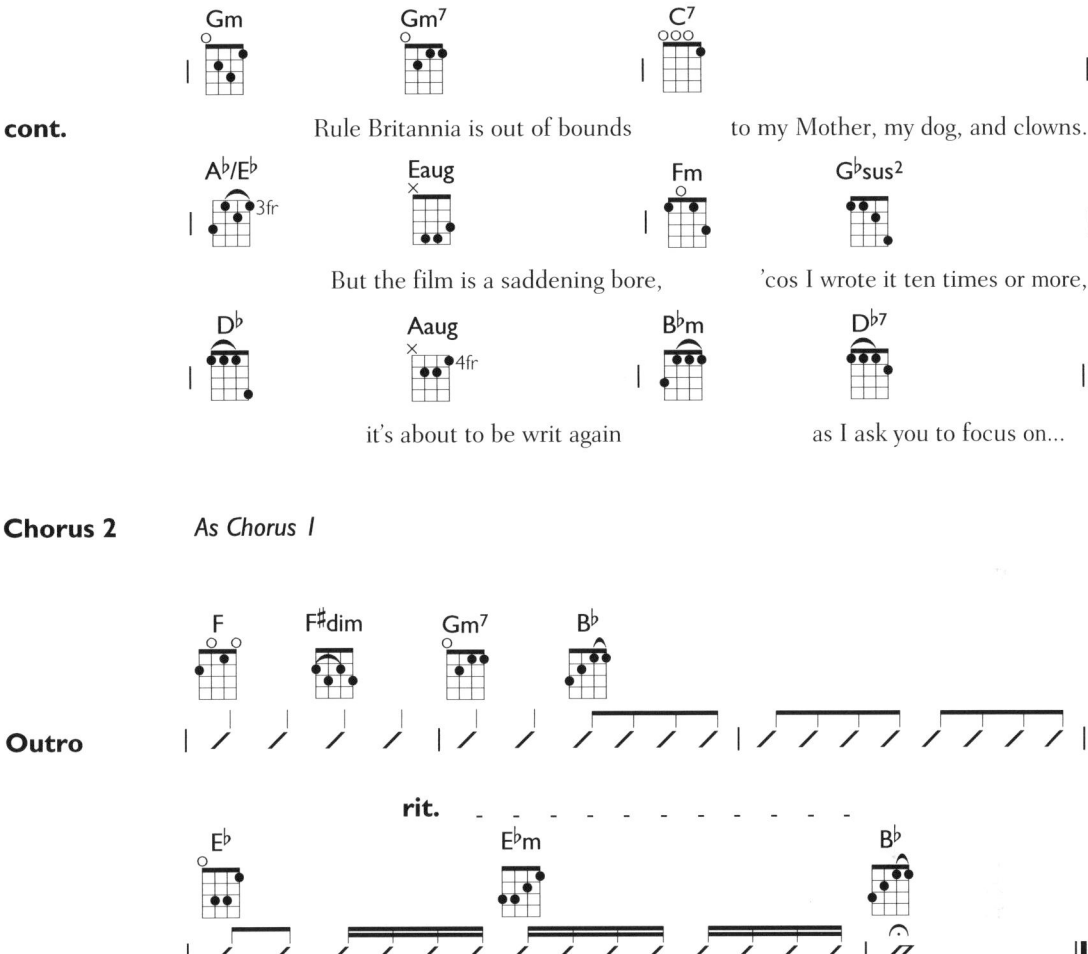

Let There Be Love

Nat 'King' Cole

Words and Music by Ian Grant and Lionel Rand

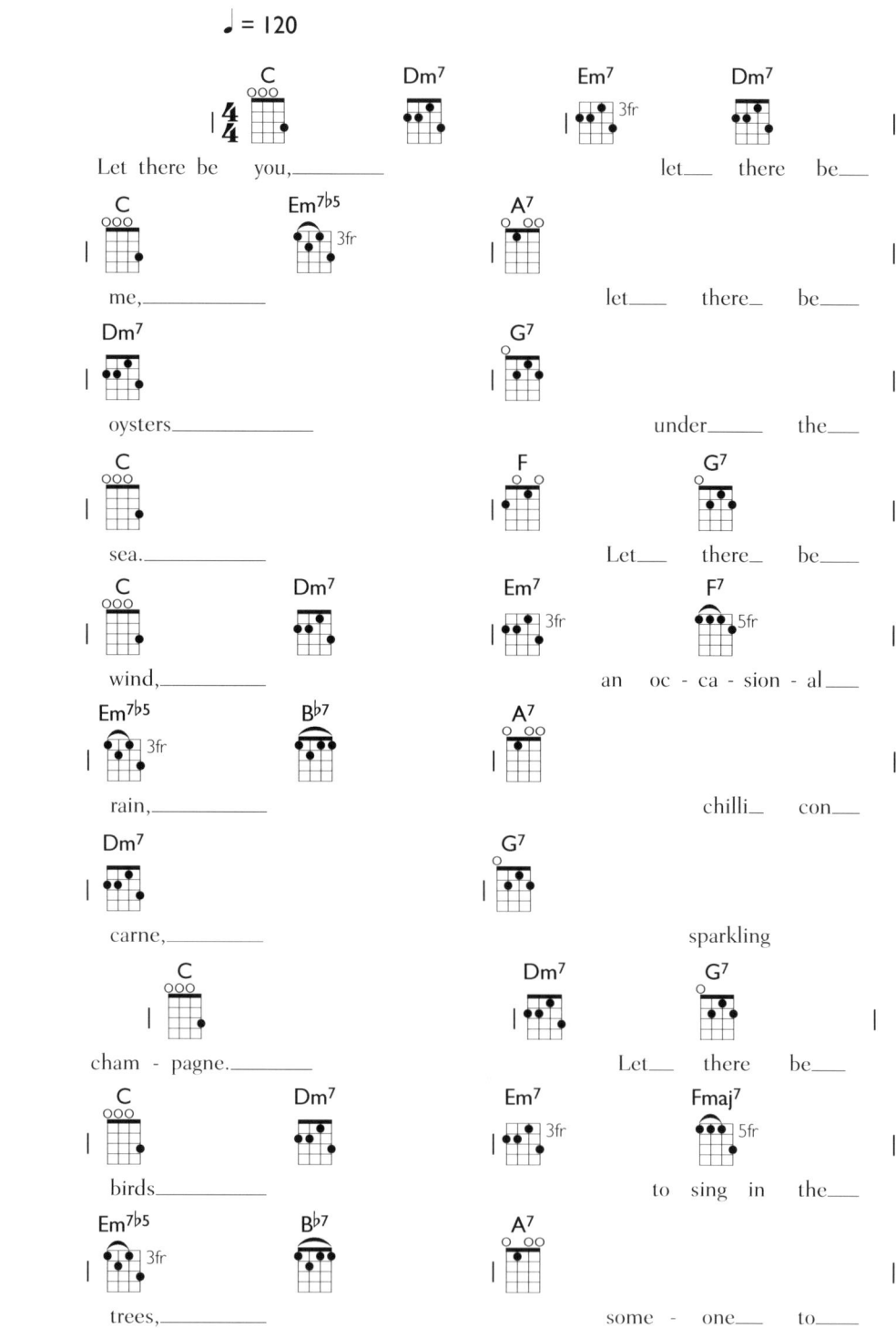

cont.

Dm7♭5		G7	D♭7	
bless me		when-ever	I	
C6	F7	C6	G7	
sneeze.		Let	there be	
C	Dm7	Em7		
cuckoos,			a lark and a	
A7	Em7	A7		
dove,		but first of all,		
Dm7		G7		
please		let there be		
C	F7	C	C	
love.				

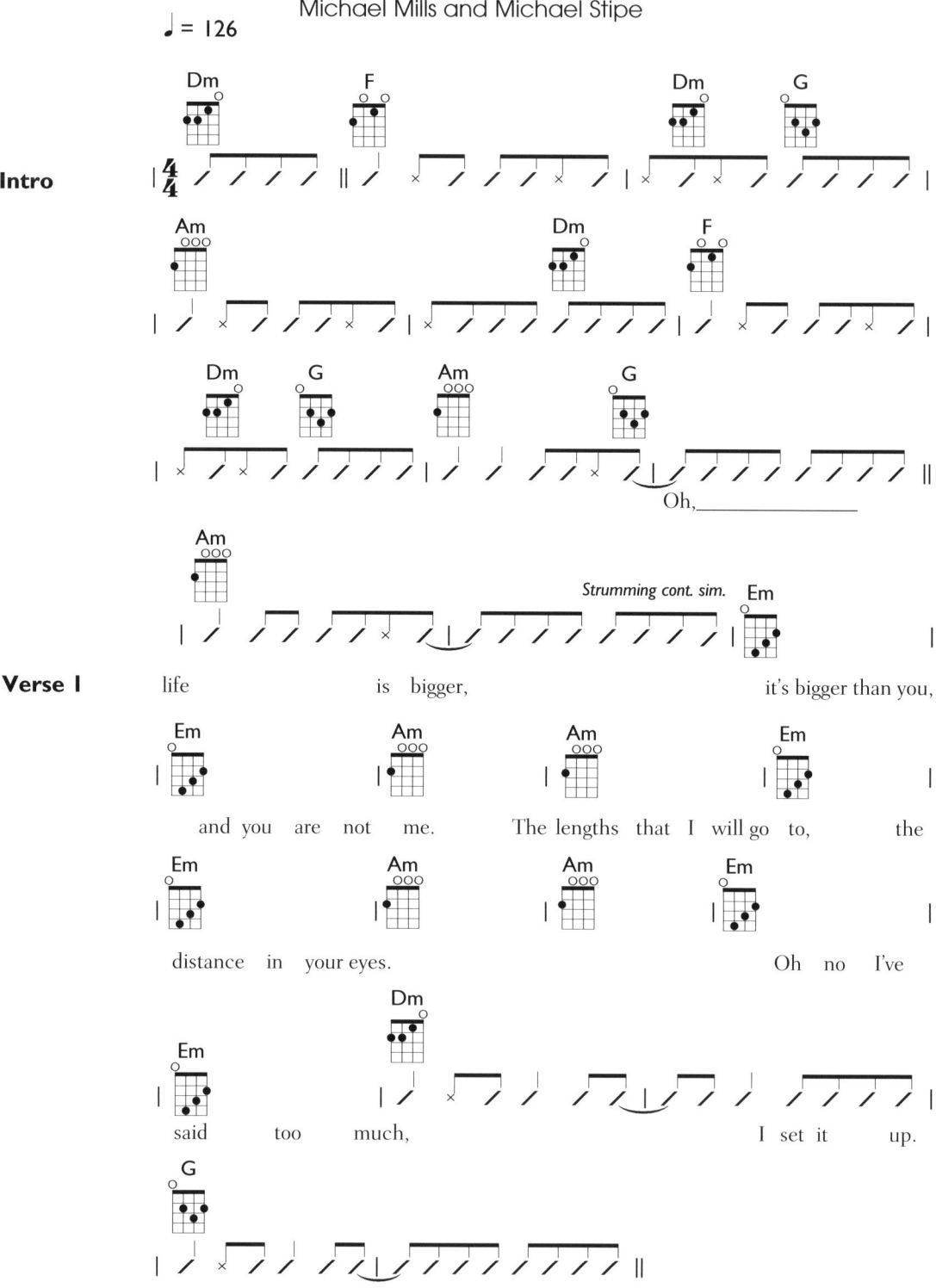

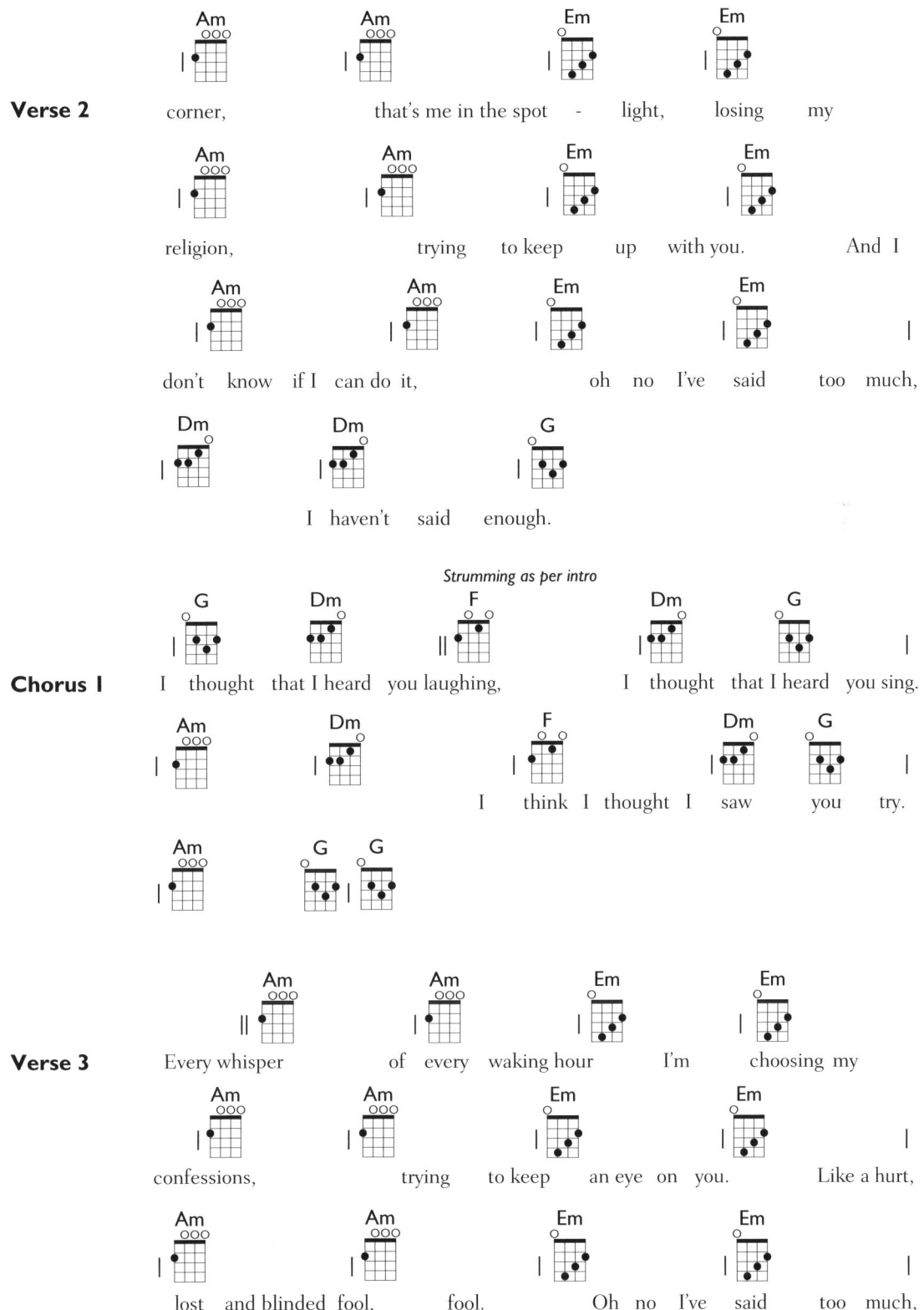

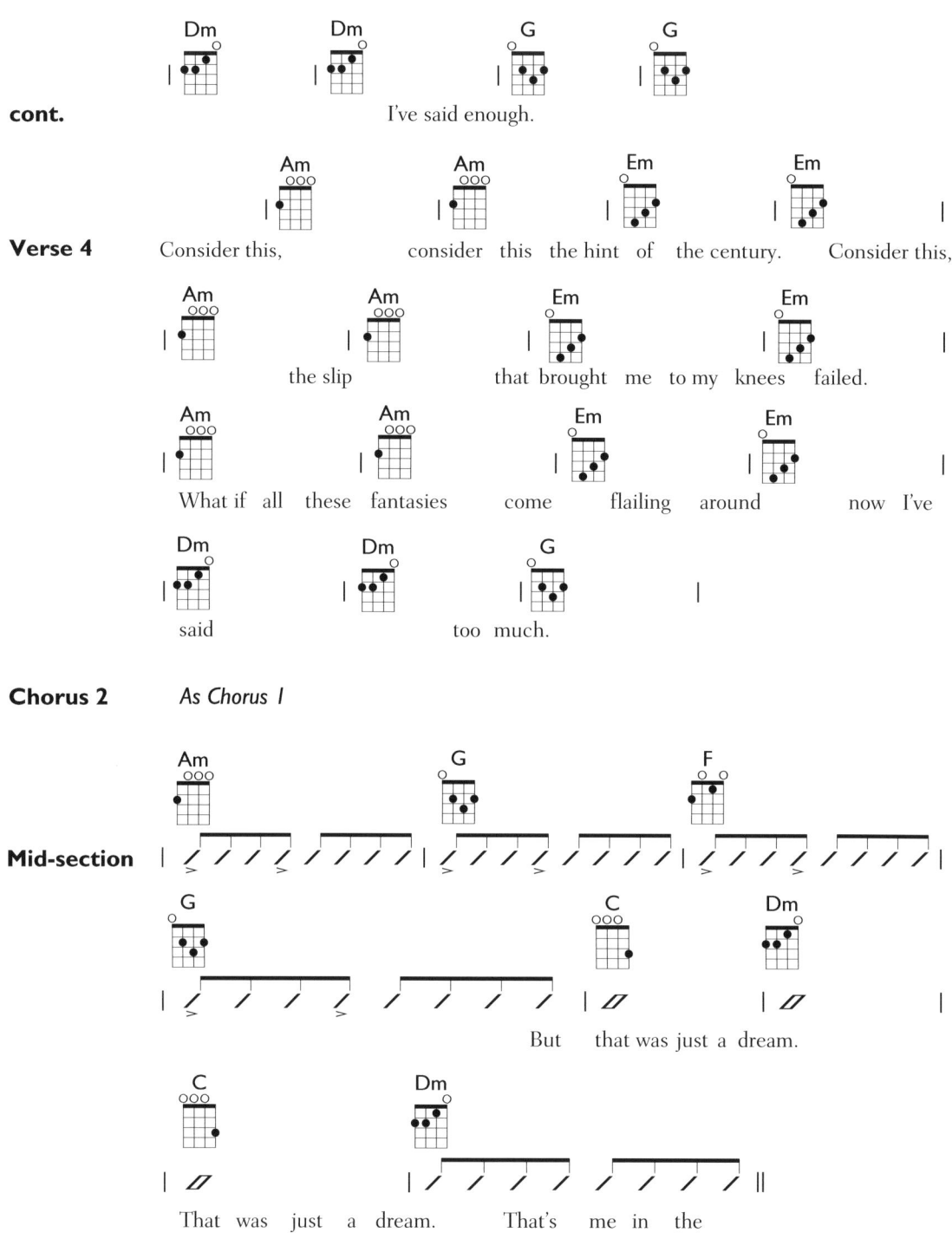

105

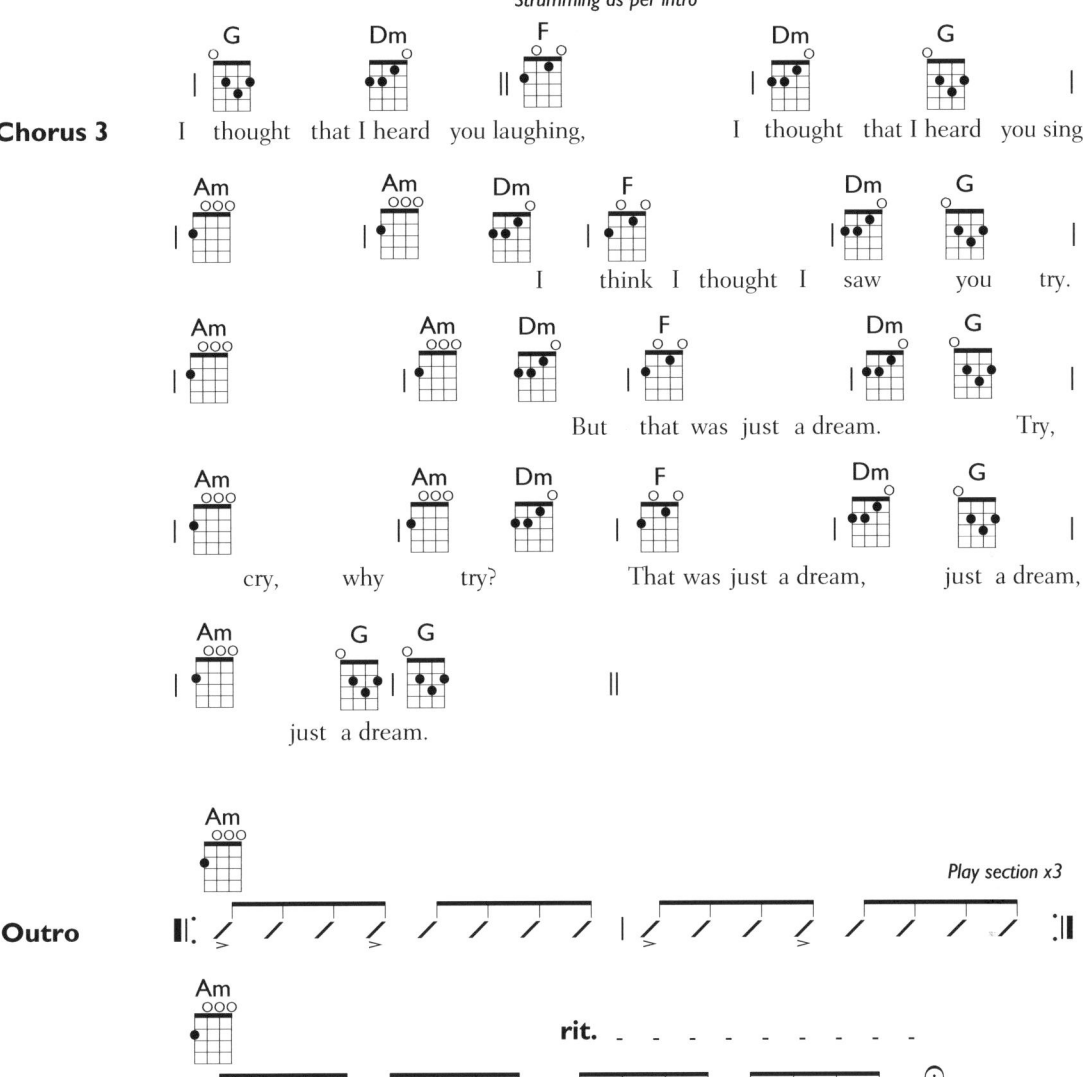

Traditional

Little Brown Jug
Words and Music by Joseph Winner

♩ = 100

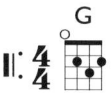   

Verses Me and my wife live all a-lone in a little log hut we call our own.

She loves gin and I love rum, and don't we have a lot of fun!

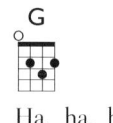

Chorus Ha, ha, ha, you and me, Little brown jug, don't I love thee!

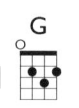 

Ha, ha, ha, you and me, Little brown jug, don't I love thee!

Verse 2

When I go toiling on the farm
I take the little jug under my arm
Place it under a shady tree
Little brown jug, 'tis you and me

Verse 3

'Tis you that makes me friends and foes
'Tis you that makes me wear old clothes
But, seeing you're so near my nose
Tip her up and down she goes

Verse 4

If all the folks in Adam's race
Were gathered together in one place
I'd let them go without a tear
Before I'd part from you, my dear

Verse 5

If I'd a cow that gave such milk
I'd dress her in the finest silk
Feed her up on oats and hay
And milk her twenty times a day

Verse 6

I bought a cow from Farmer Jones
And she was nothing but skin and bones
I fed her up as fine as silk
She jumped the fence and strained her milk

Verse 7

And when I die don't bury me at all
Just pickle my bones in alcohol
Put a bottle o' booze at my head and feet
And then I know that I will keep...

Verse 8

The rose is red, my nose is too
The violet's blue and so are you
And yet, I guess, before I stop
We'd better take another drop

© 2014 Faber Music Ltd
All Rights Reserved.

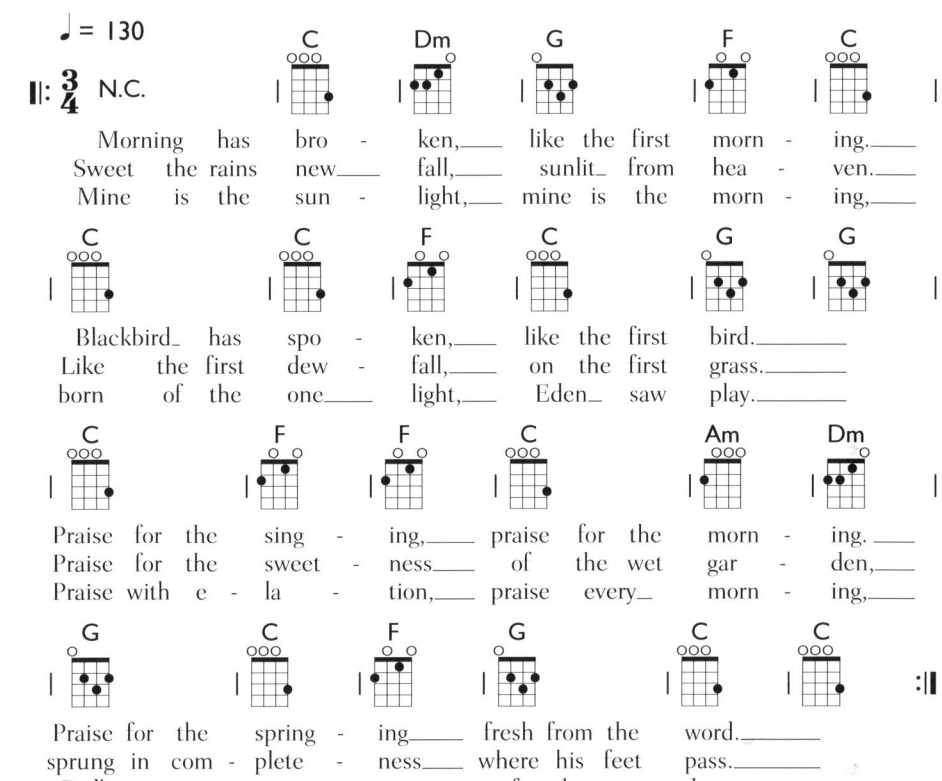

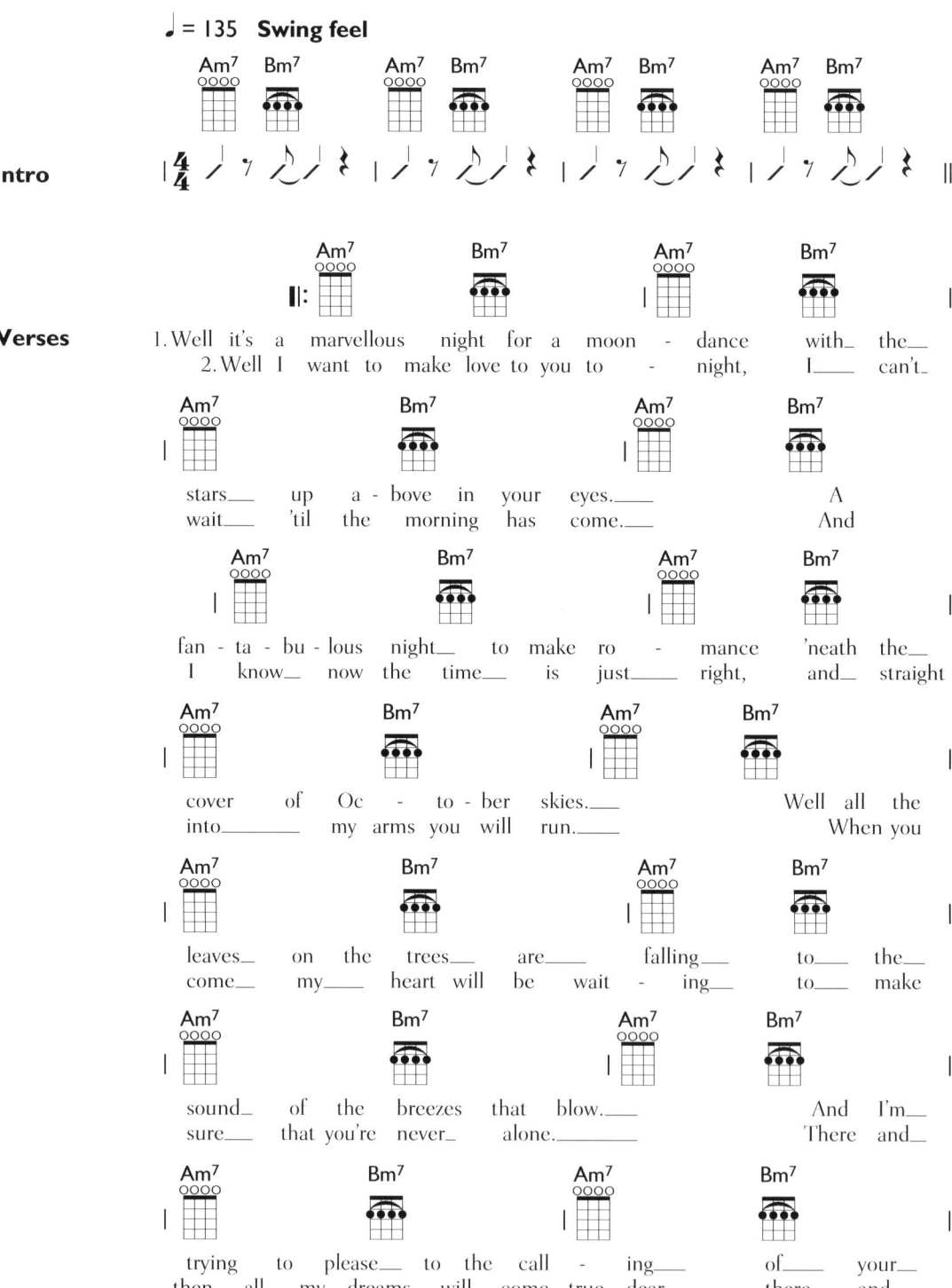

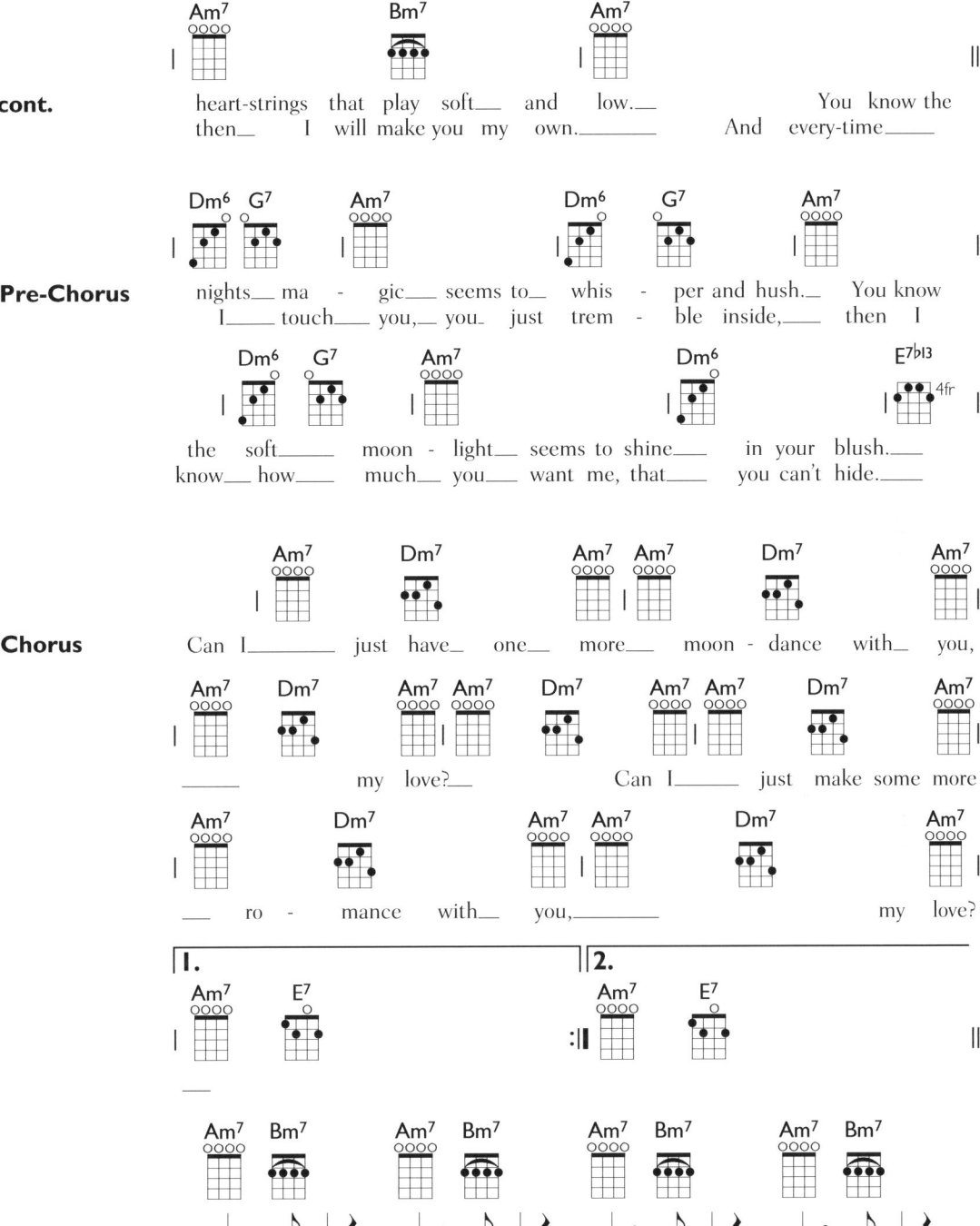

Traditional

My Grandfather's Clock
Words and Music Traditional

Verses

D	A	D	G

1. My grand-father's clock was too large for the shelf, so it
2. In watch-ing its pendulum swing to and fro, many

D	A	D	

stood nine-ty years on the floor. It was
years had he spent while a boy. And in

D	A	D	G

tal - ler by half than the old man him-self, though it
child - hood and man - hood the clock seemed to know and to

D	A	D	

weighed not a pen-ny-weight more. It was
share both his grief and his joy. For it

D		G	D

bought on the morn of the day that he was born, and was
struck twen-ty-four when he entered at the door, with a

D	A		

al - ways his trea - sure and pride. ⎞ But it
bloom - ing and beau - ti - ful bride, ⎠

D	A	D	G

stopped, short, ne - ver to go a - gain when the

D	A	D	

old man died.

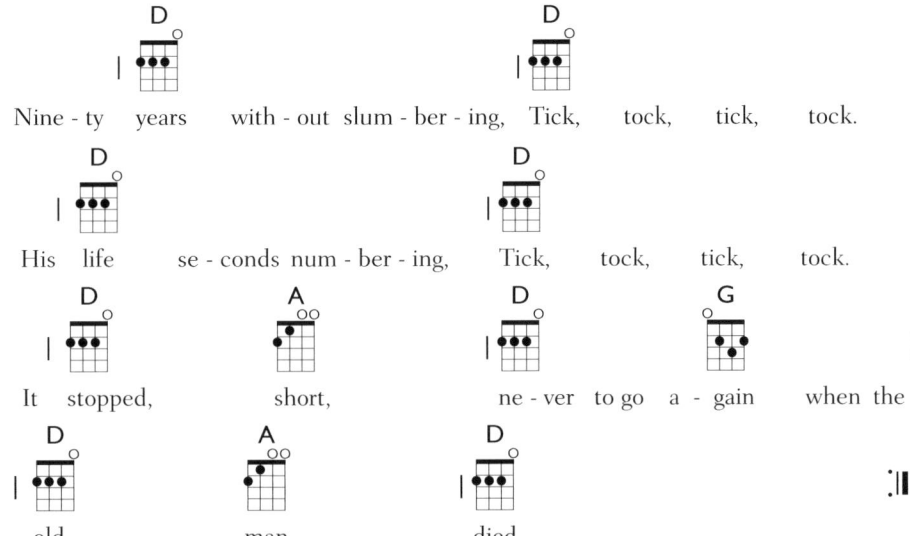

Chorus

Nine-ty years with-out slum-ber-ing, Tick, tock, tick, tock.
His life se-conds num-ber-ing, Tick, tock, tick, tock.
It stopped, short, ne-ver to go a-gain when the old man died.

Verse 3

My grandfather said that of those he could hire
Not a servant so faithful he found.
For it wasted no time and had but one desire
At the close of each week to be wound.
And it kept in its place, not a frown upon its face
And its hand never hung by its side,
But it stopped, short, never to go again
When the old man died.

Verse 4

It rang an alarm in the dead of the night
An alarm that for years had been dumb,
And we knew that his spirit was pluming for flight
That his hour of departure had come.
Still the clock kept the time with a soft and muffled chime
As we silently stood by his side,
But it stopped, short, never to go again
When the old man died.

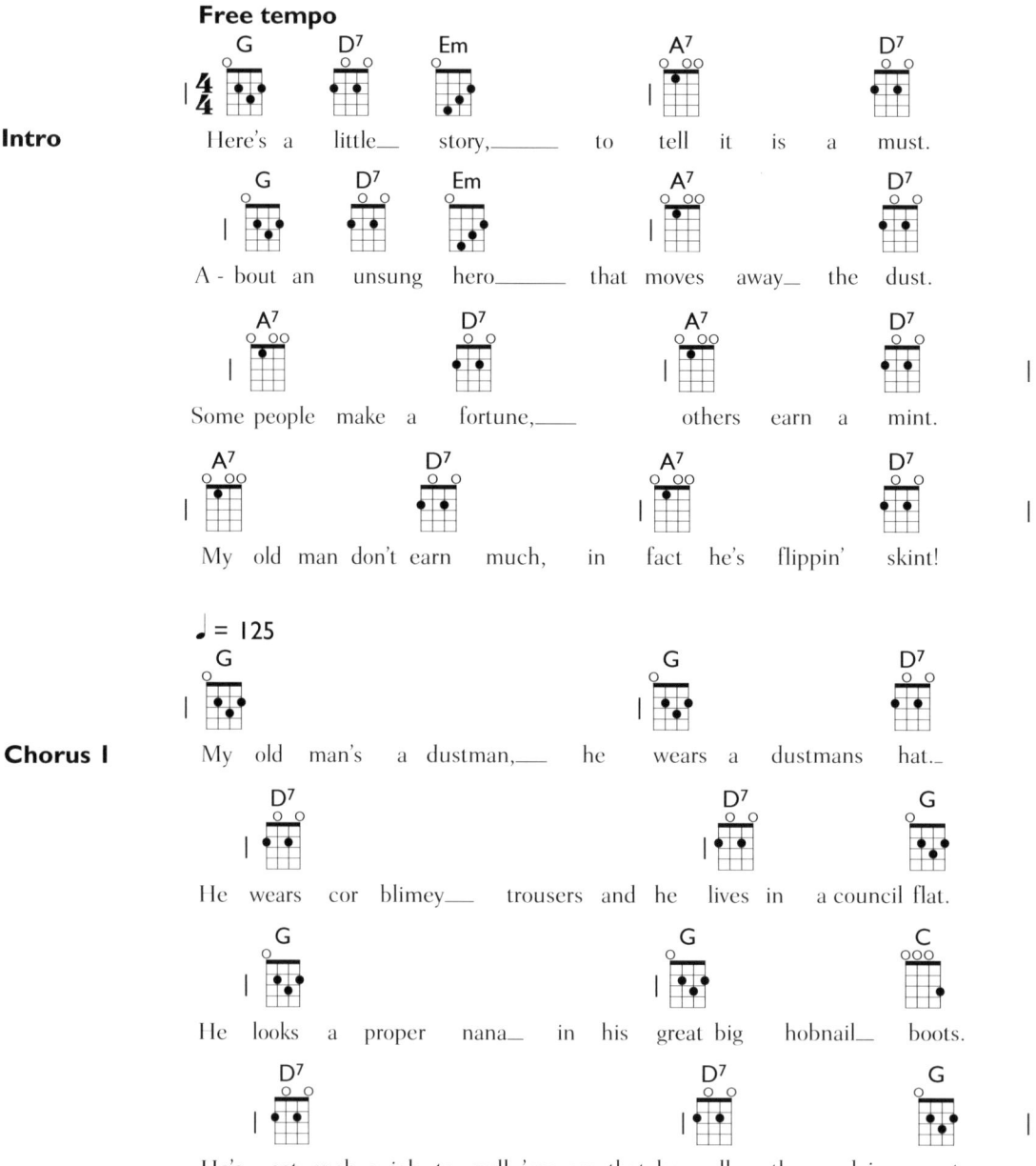

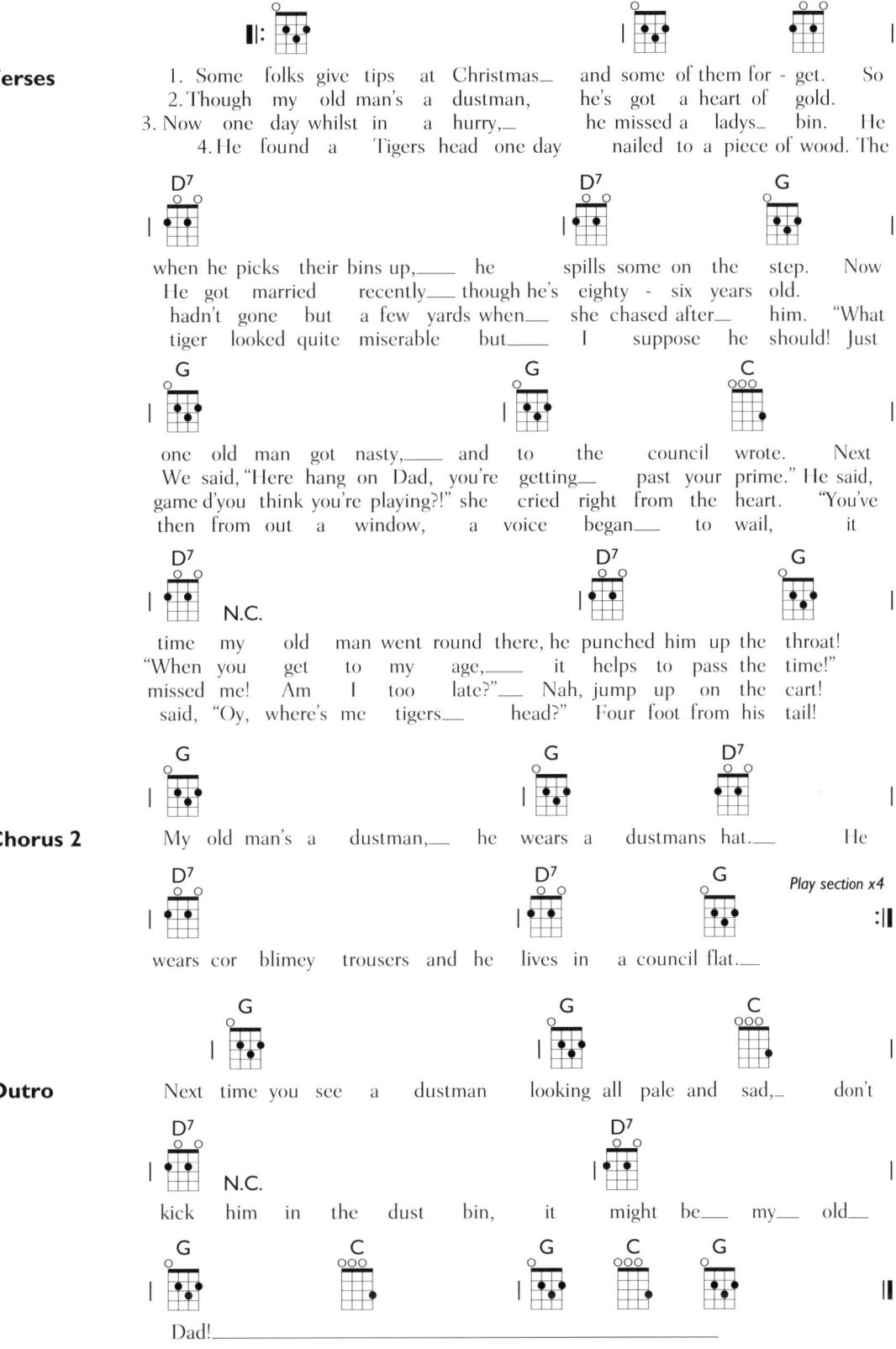

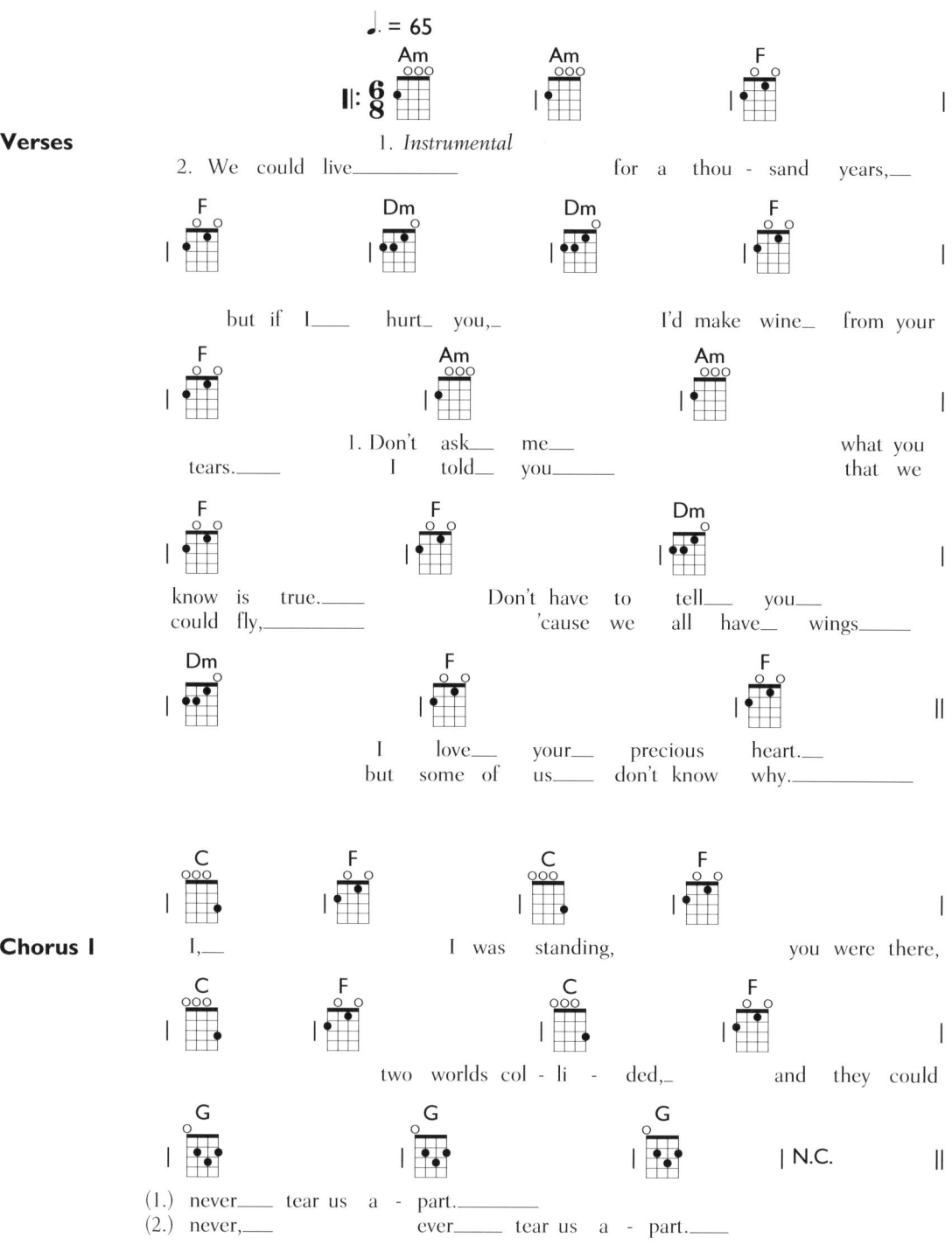

115

Bridge

Solo

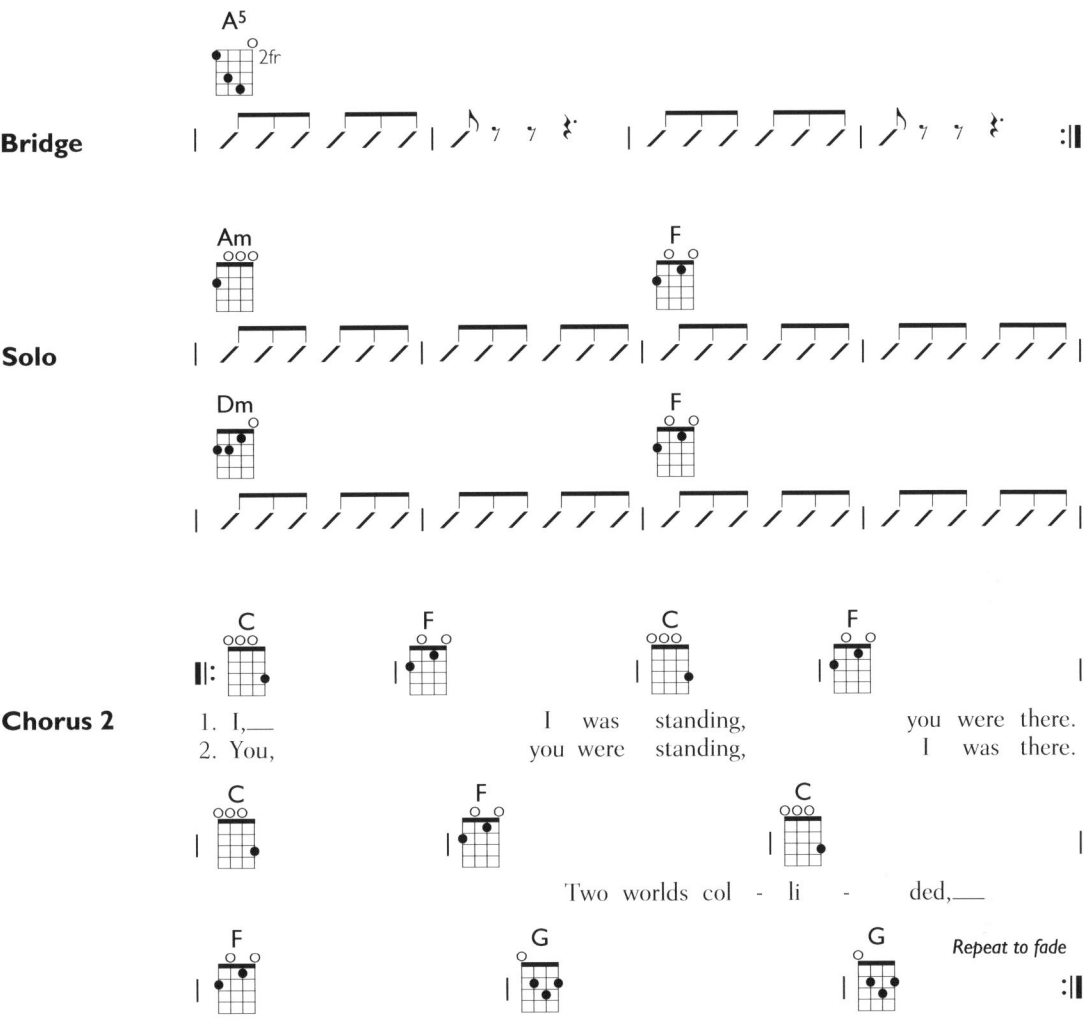

Chorus 2

1. I,   I was standing,   you were there.
2. You,   you were standing,   I was there.

Two worlds col - li - ded,

Repeat to fade

and they could never tear us a - part.

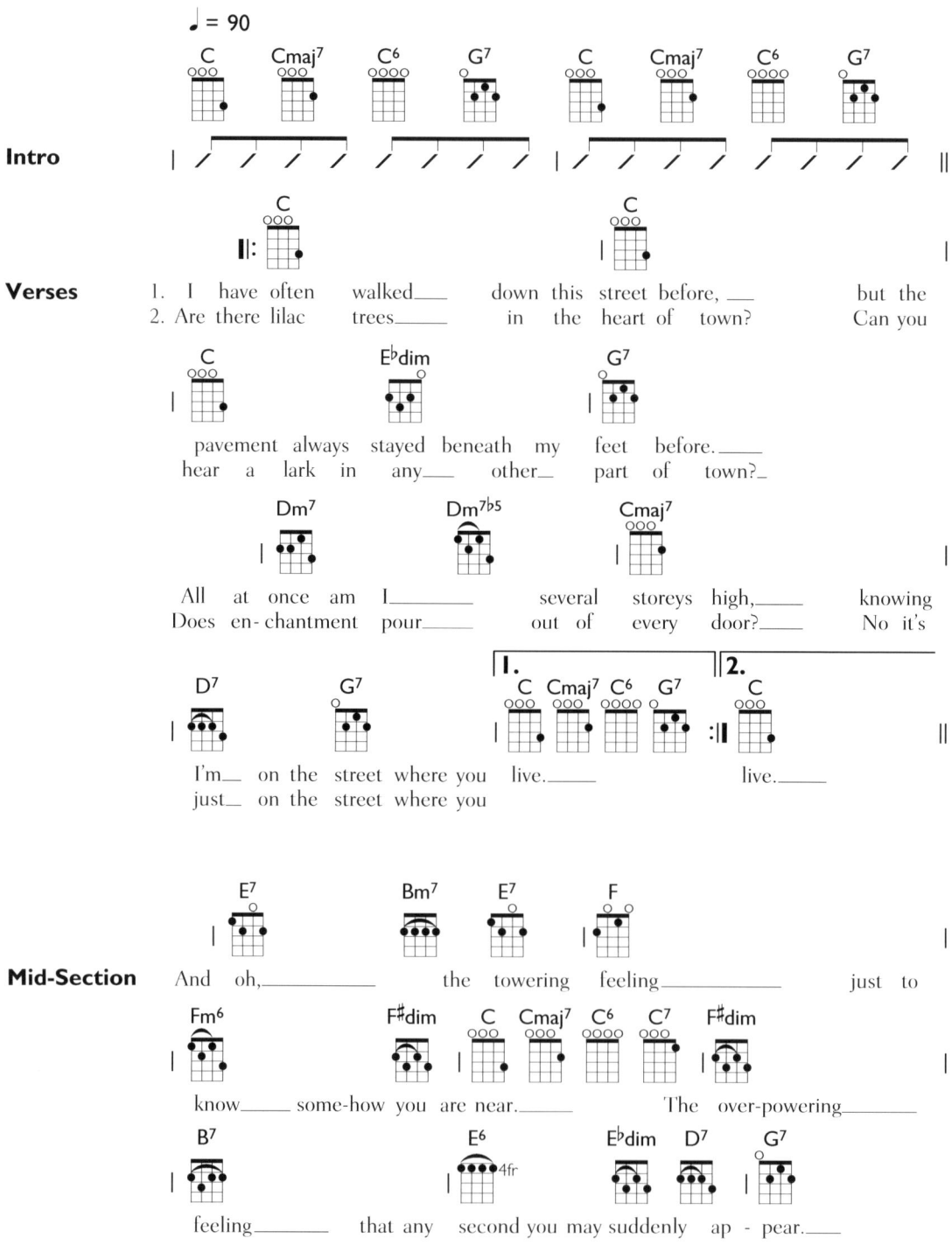

Verse 3

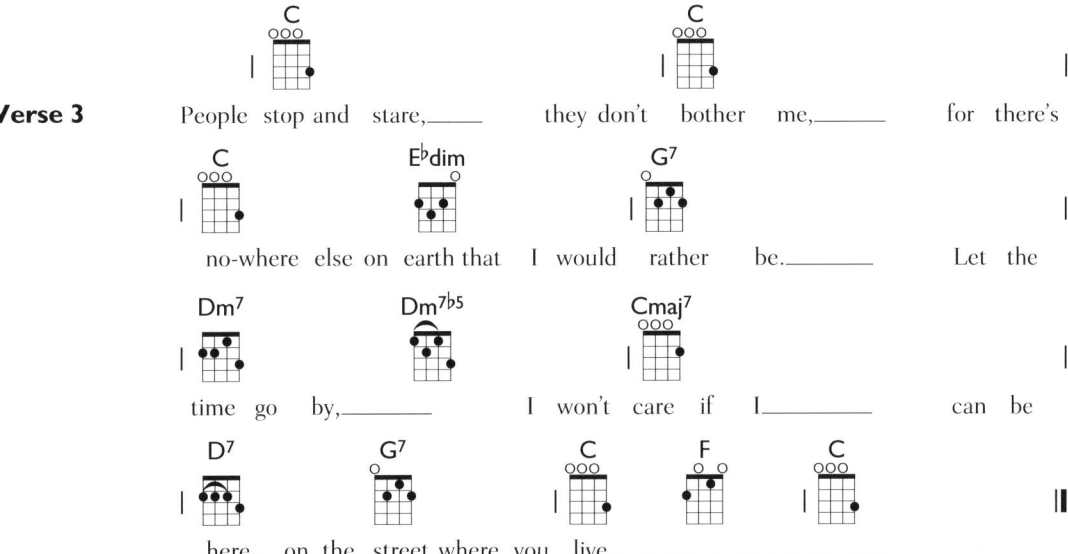

People stop and stare,_____ they don't bother me,_____ for there's no-where else on earth that I would rather be._____ Let the time go by,_____ I won't care if I_____ can be here_ on the street where you live._____

Of The Night

Bastille

Words and Music by Michael Gaffey, Francesco Bontempi, Annerley Gordon, Giorgio Spagna, Peter Glenister, Benito Benites, John Garrett III and Thea Austin

© 2013 Intersong Music Ltd, Extravaganza Publishing SRL administered by Artemis Muziekuitgeverij B.V.,
Bug Music o/b/o Bug Music Ltd, Songs Of Logic Verlags GmbH and Hanseatic Musikverlag GmbH & Co KG
This arrangement © 2014 Intersong Music Ltd, Extravaganza Publishing SRL administered by Artemis Muziekuitgeverij B.V.,
Bug Music o/b/o Bug Music Ltd, Songs Of Logic Verlags GmbH and Hanseatic Musikverlag GmbH & Co KG
All Rights for Bug Music Administered by Bug Music, Inc., a BMG Chrysalis Company
All Rights for Intersong Music Ltd and Extravaganza Publishing SRL Administered by WB Music Corp.
All Rights Reserved. Used by Permission
Reprinted by Permission of Hal Leonard Corporation
(This song contains elements of "THE RHYTHM OF THE NIGHT" by Gaffey/Bontempi/Gordon/Spagna/Glenister
© Intersong Music Ltd, Extravaganza Publishing SRL administered by Artemis Muziekuitgeverij B.V. & Bug Music Ltd
and "RHYTHM IS A DANCER" by Benites/Garrett III/Austin © Songs Of Logic Verlags GmbH
& Hanseatic Musikverlag GmbH & Co KG)

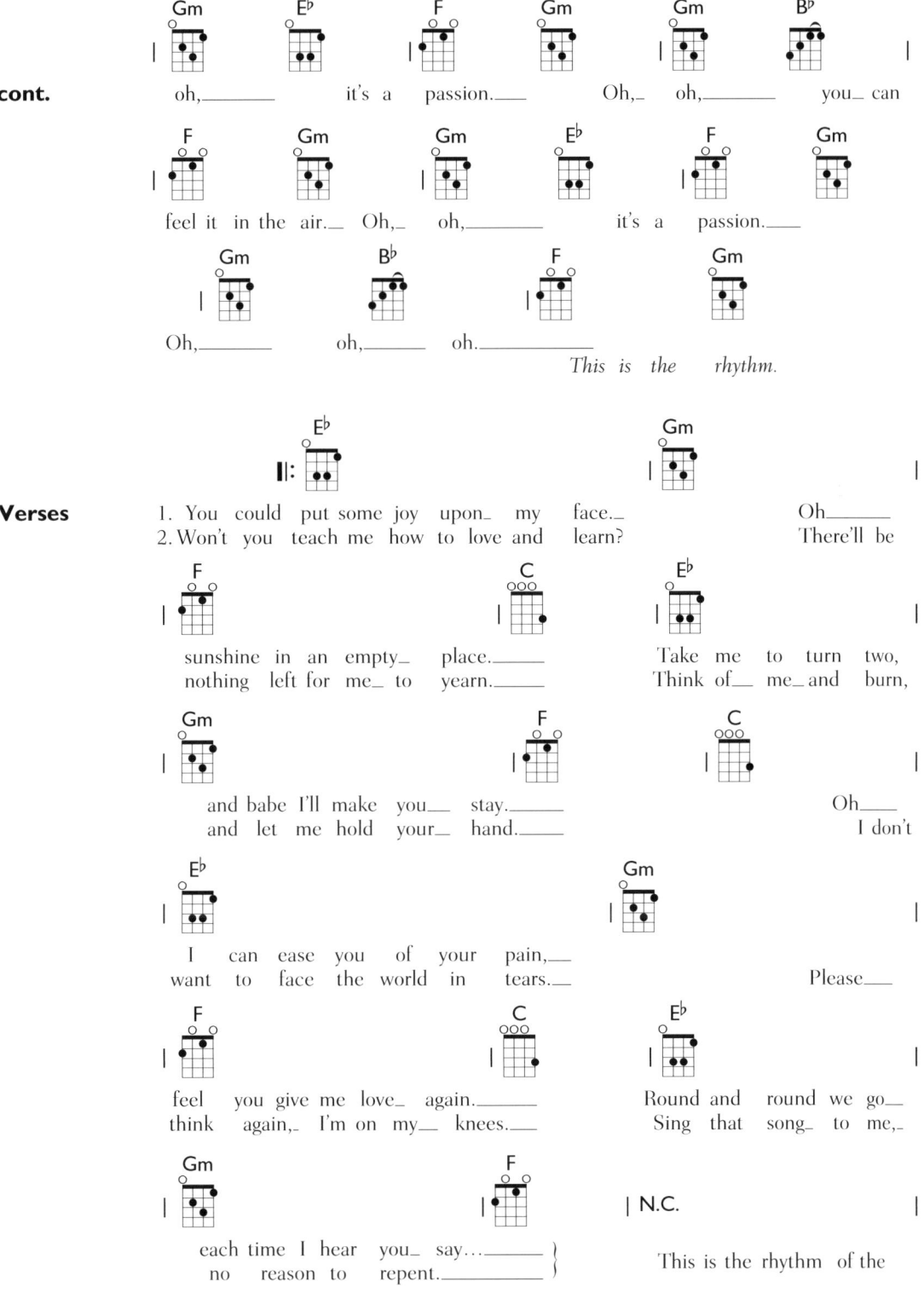

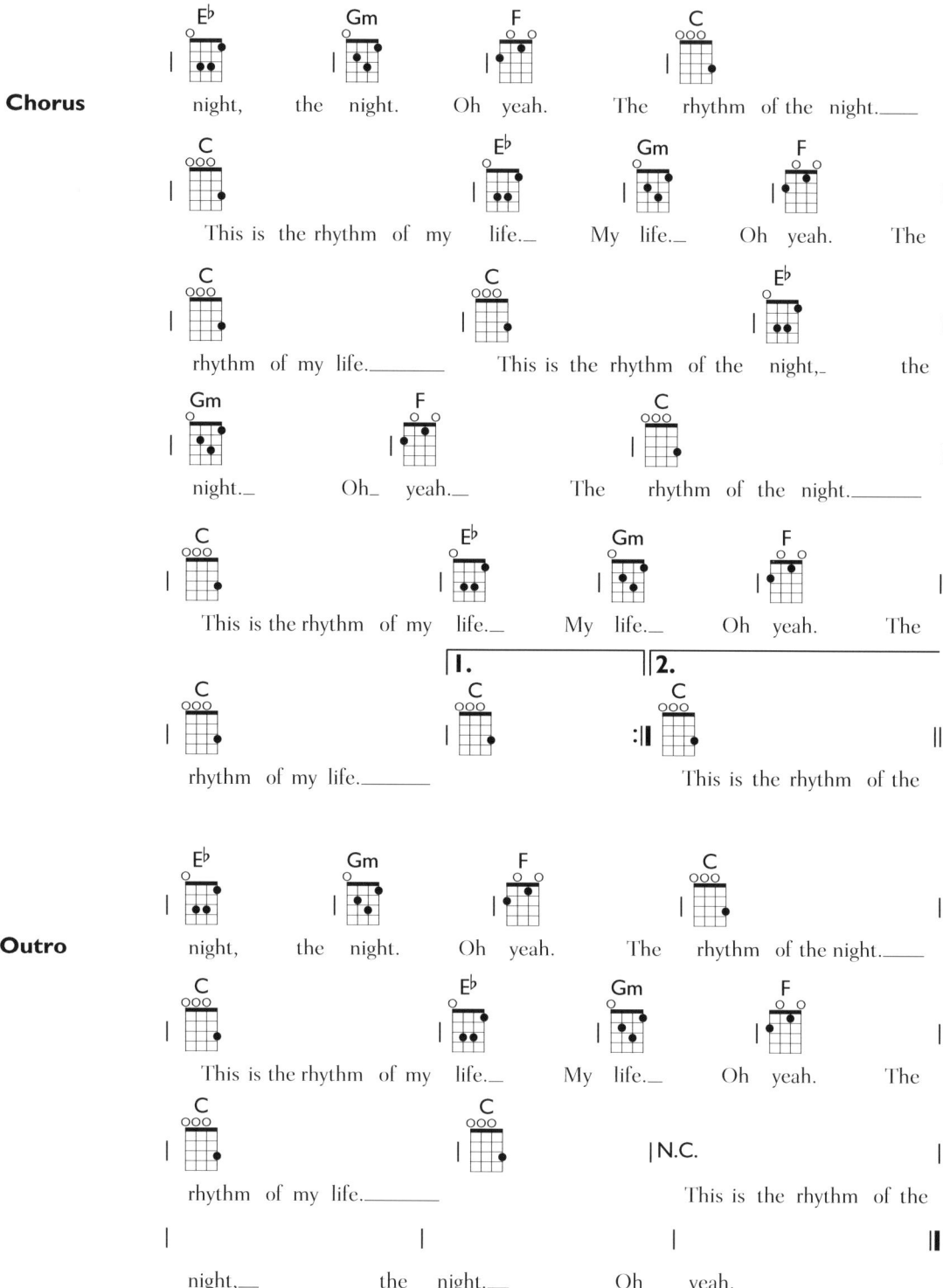

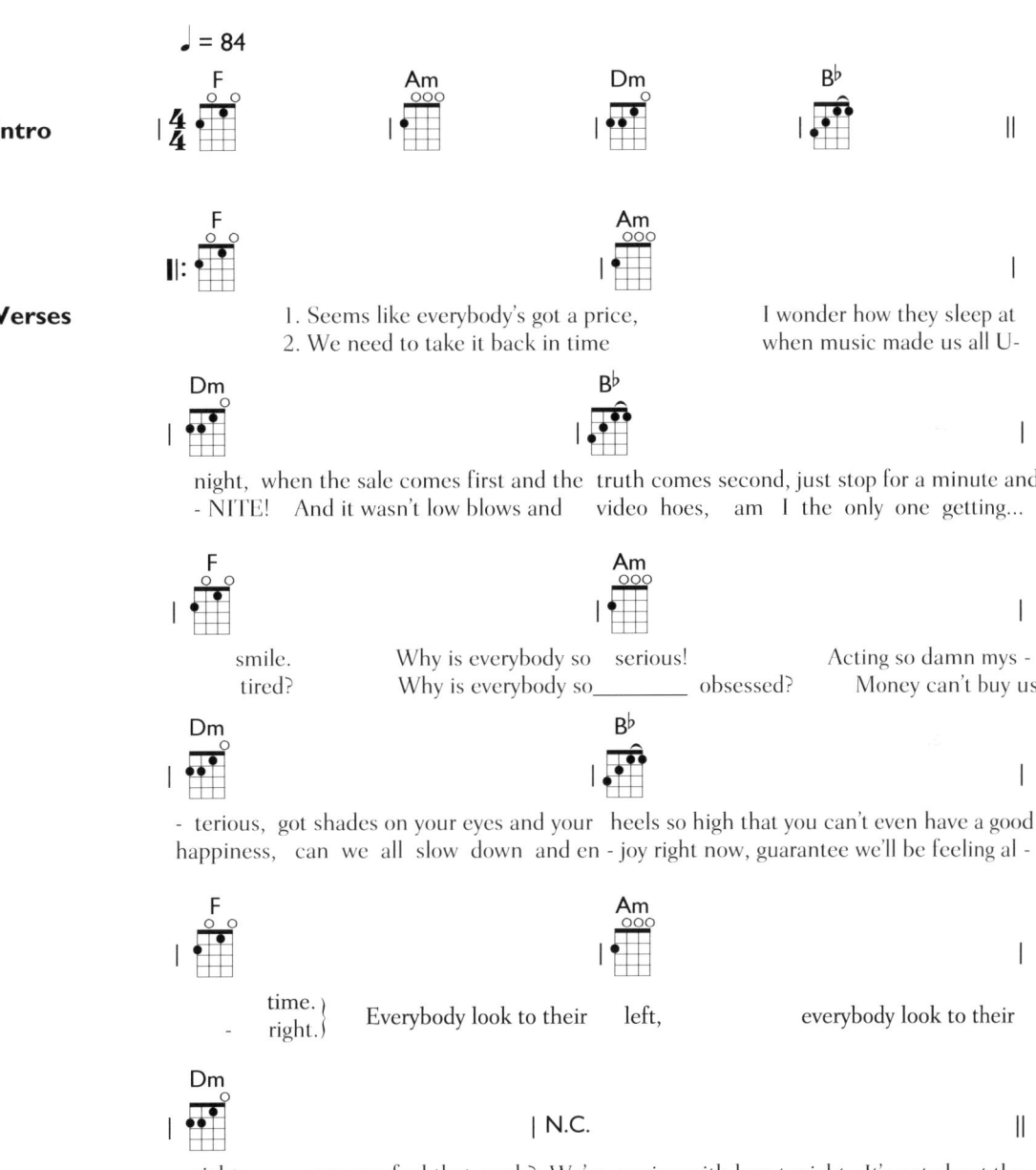

Chorus 2

Outro

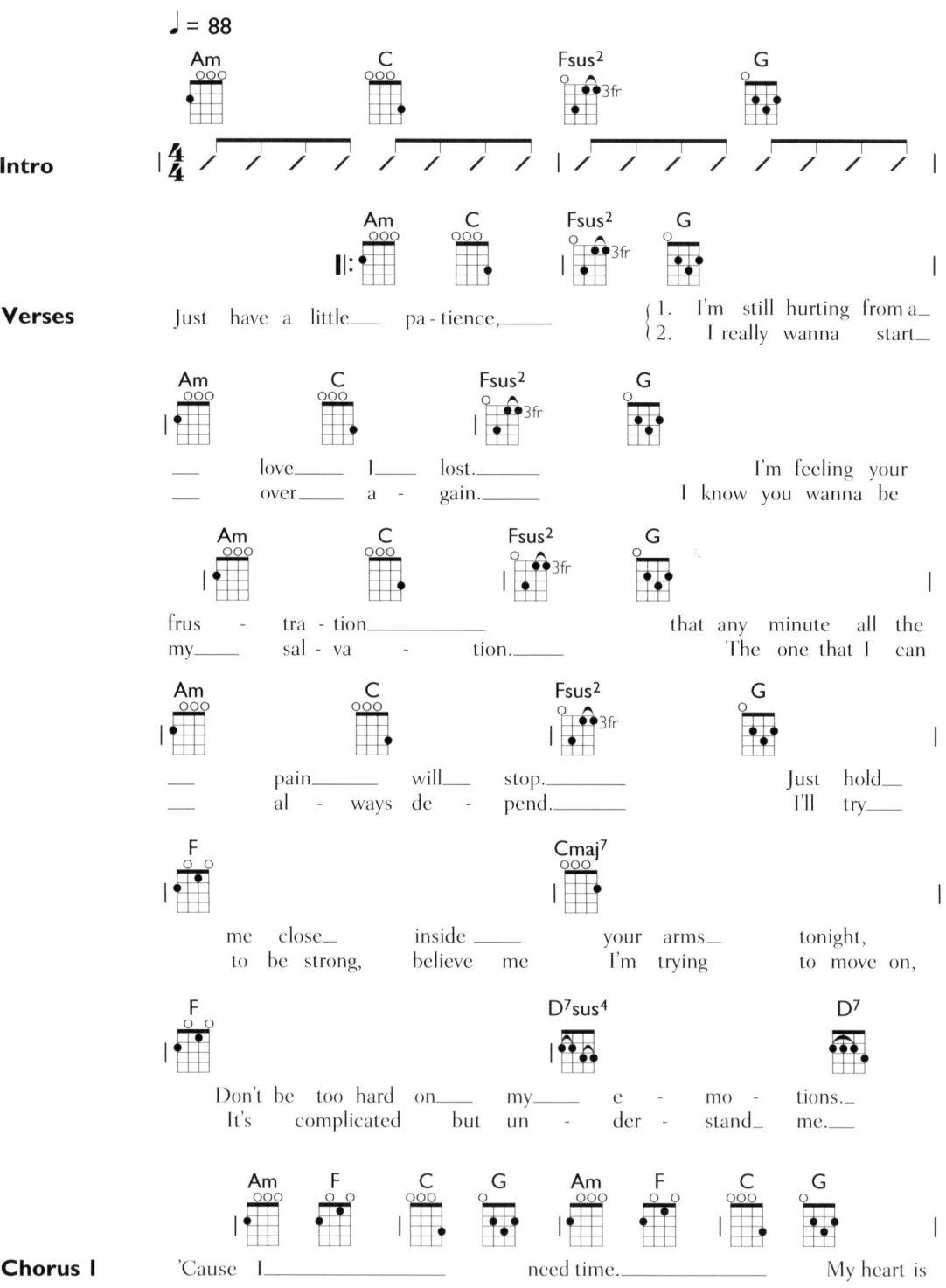

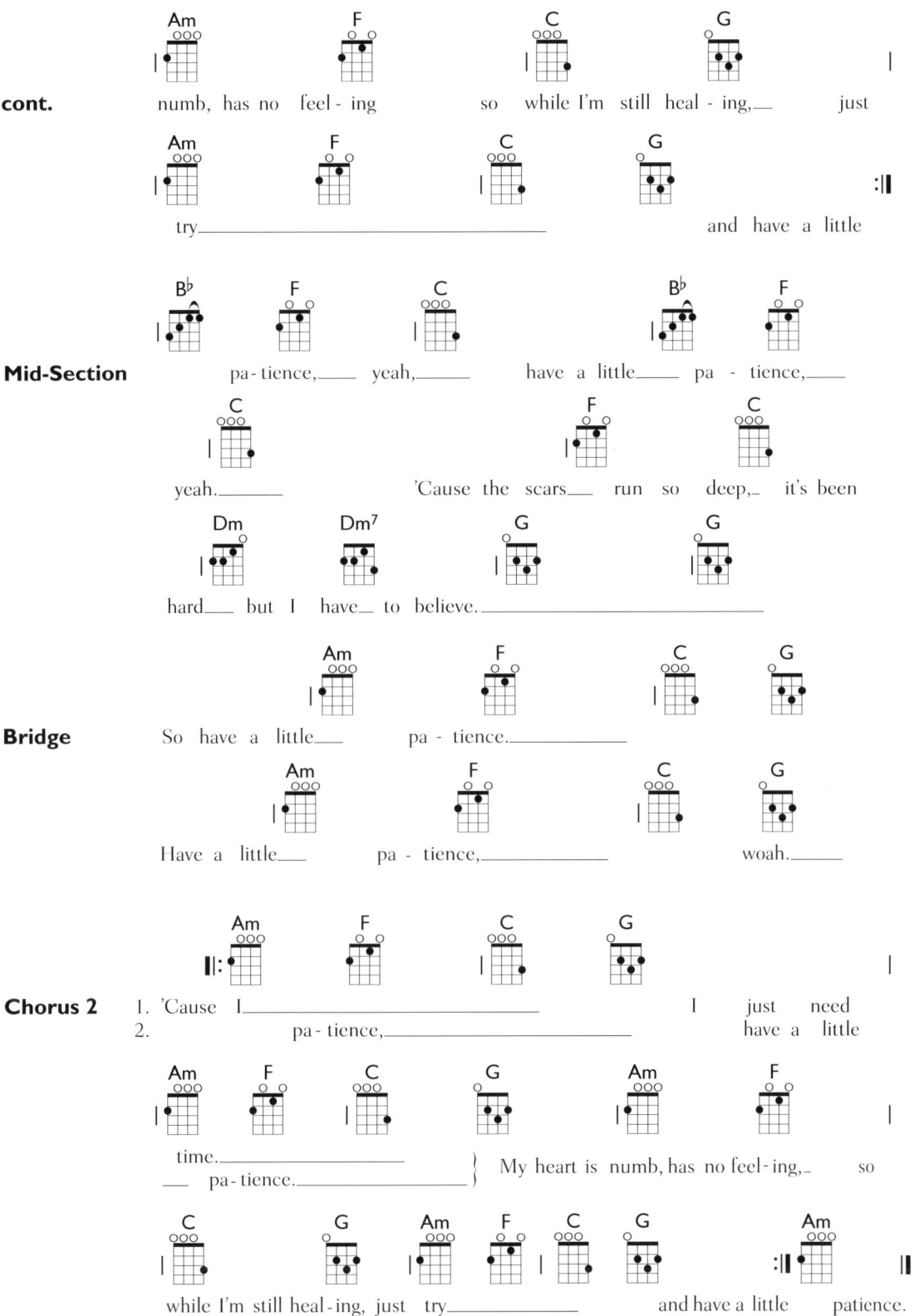

Puff The Magic Dragon

Words and Music by Peter Yarrow and Leonard Lipton

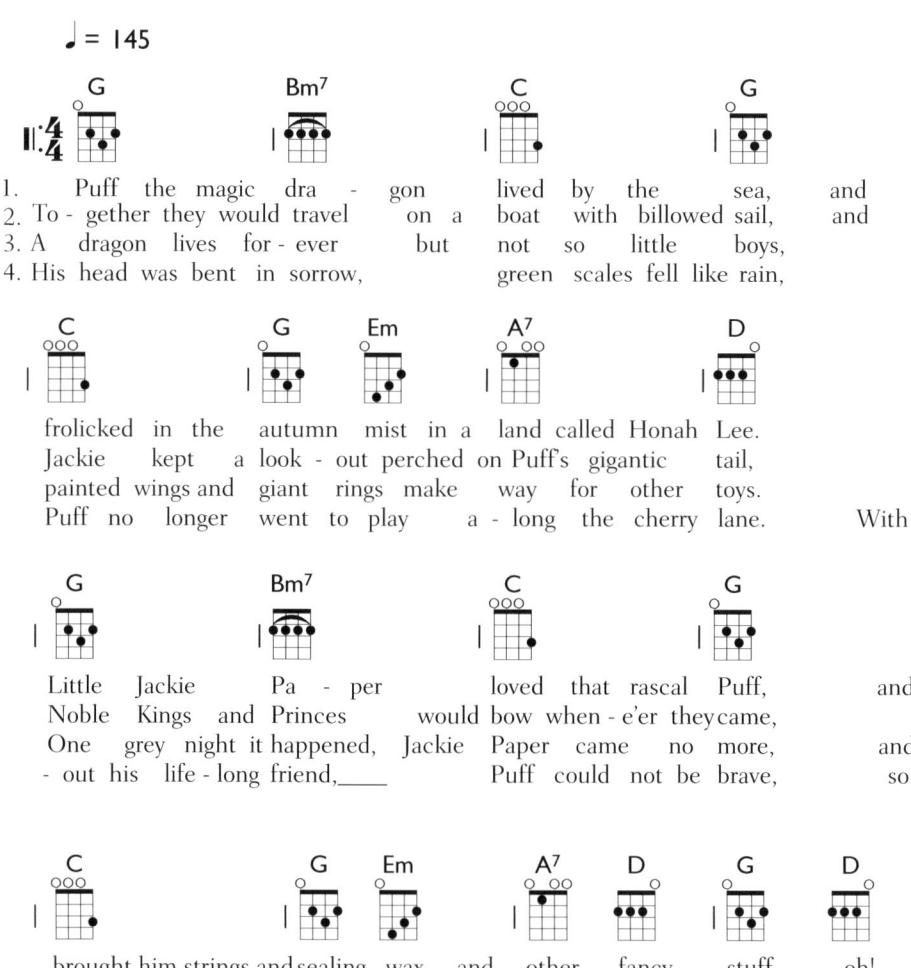

♩ = 145

Verses

1. Puff the magic dra - gon lived by the sea, and frolicked in the autumn mist in a land called Honah Lee. Little Jackie Pa - per loved that rascal Puff, and brought him strings and sealing wax and other fancy stuff, oh!
2. To - gether they would travel on a boat with billowed sail, and Jackie kept a look - out perched on Puff's gigantic tail, Noble Kings and Princes would bow when - e'er they came, and pirate ships would lower their flags when Puff roared out his name, oh!
3. A dragon lives for - ever but not so little boys, painted wings and giant rings make way for other toys. One grey night it happened, Jackie Paper came no more, and Puff that mighty dragon, he ceased his fearless roar, oh!
4. His head was bent in sorrow, green scales fell like rain, Puff no longer went to play a - long the cherry lane. With - out his life - long friend, Puff could not be brave, so Puff that mighty dragon sadly slipped into his cave, oh!

© 1963 (Renewed 1991) Silver Dawn Music and Honalee Melodies
This arrangement 2014 Silver Dawn Music and Honalee Melodies
Worldwide Rights for Silver Dawn Music Administered by WB Music Corp
Worldwide Rights for Honalee Music Administered by BMG Rights Management (US) LLC
International Copyright Secured All Rights Reserved.
Reprinted by Permission of Hal Leonard Corporation

127

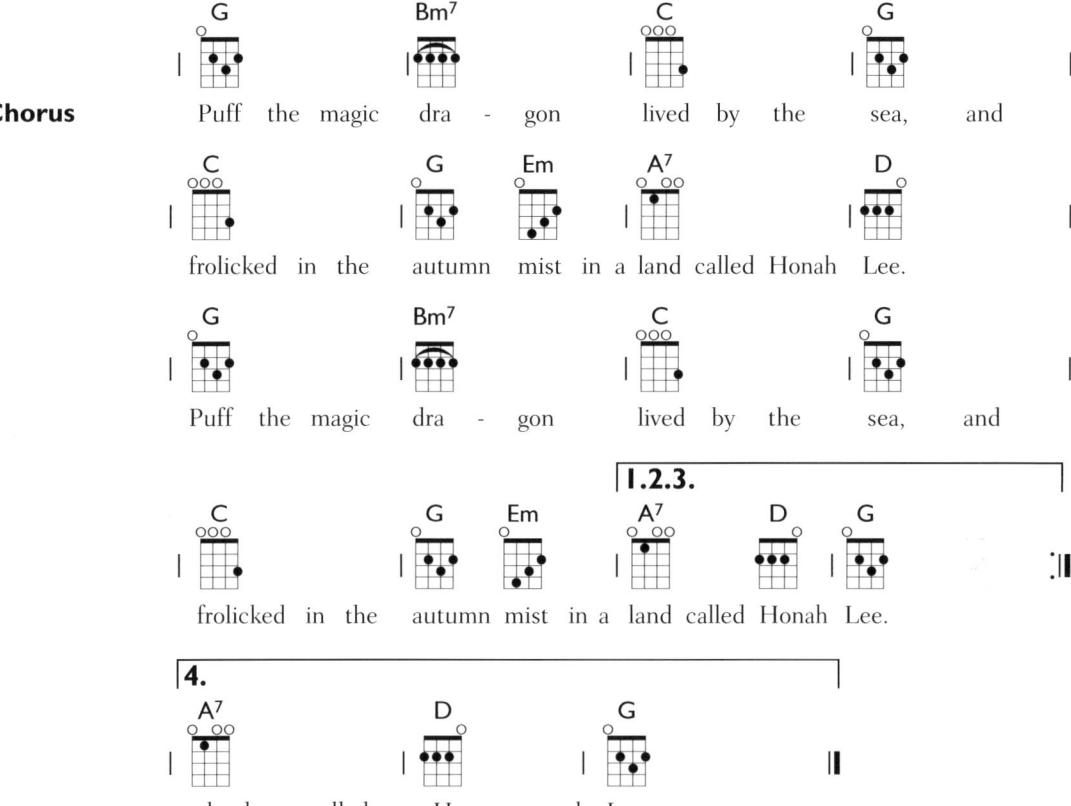

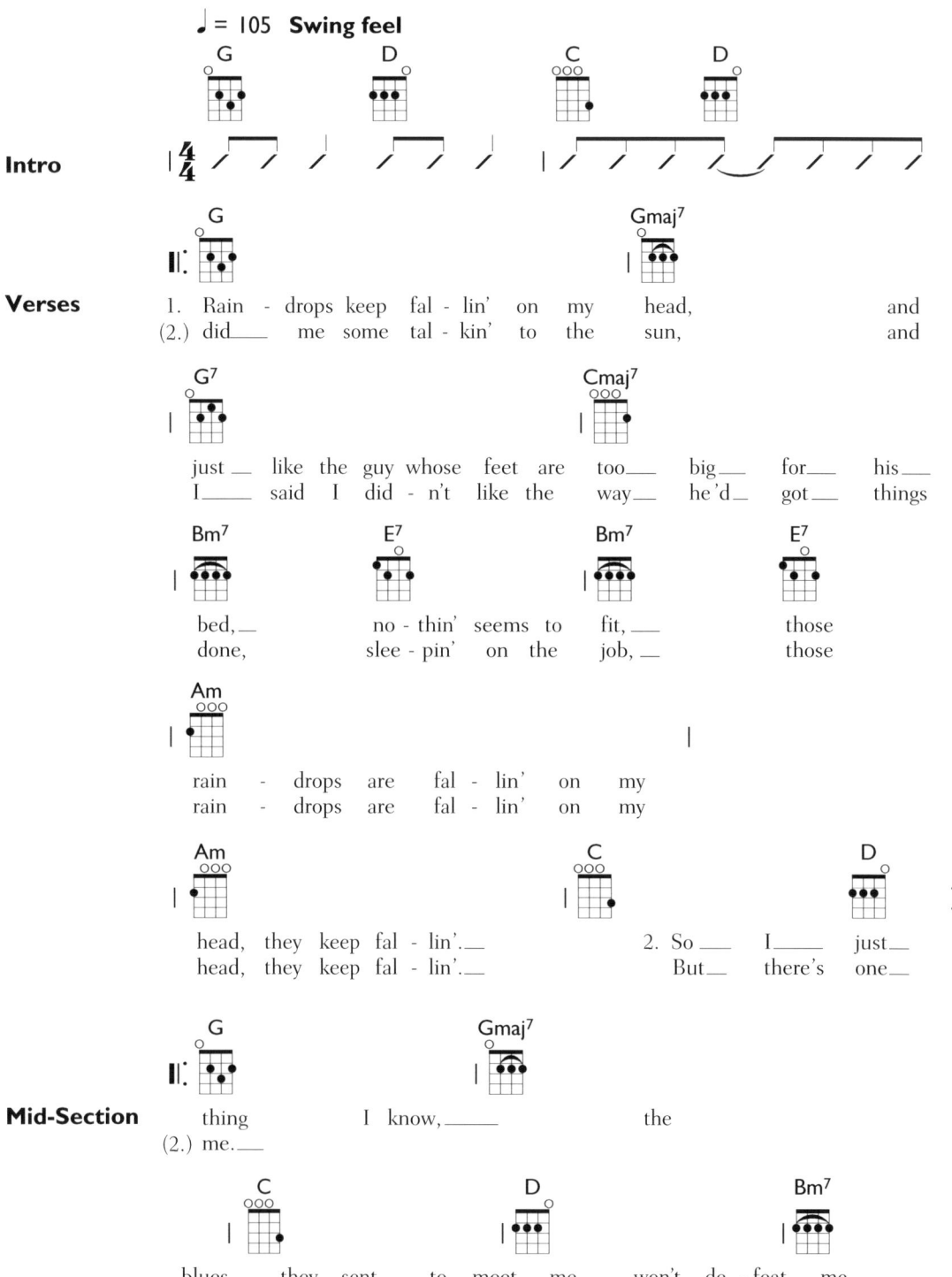

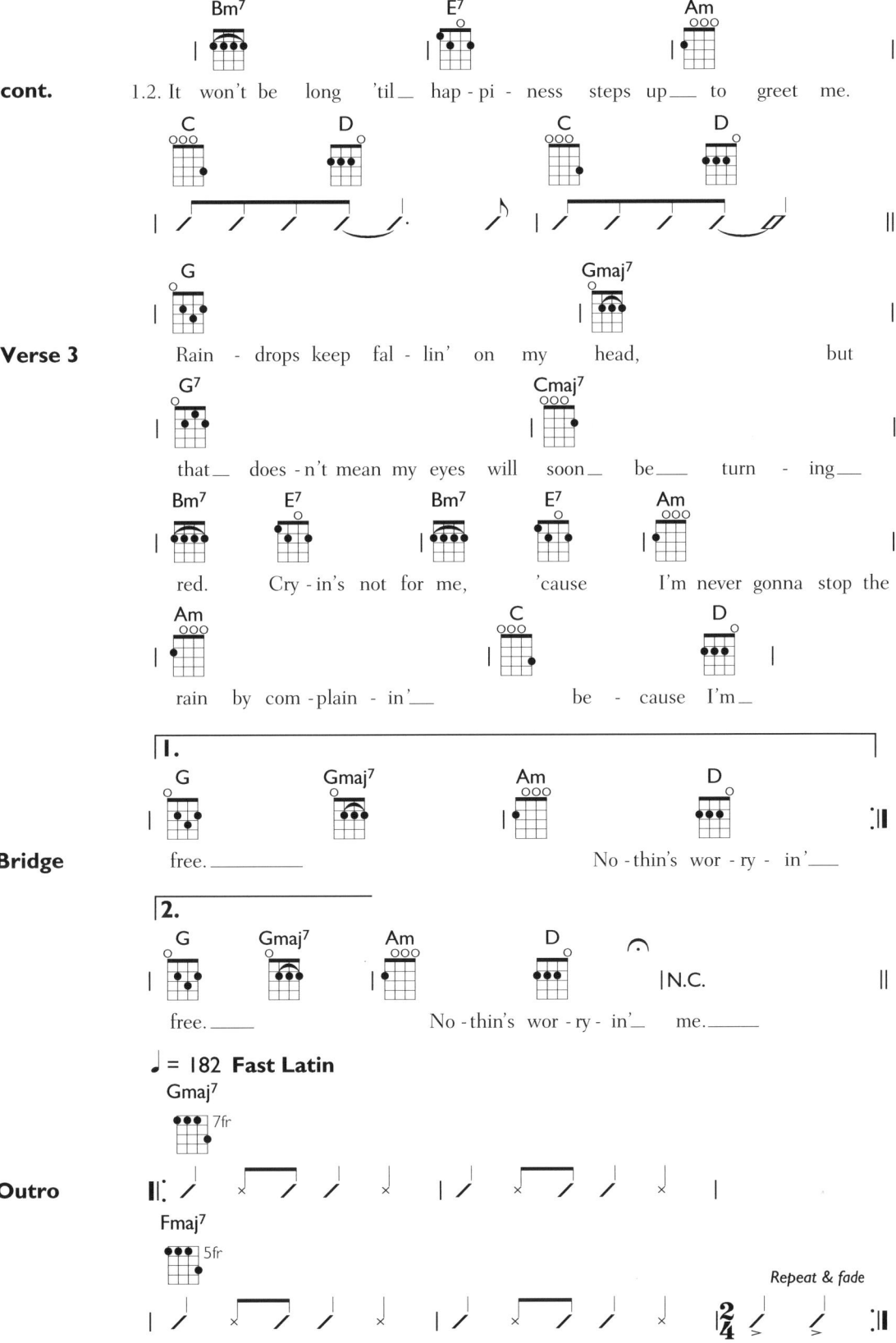

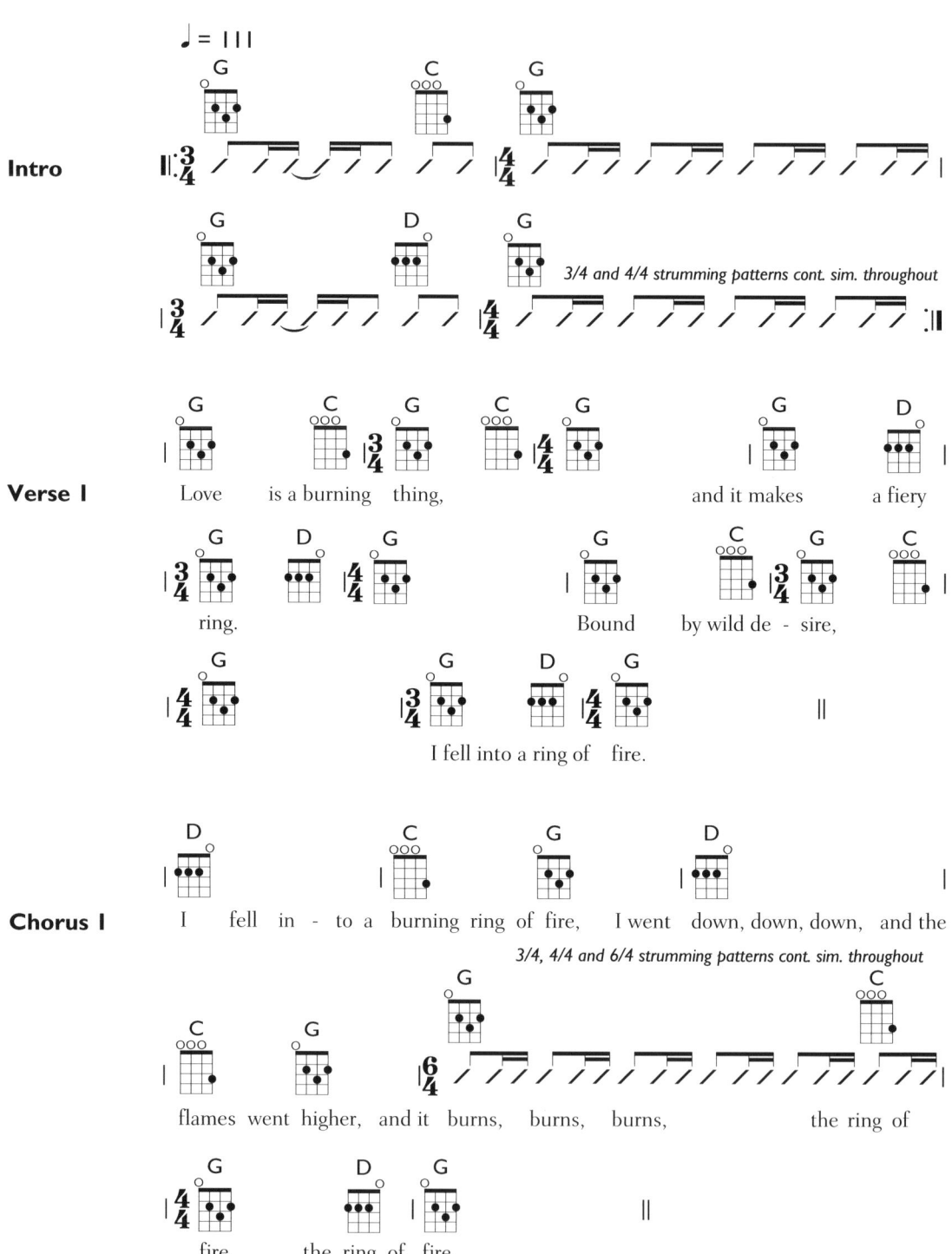

Bridge   *As Intro*

Chorus 2   *As Chorus 1*

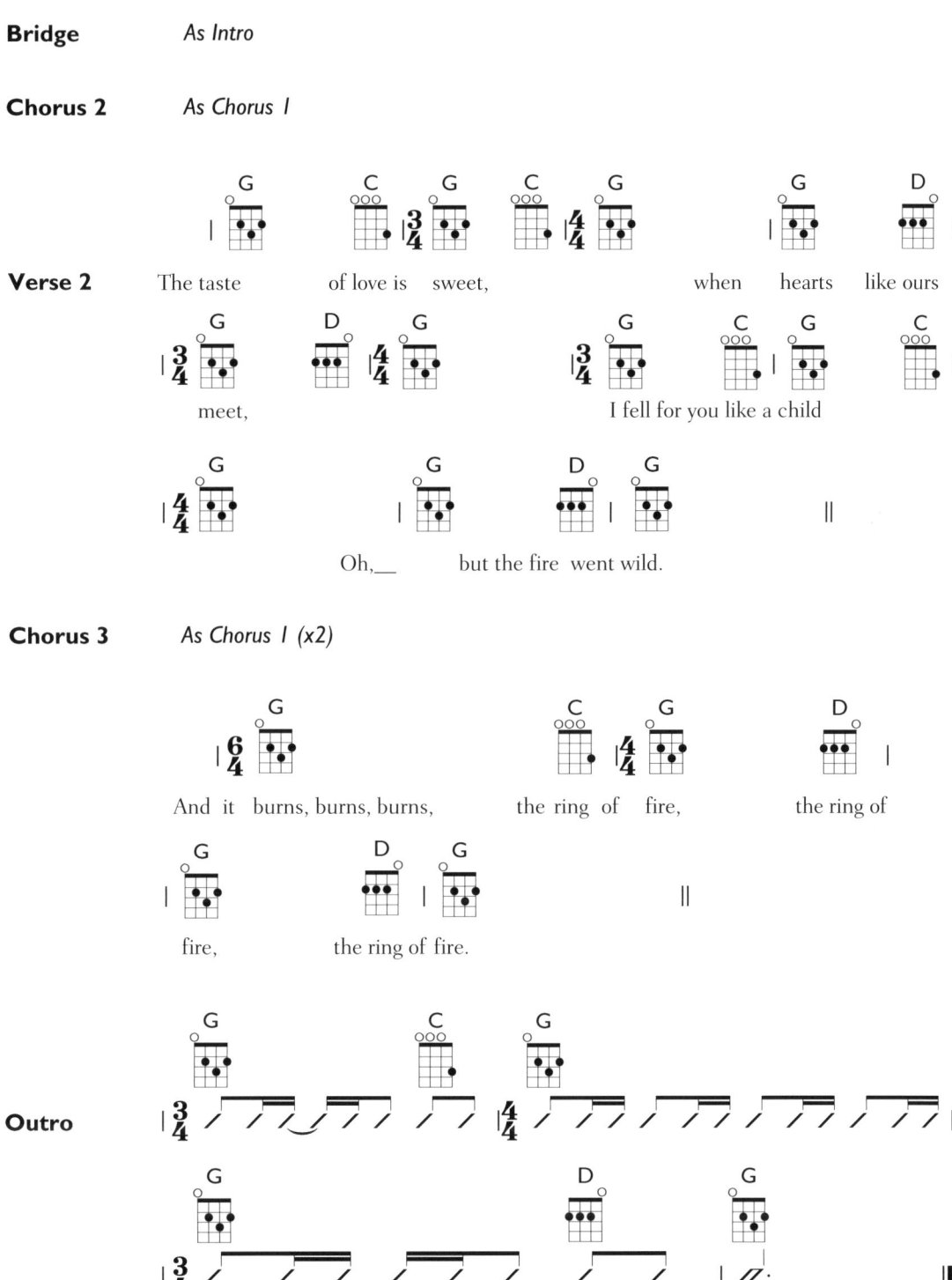

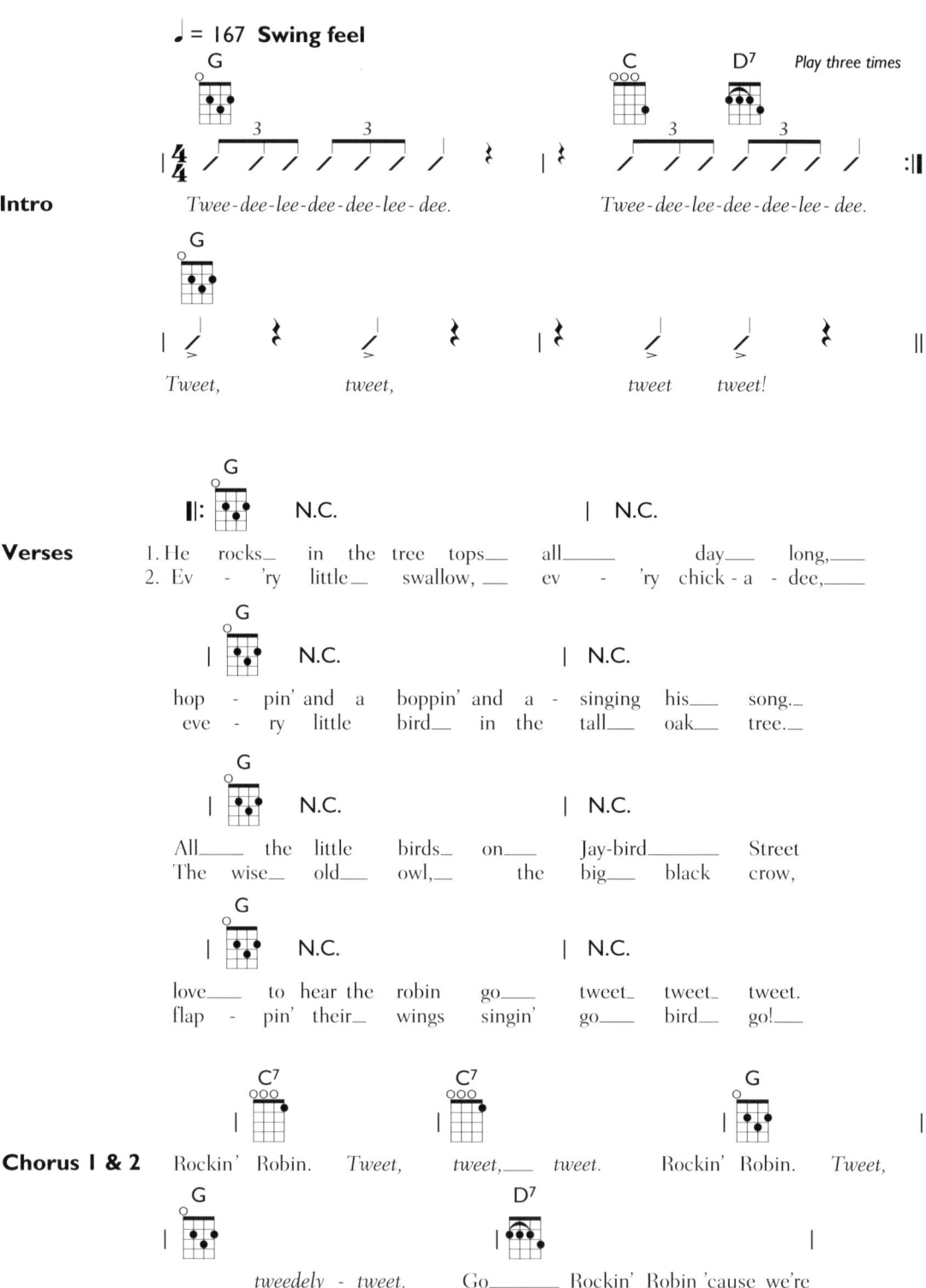

cont.

| D7 | G | G :||

really gonna rock_ tonight.______

Instrumental

G			G7
//// ////	//// ////	//// ////	//// ////

C		G	
//// ////	//// ////	//// ////	//// ////

D7	C7	G	
//// ////	//// ////	//// ////	//// //// ‖

Mid-Section

||: C | C | G |

A pretty little raven at the bird band stand_ taught him how to do the bop and

| G | C | C |

it__ was grand. They started going steady and bless my soul, he

| D7 N.C. | N.C. ‖

out - bopped the buzzard and the__ oriole!_

Verse 3 *As Verse 1*

Chorus 3 ||: *As Chorus 1 & 2* :||

Outro *As Intro*

134　　　　　　　　　　　　　　　　　　　　　　　　　　　　　　　　　　　　　　　Traditional

Scarborough Fair
Words and Music Traditional

Verses

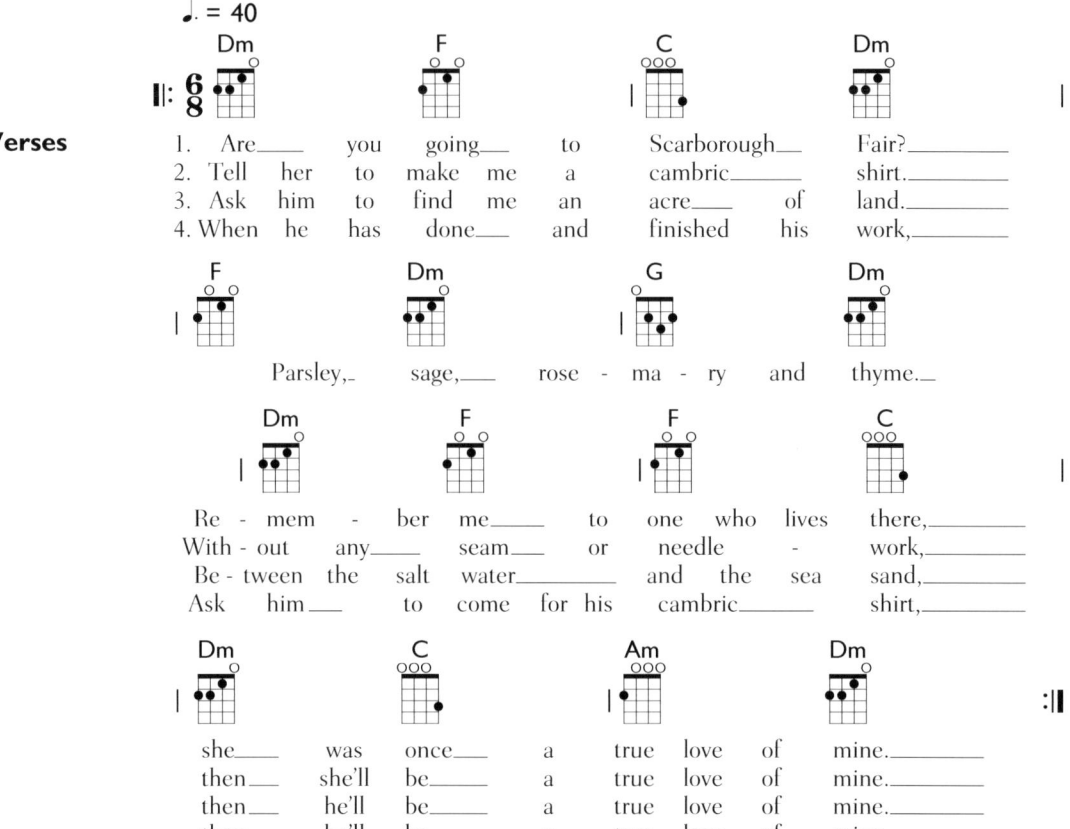

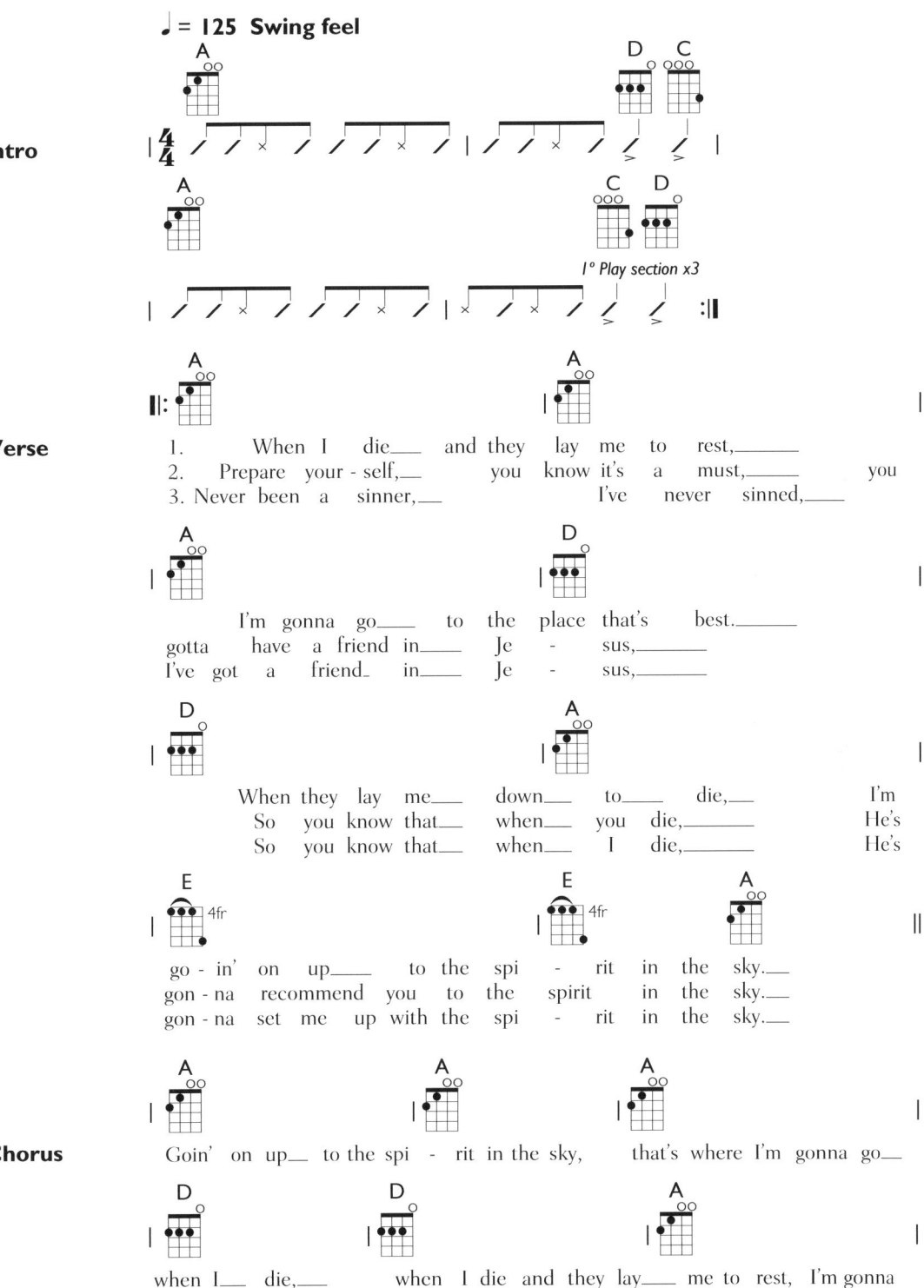

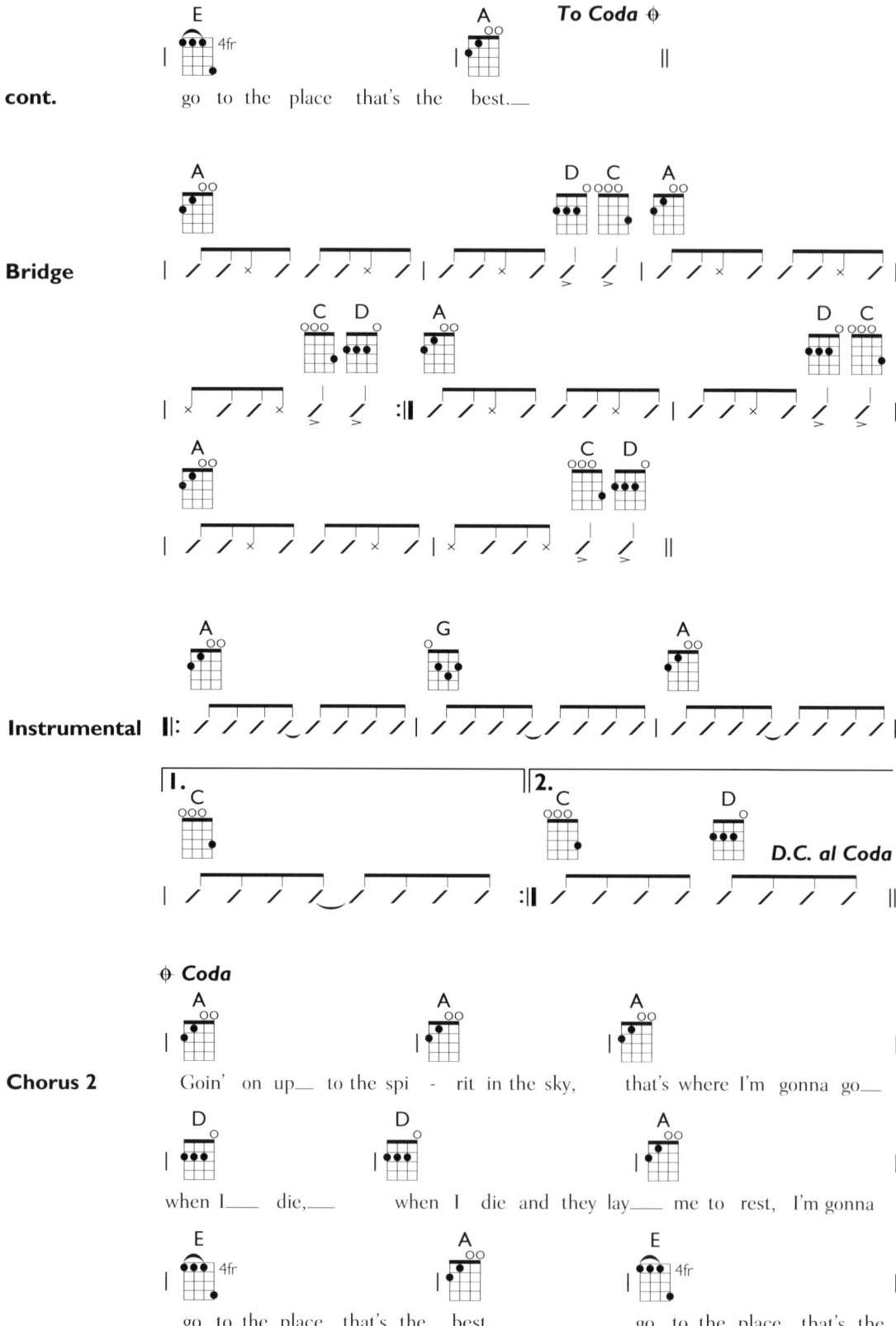

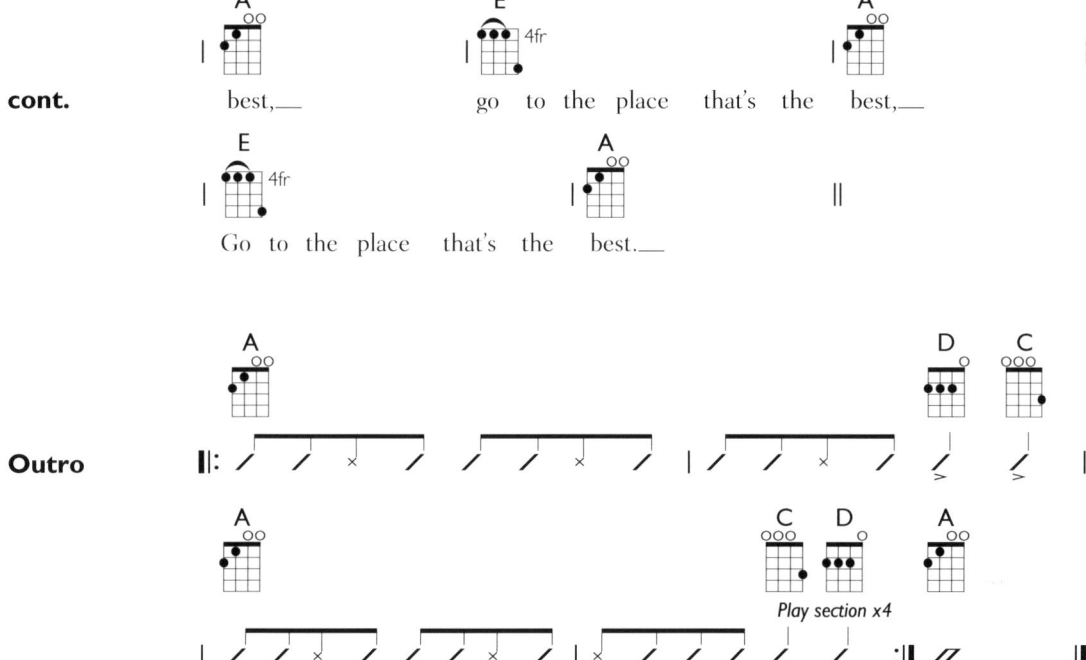

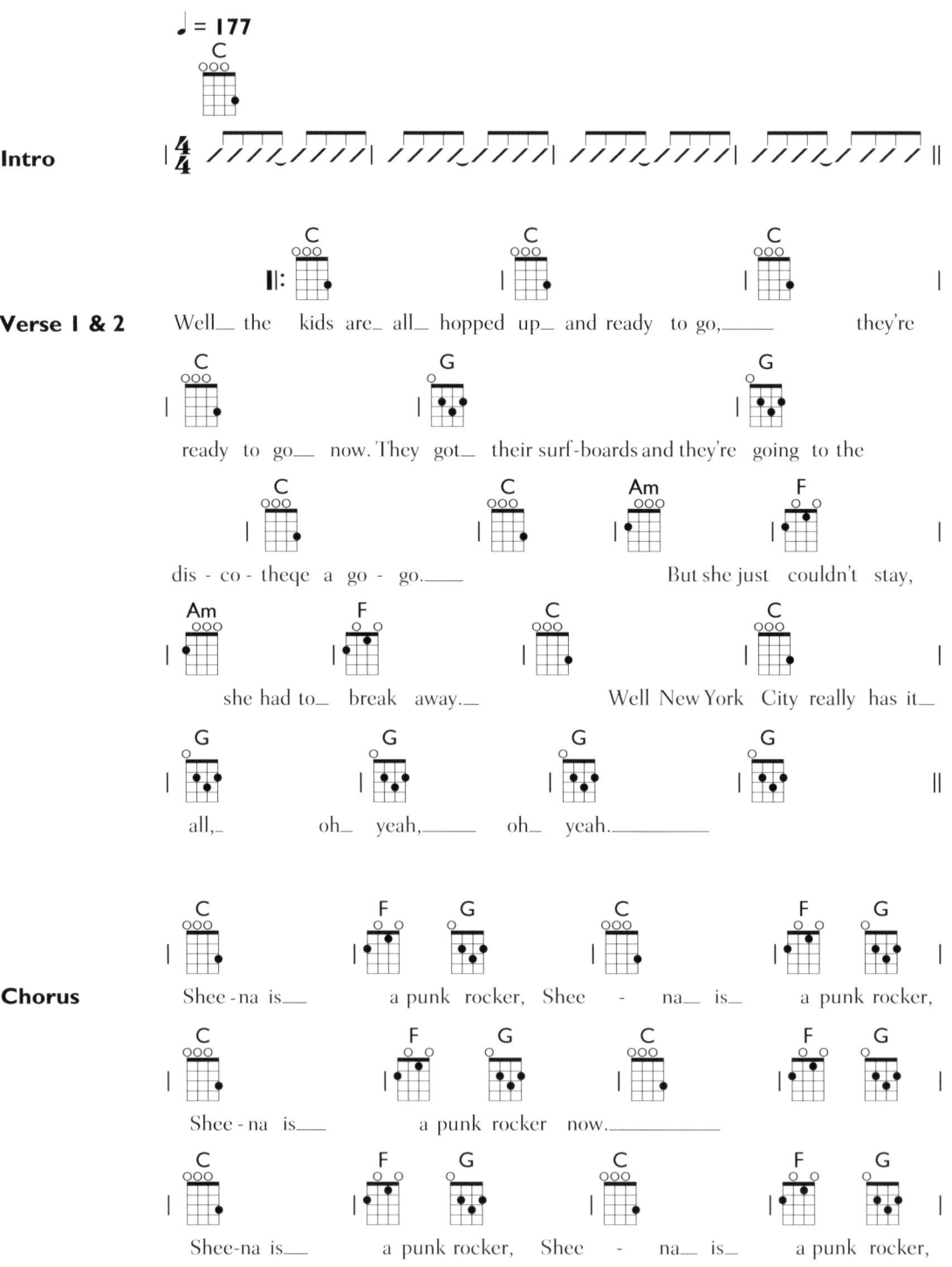

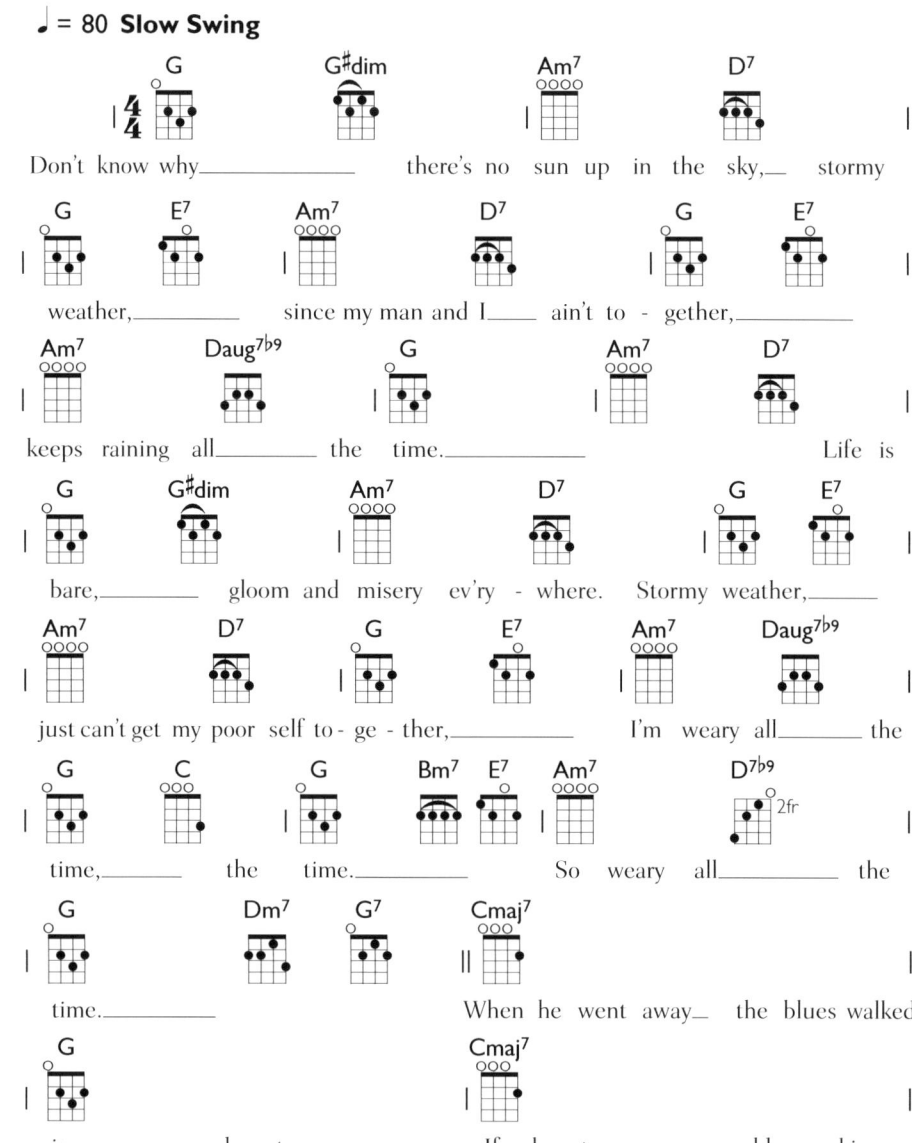

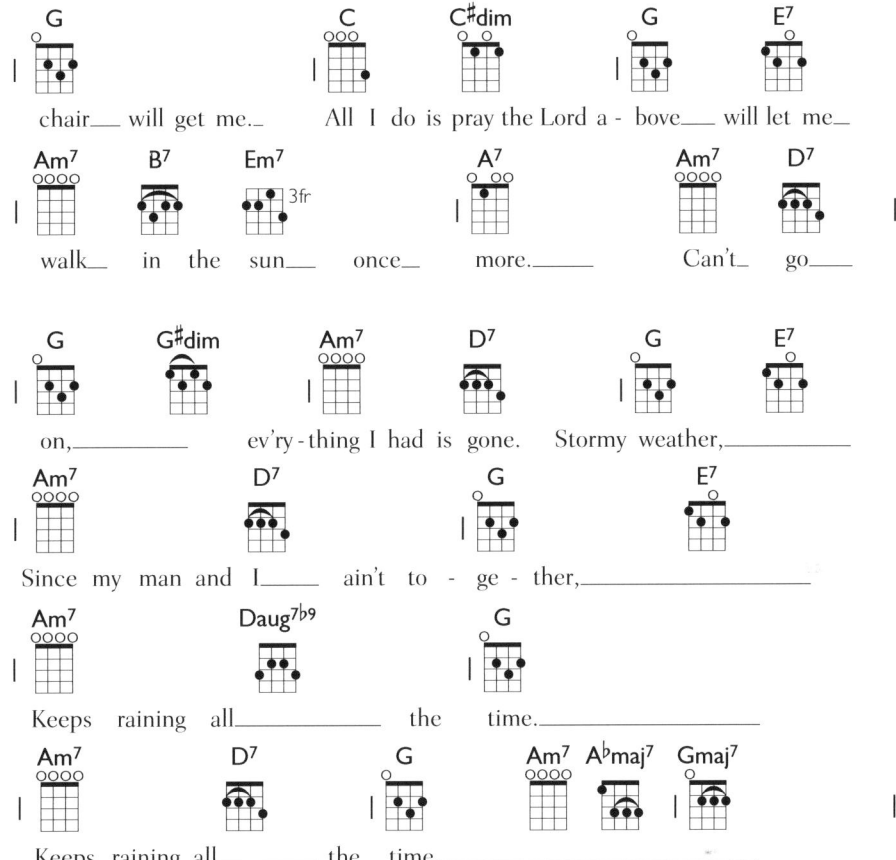

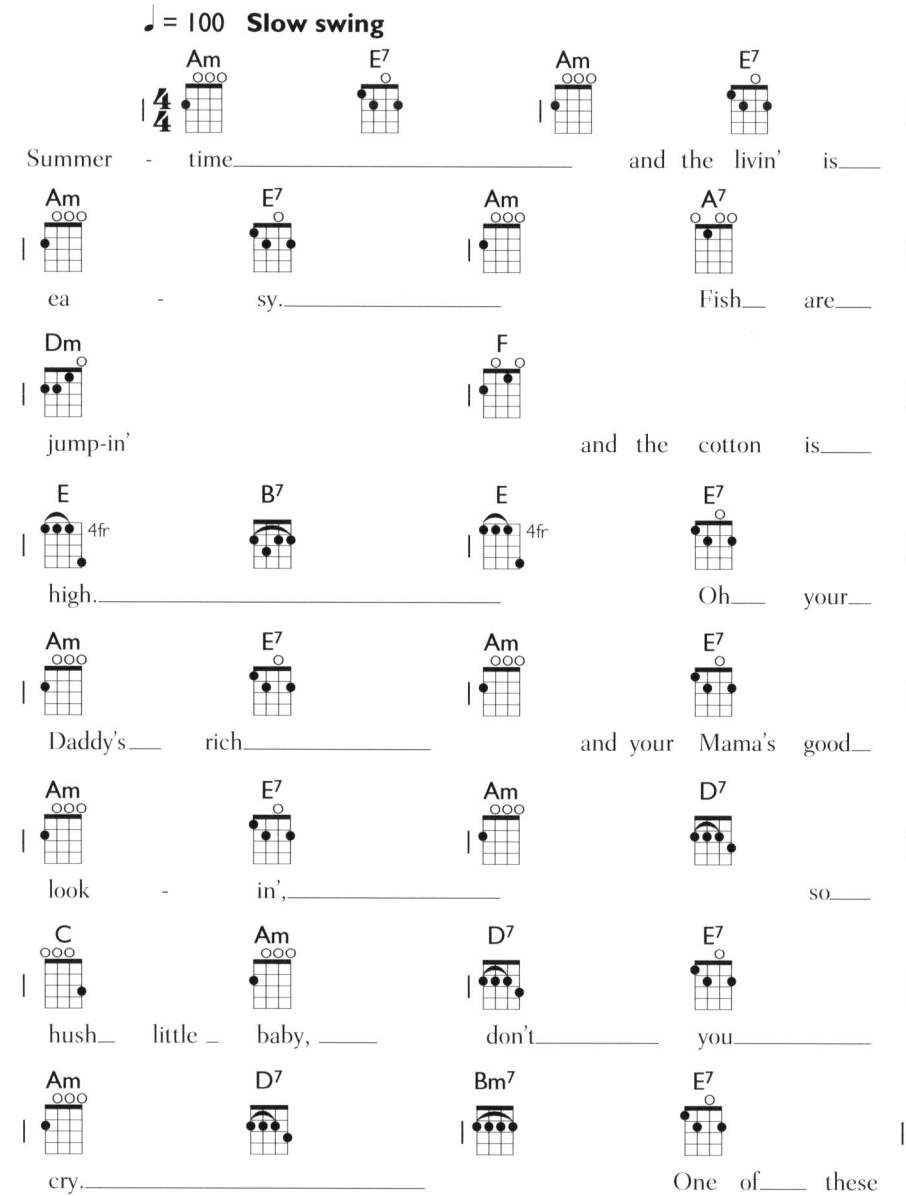

From 'Mary Poppins'

A Spoonful Of Sugar

Words and Music by Richard M. Sherman and Robert B. Sherman

♩ = 110

Verses

1. In every job that must be done there is an element of fun, you
2. A robin feathering his nest has very little time to rest while
3. The honey bees that fetch the nectar from the flowers to the comb never

find the fun and snap! The job's a game.   And every
gathering his bits of twine and twig.   Though quite in -
tire of ever buzzing to and fro.   Because they

task you under - take be - comes a piece of cake. A
- tent in his pur - suit he has a merry tune to toot. He
take a little nip from every flower that they sip, and

lark! A spree! It's very clear to see... That a
knows a song will move the job a - long... For a
hence, they find their task is not a grind... Just a

Chorus

spoonful of sugar helps the   medicine go down,   the

medicine go down,   medicine go down. Just a

spoonful of sugar helps the   medicine go down,

|1.2. |3.

in a most delight - ful   way.   way.

© 1964 Wonderland Music Company Inc administered by Artemis Muziekuitgeverij B.V.
Warner/Chappell Artemis Music Ltd
All Rights Reserved.

Julie Fowlis 145

Touch The Sky (from 'Brave')
Words by Alex Mandel and Mark Andrews
Music by Alex Mandel

♩ = 234 **Fast folk**

Intro

: D	D	D	D :
D	D	D	D	D
D	D	D	Dsus²	Dsus²	
: D	D	D	Csus⁴ :| *Repeat x3*

Verse 1

| Am | Am | Am | Am |
| | | | When the |

| D | D | G | G |
| cold wind____ | is a-call-ing | | and the |

| D | D | G | G |
| sky is____ | clear and | bright, | misty |

| Bm⁷ | Bm⁷ | G⁶⁄₉ | G⁶⁄₉ |
| mountains | sing and | beckon, | lead me out____ |

| D | D | A | A ||
| ____ | into the | light.____ | I will____ |

© 2012 Pixar Talking Pictures administered by Artemis Muziekuitgeverij B.V.
Warner/Chappell Artemis Music Ltd

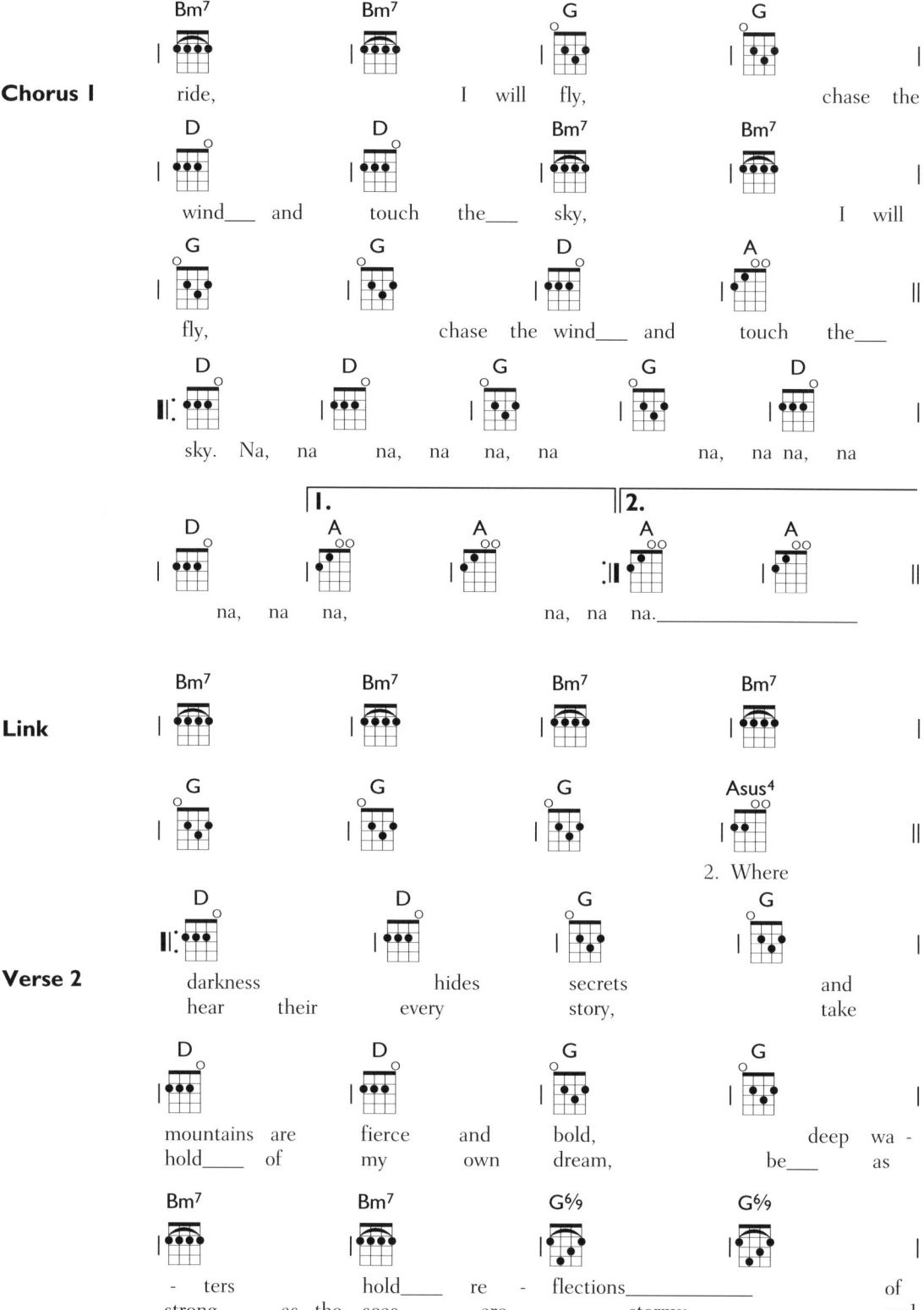

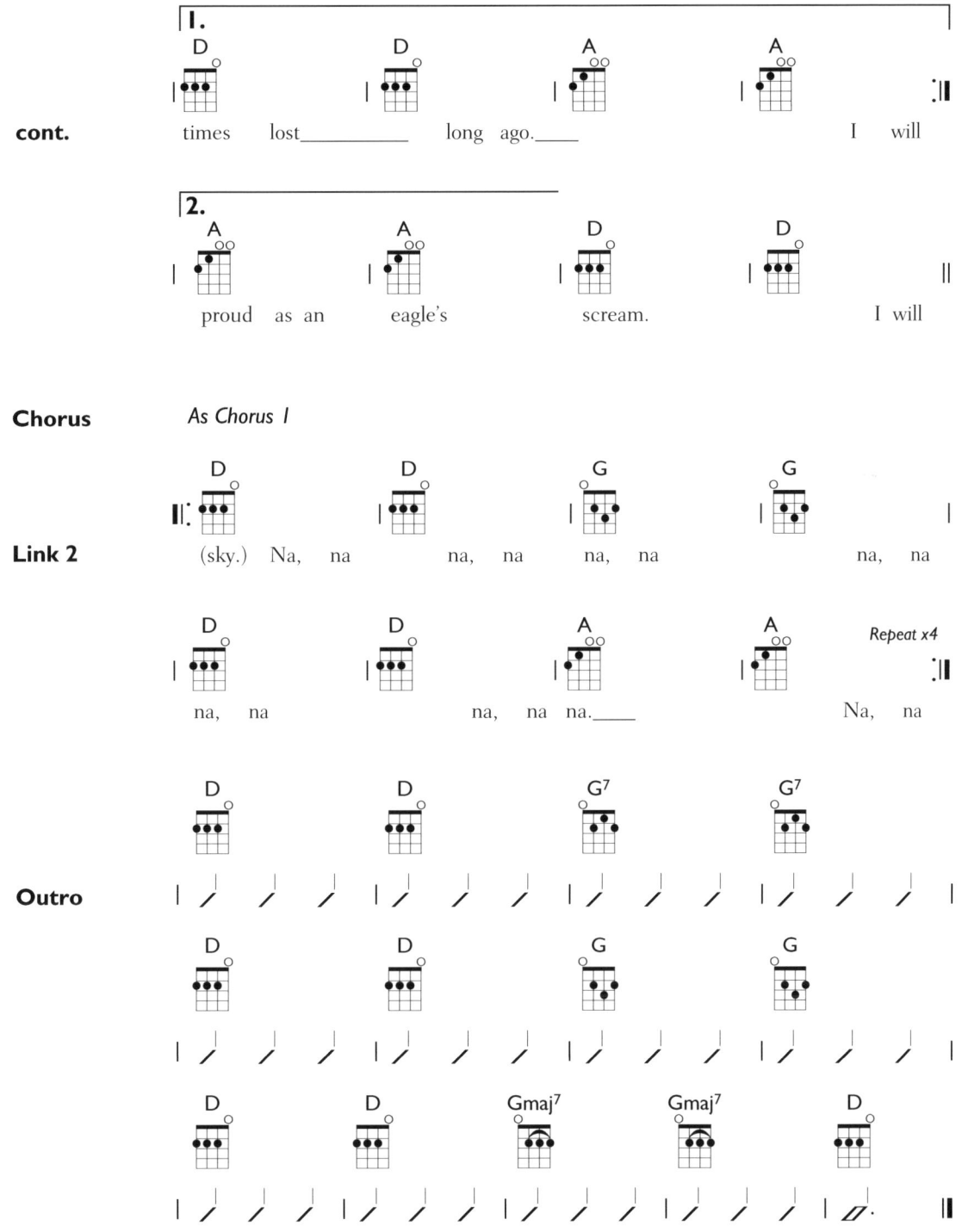

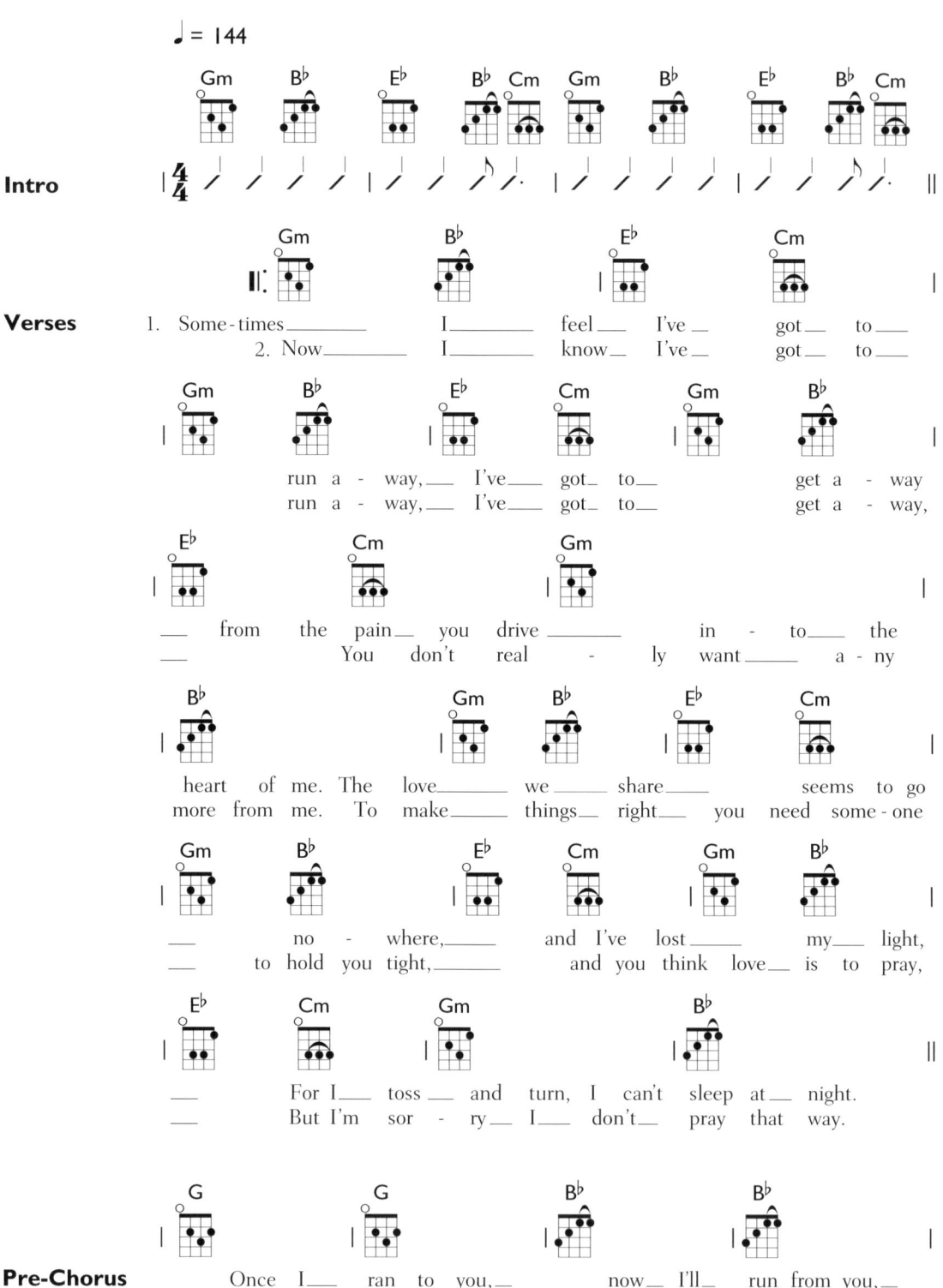

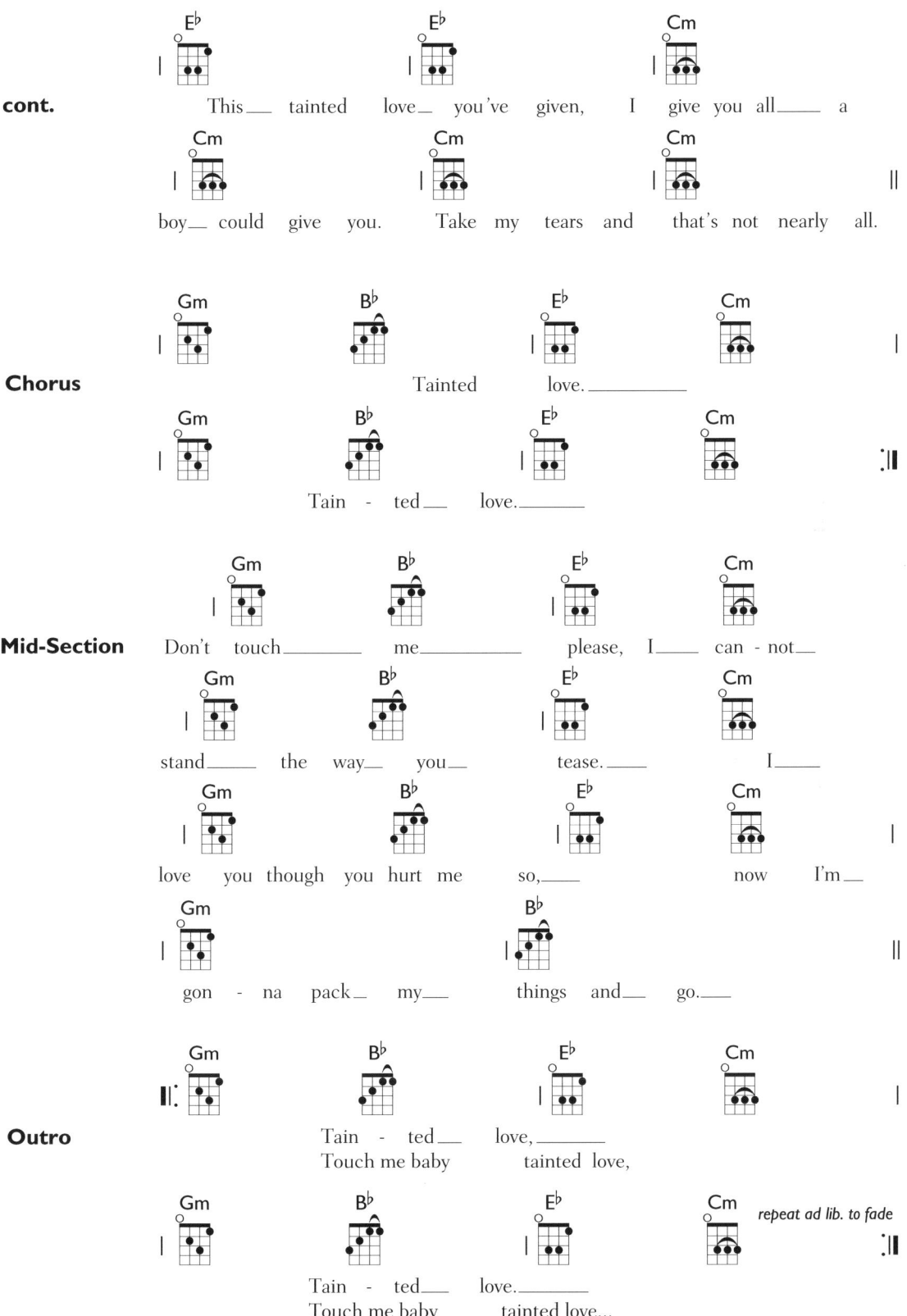

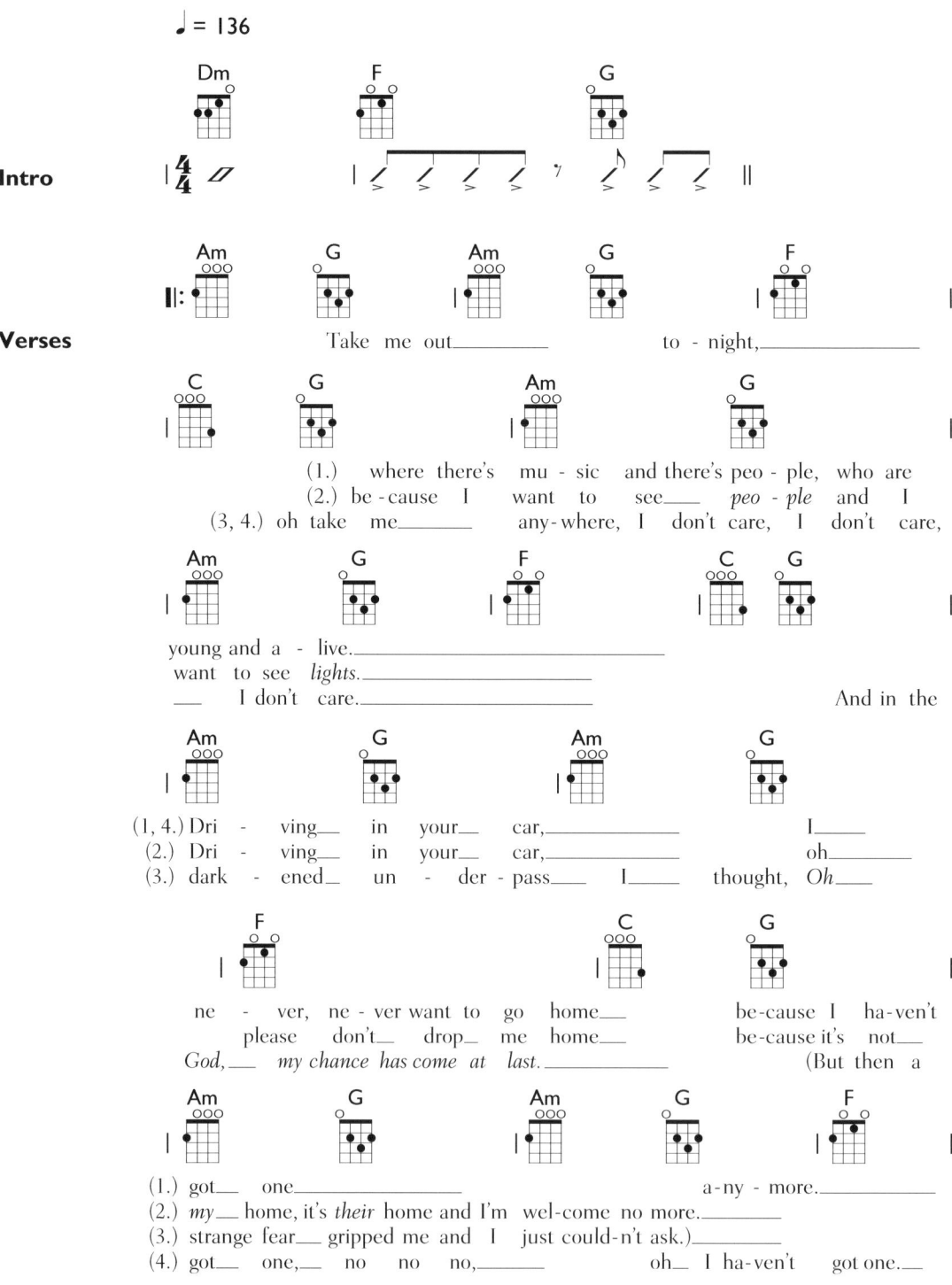

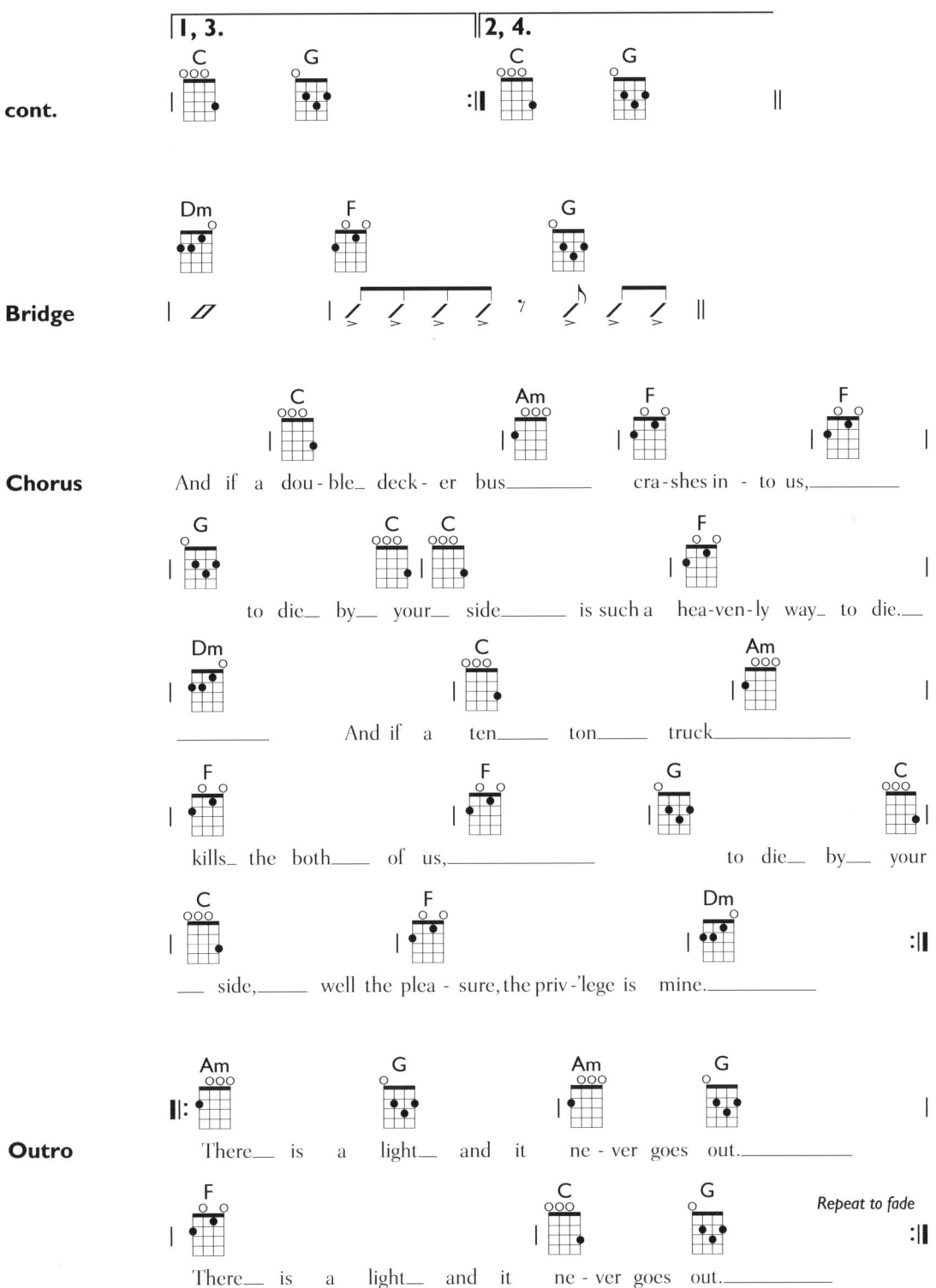

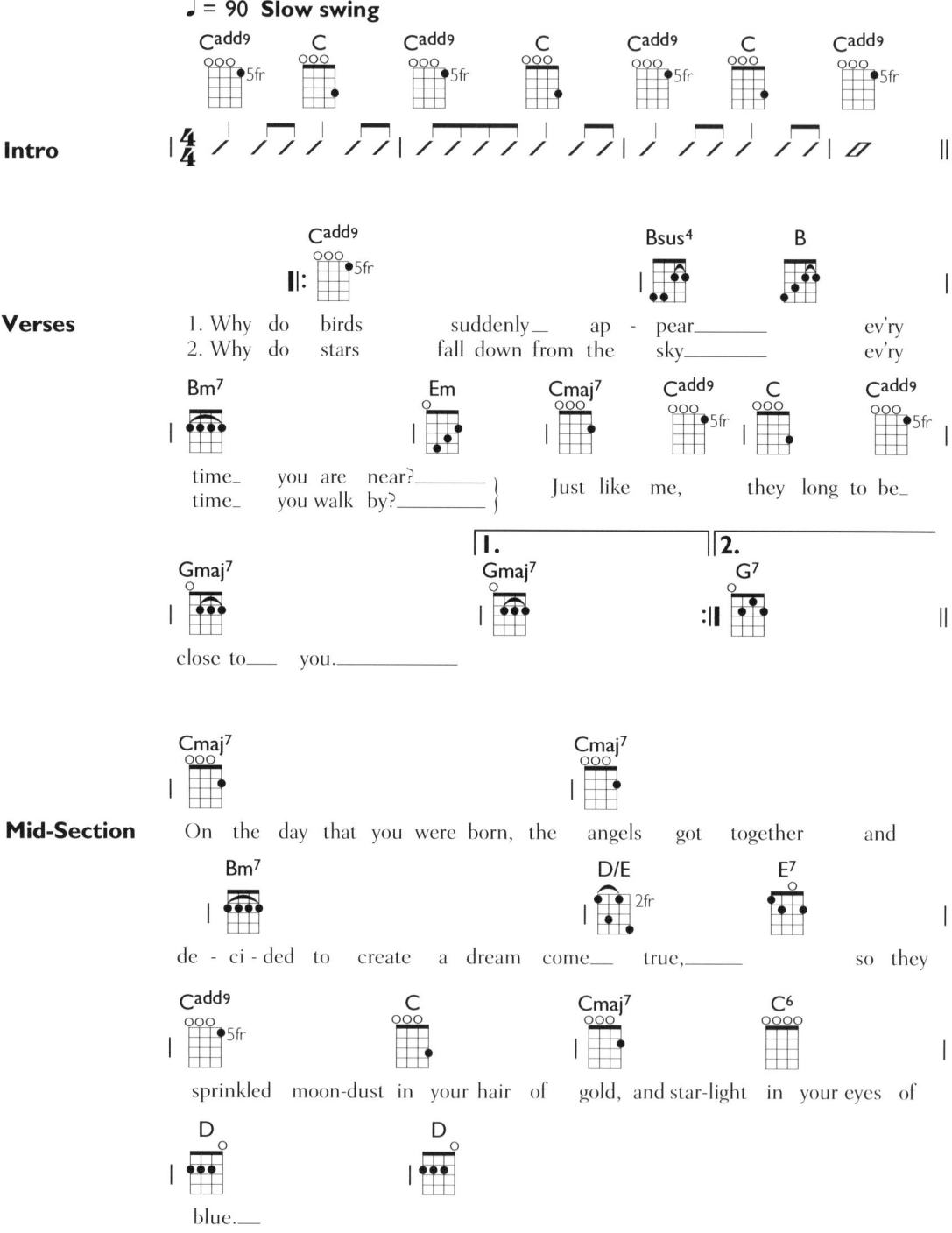

Verse 3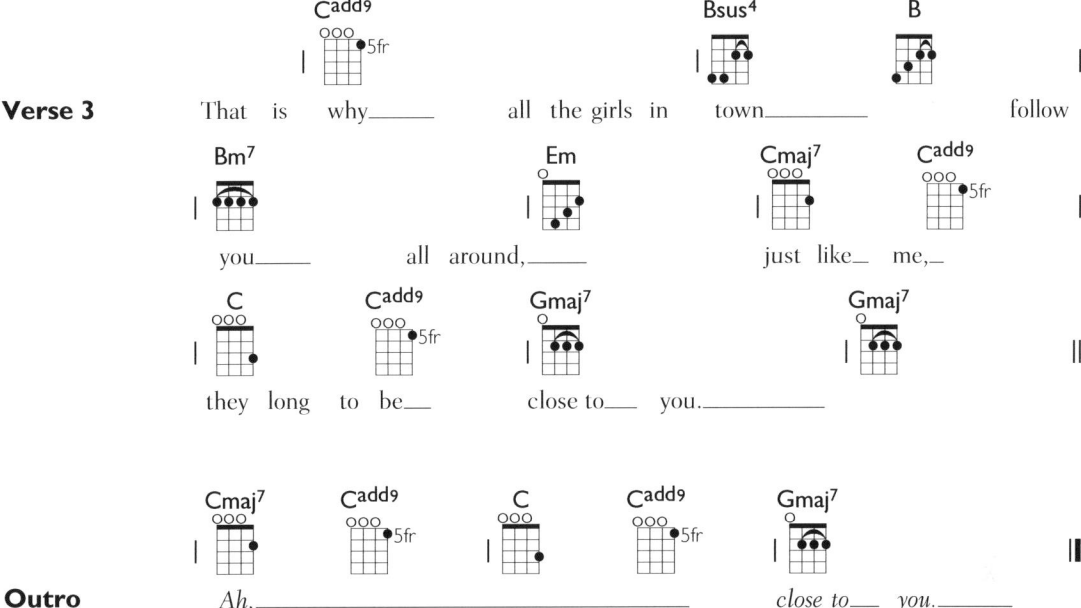

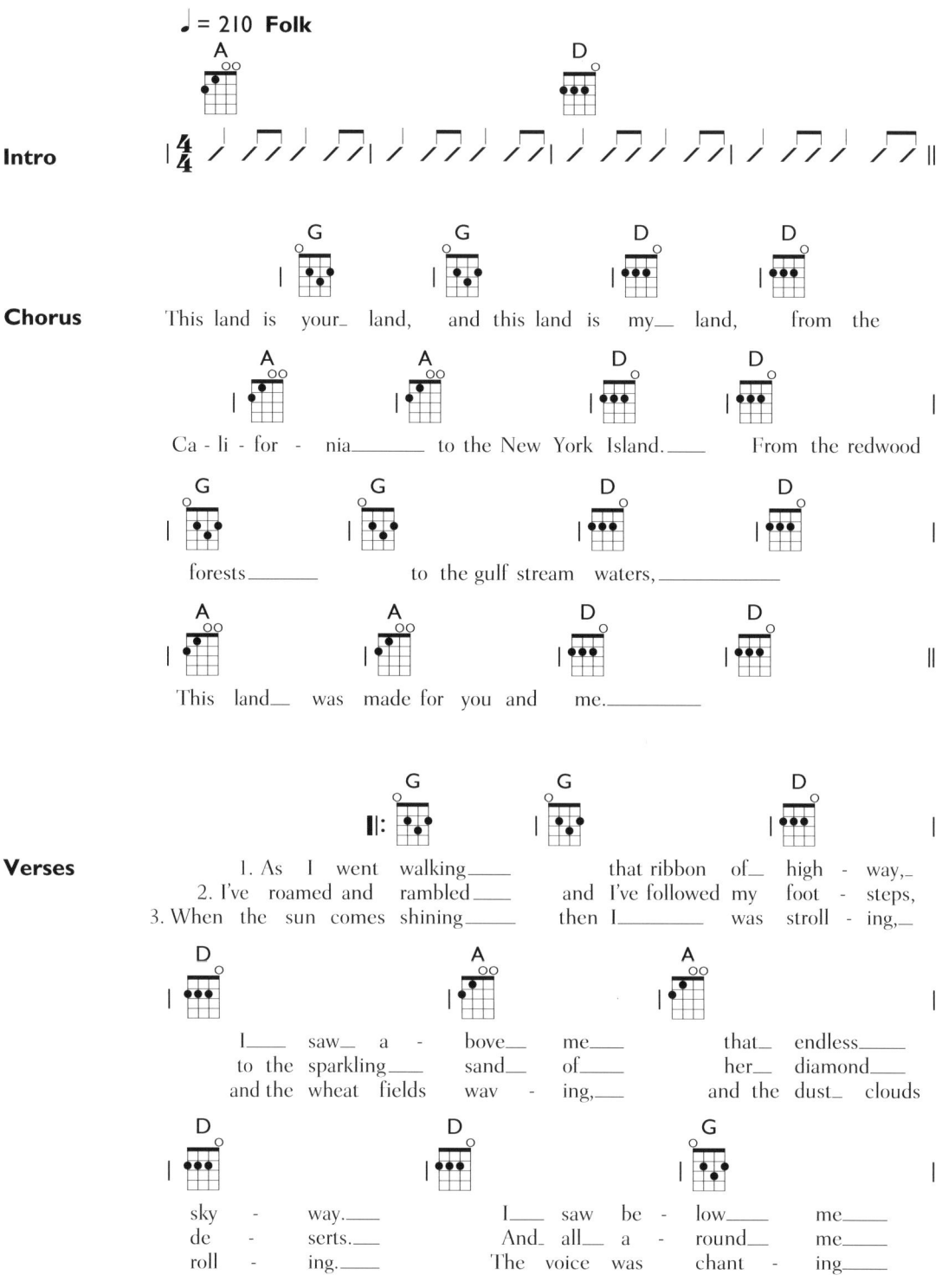

cont.

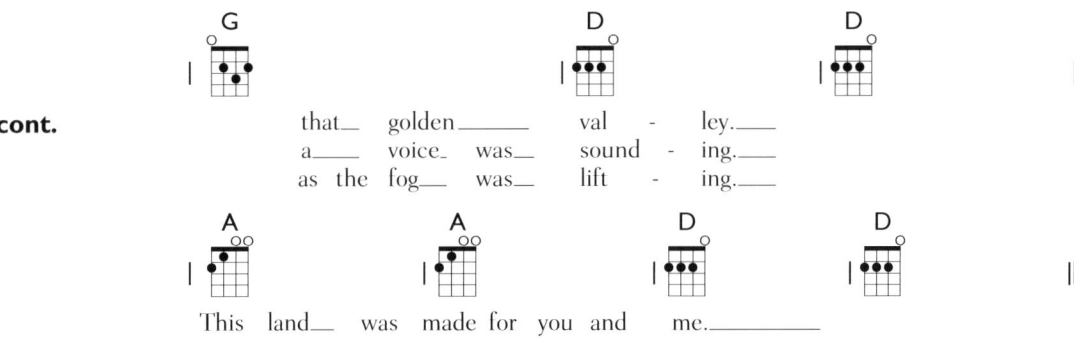

	G		D	D
	that golden		val - ley.	
	a voice was		sound - ing.	
	as the fog was		lift - ing.	

A	A	D	D
This land was	made for	you and	me.

Chorus 2   ‖: *As Chorus 1*   *Play three times* :‖

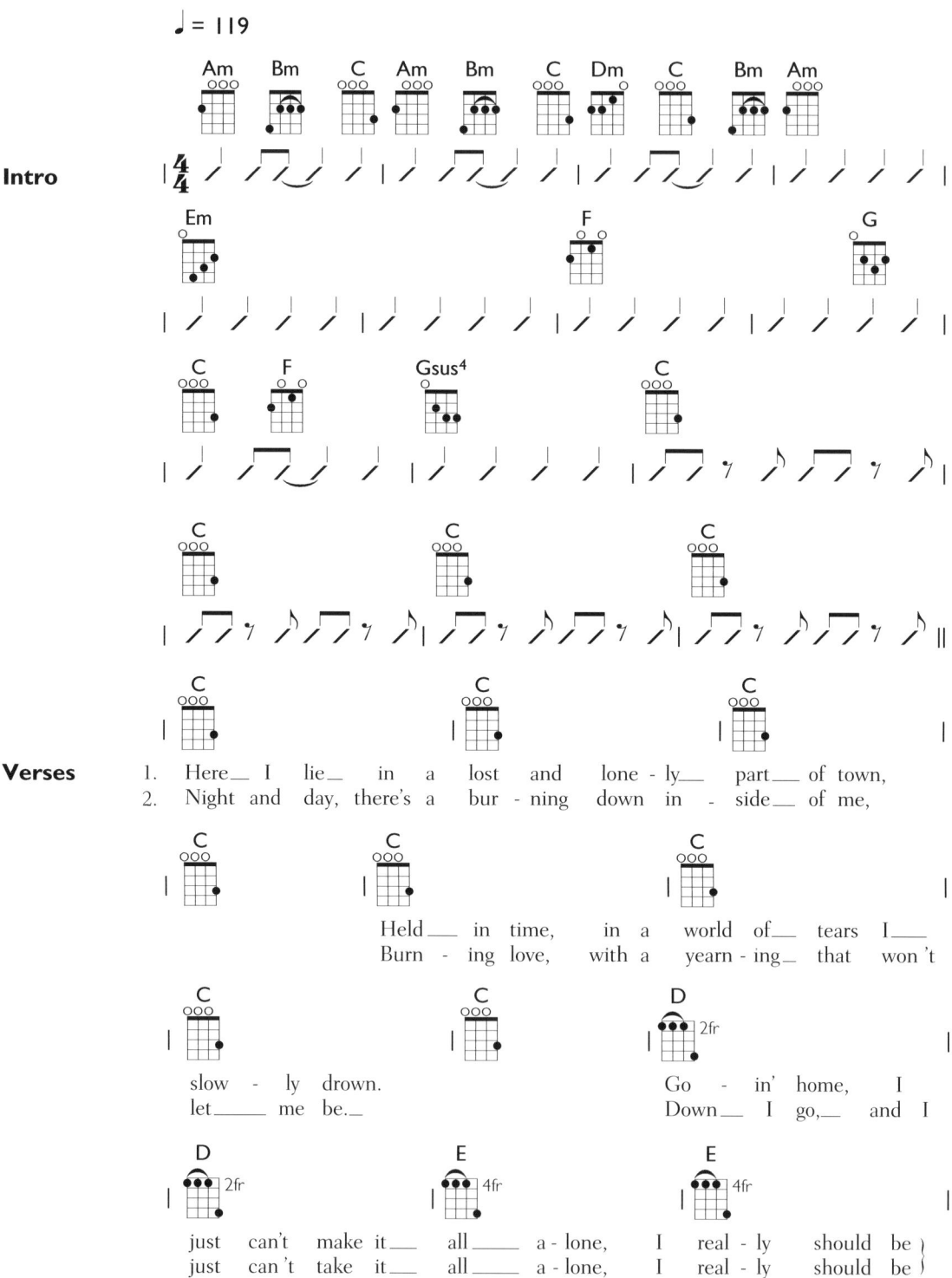

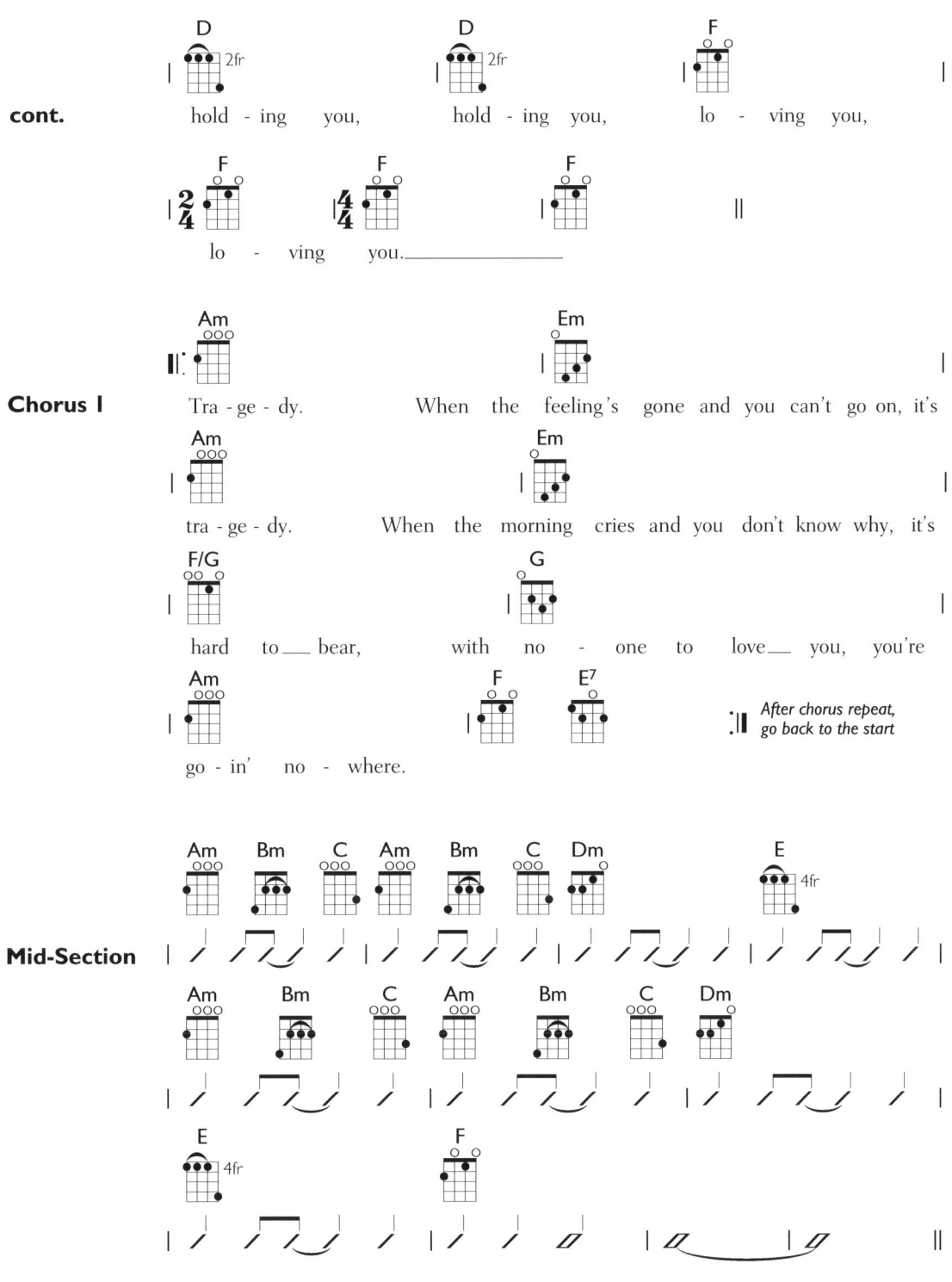

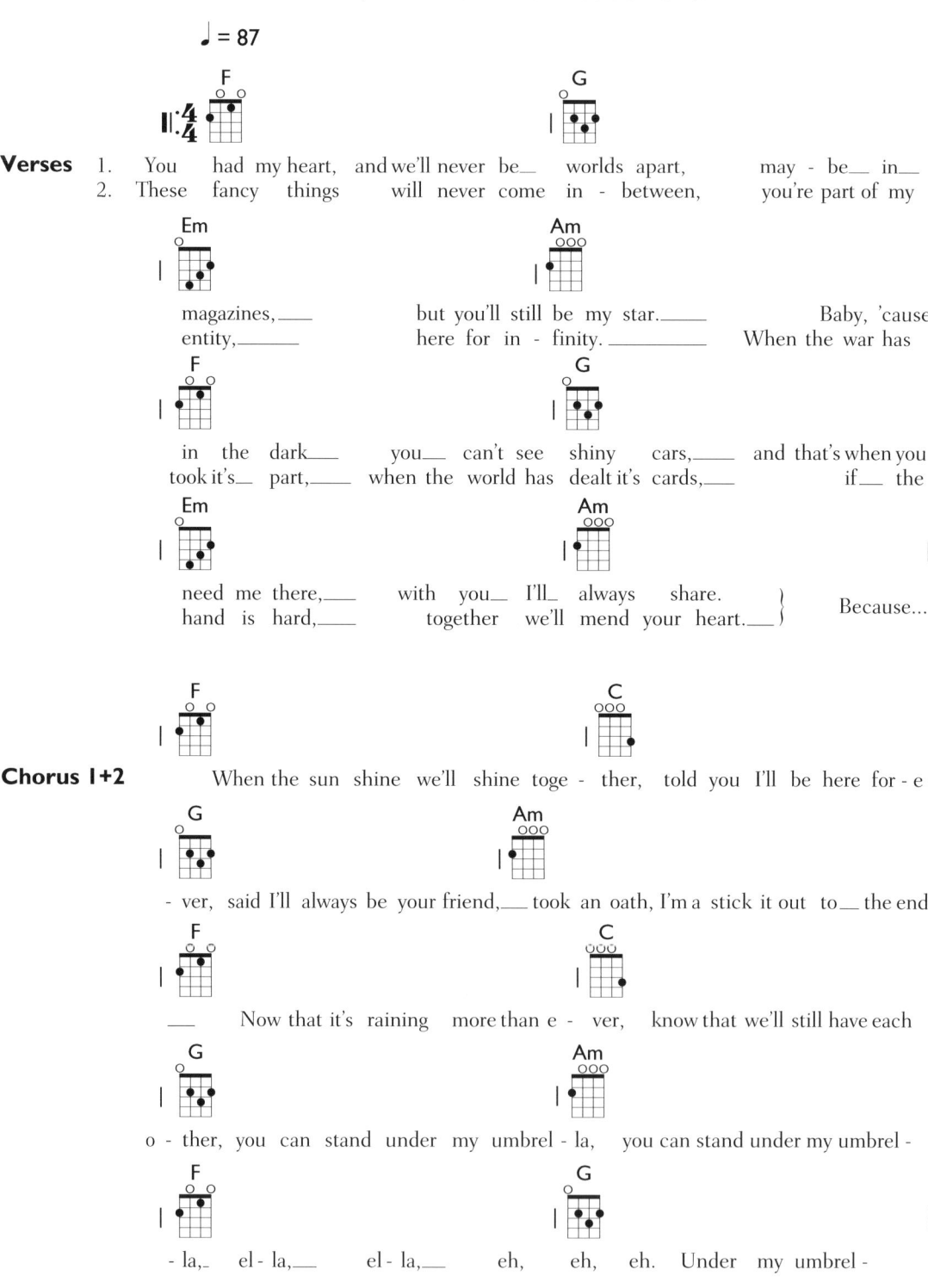

159

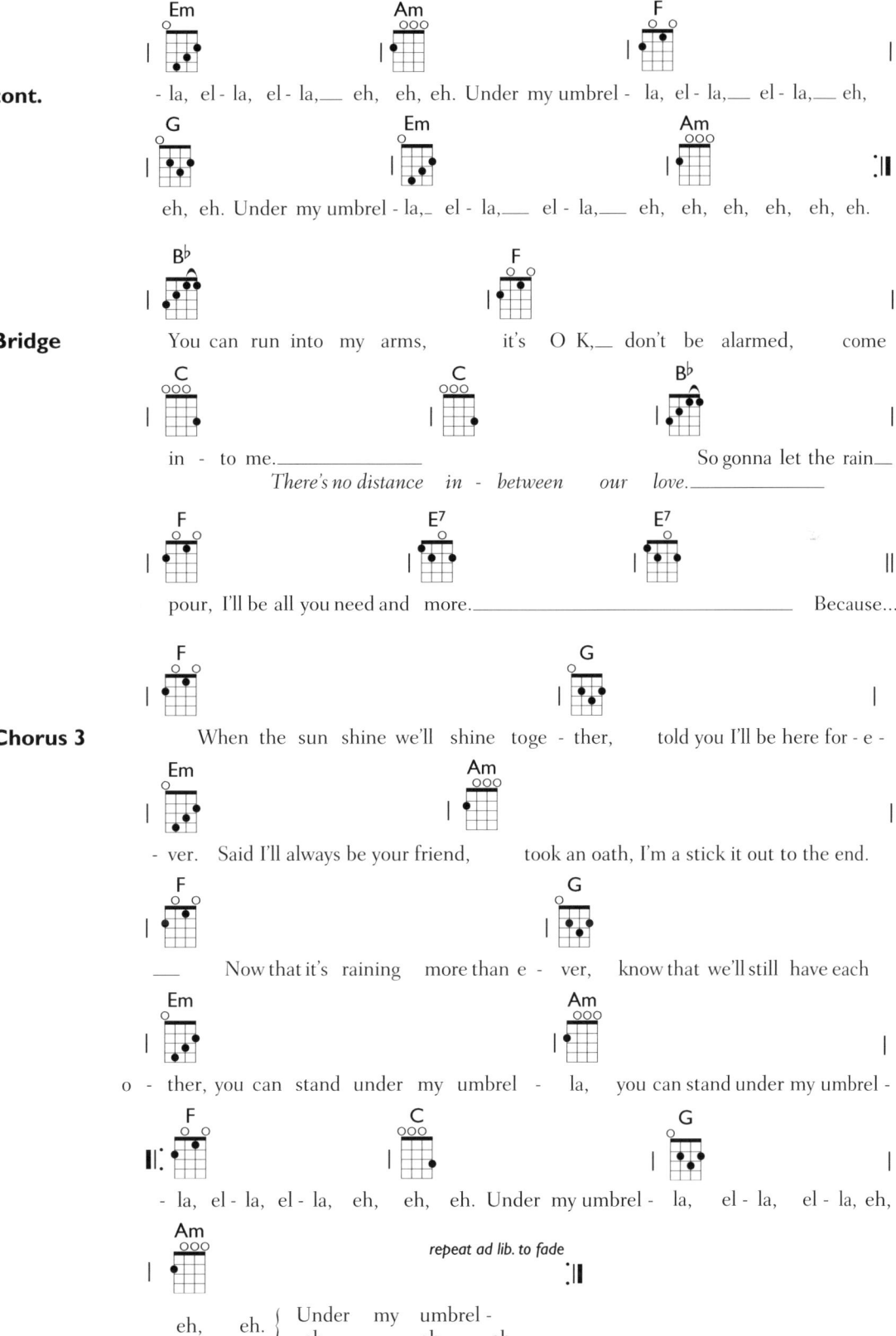

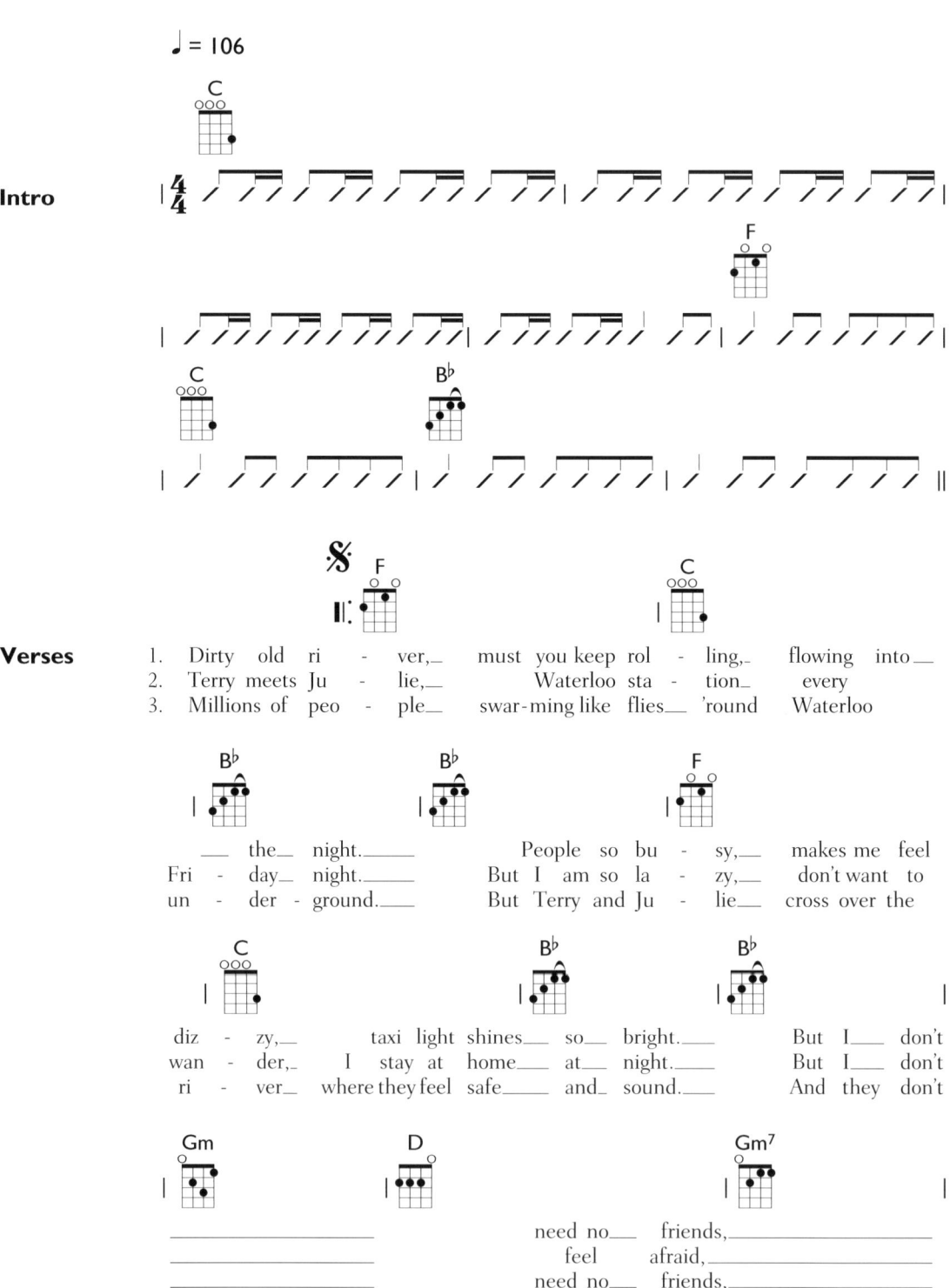

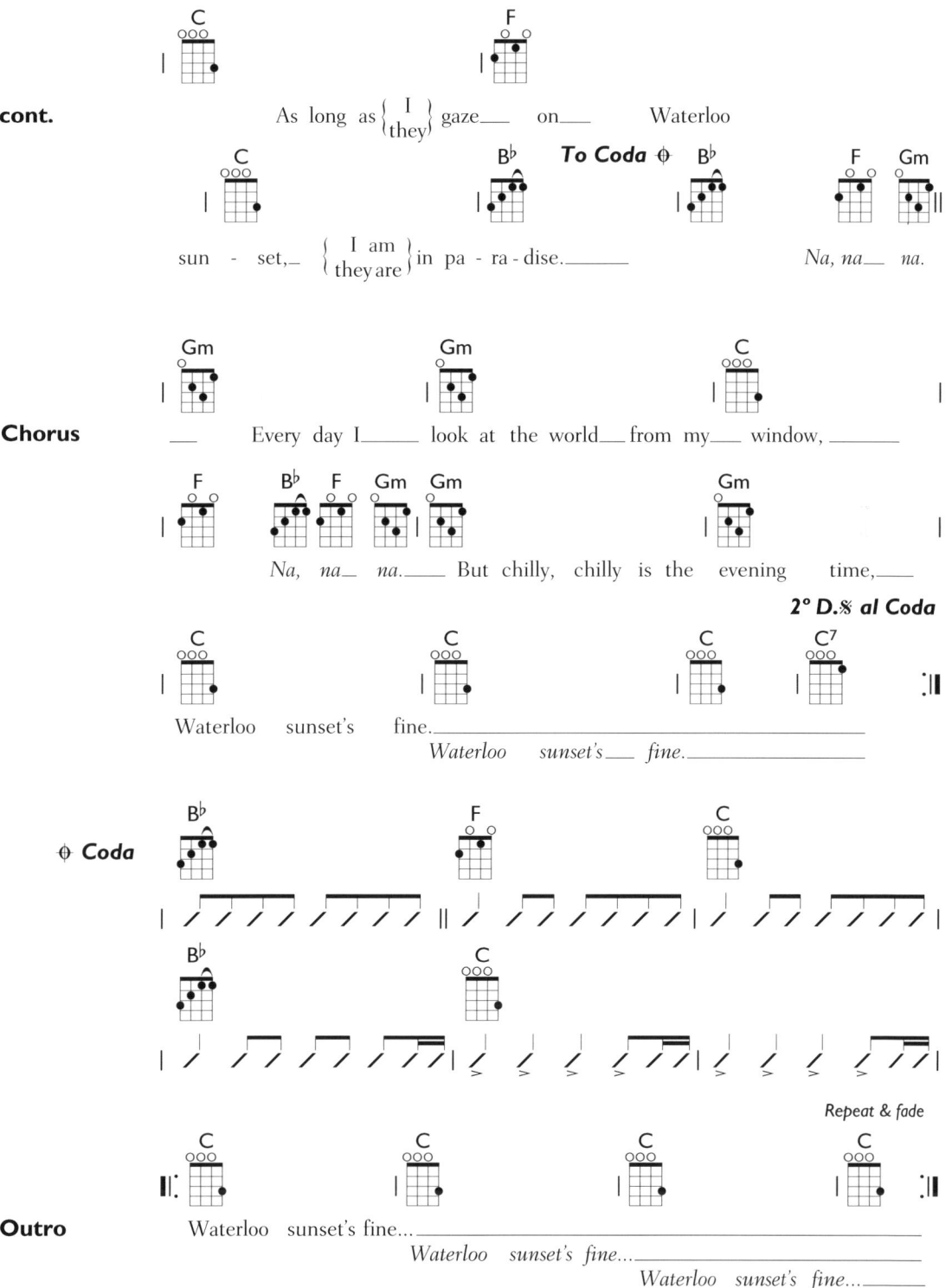

The Way You Look Tonight

Frank Sinatra

Words by Dorothy Fields
Music by Jerome Kern

Ballad

Verses

| Gmaj7 | Em7 | Am7 | D7 |

1. Some—— day—— when I'm awfully low,——
(2.) love - ly,—— with your smile so warm,——

| Gmaj7 | Em7 | Am7 |

when the world is cold,—— I will feel a
and your cheek so soft,—— there is nothing

| D7 | Dm11 | G7 | Cmaj7 |

glow just thinking of—— you,—— and the way you
for me but to love—— you,—— just the way you

| Am7 | D7 | Gmaj7 | Em7 | Am7 | D7 |

look—— to - night.——
look—— to - night.——

1. | Am7 | D7 :||
2. | Cm7 | F7 ||

| Gmaj7 | Em7 |

2. Oh but you're

| Bbmaj7 | Bdim7 | Cm7 | F7 |

With each word your tenderness grows,——

| Bbmaj7 | Dm7 | C#dim7 | Cm7 | F7 |

tearing—— my fear—— a - part.——

© 1936 T B Harms Company
Chappell Music Ltd, Shapiro Bernstein & Co Limited and Universal Music Publishing Ltd
All Rights Reserved.

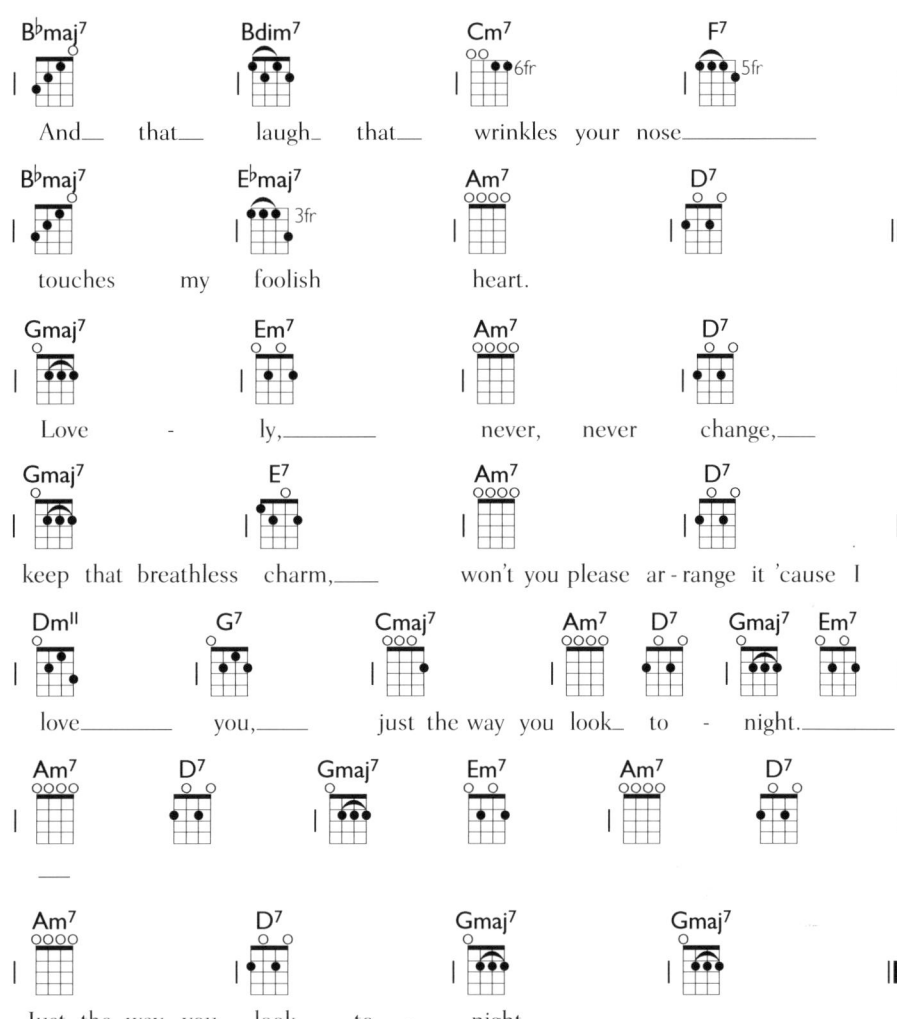

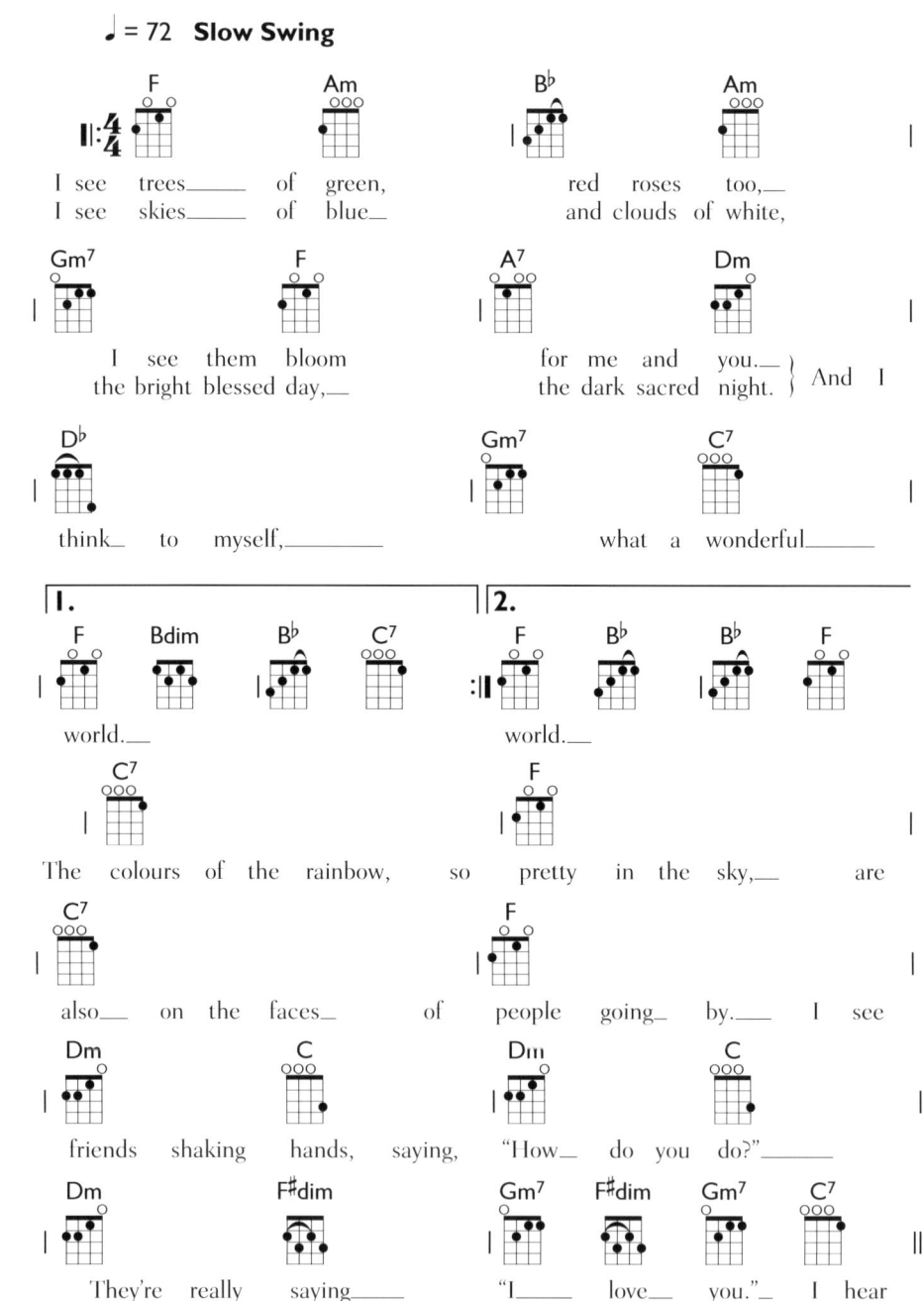

cont.

F	Am	B♭	Am

babies_____ cry,_____   I watch them grow,_____

Gm7	F	A7	Dm

They'll learn much more_____ than I'll_____ ever_____ know. And I

D♭		Gm7	C7

think_ to myself,_____   what a wonderful_____

F	Am7♭5	D7	

world._____   Yes_ I_____

Gm7		C7	

think_ to myself,_____   what a wonderful_____

F	B♭6	F	

world._____

Traditional

Waltzing Matilda
Words and Music Traditional

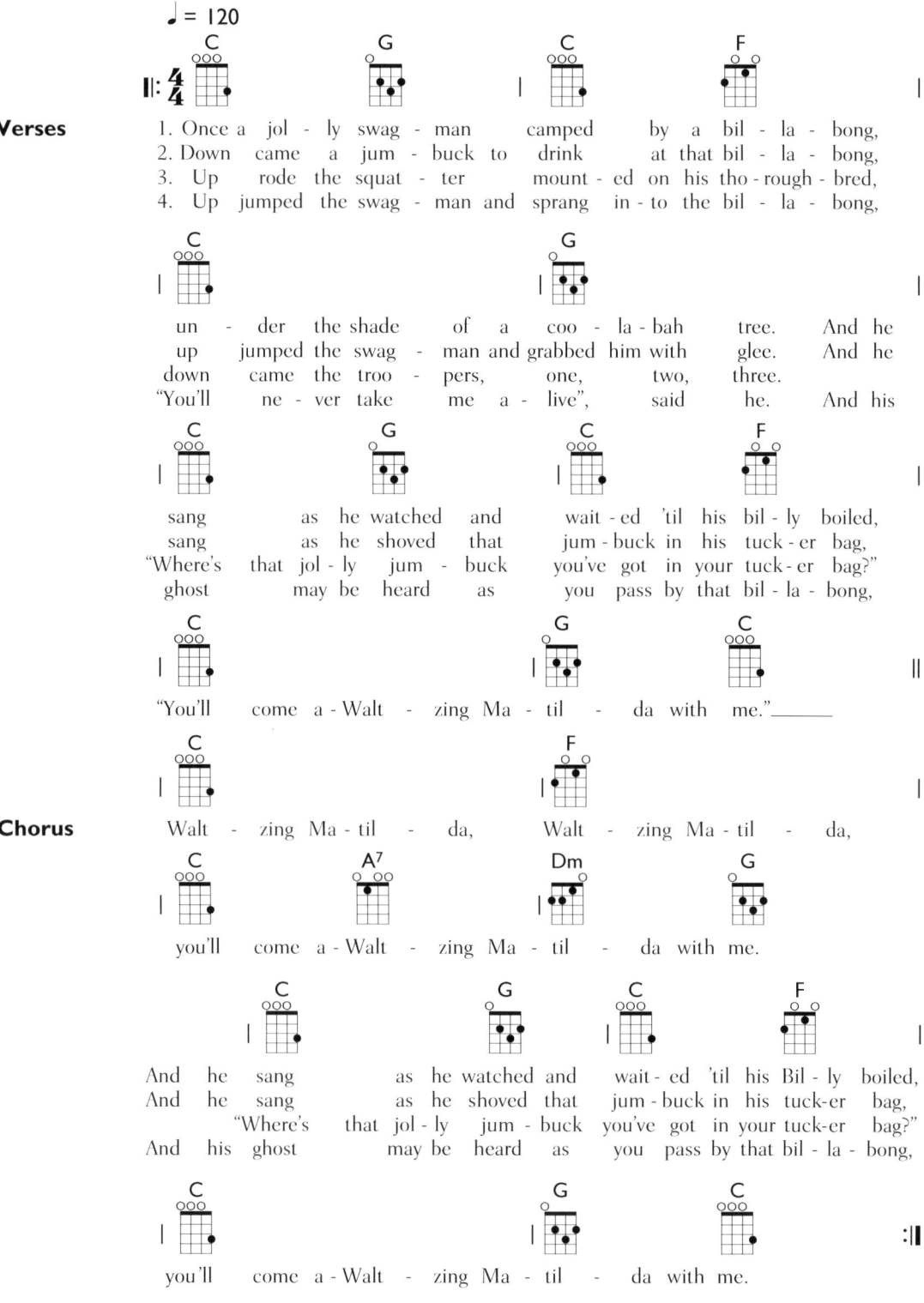

Traditional

What Shall We Do With The Drunken Sailor?

Words and Music Traditional

♩ = 112

Verses

|: Em — What shall we do with a drunken sailor? D — What shall we do with a drunken sailor?
Put him in the long boat till he's sober, put him in the long boat till he's sober,
Shave his belly with a rusty razor, shave his belly with a rusty razor,
Put him in the scuppers with a hose pipe on him, put him in the scuppers with a hose pipe on him,
Pull out the plug and wet him all over, pull out the plug and wet him all over,
Lock him in the guard room till he's sober, lock him in the guard room till he's sober,
That's what we do with a drunken sailor, that's what we do with a drunken sailor,

Em
What shall we do with a drunken sailor
put him in the long boat till he's sober,
shave his belly with a rusty razor,
put him in the scuppers with a hose pipe on him,   } Bm D Em — early in the morning. ‖
pull out the plug and wet him all over,
lock him in the guard room till he's sober,
that's what we do with a drunken sailor,

Refrain

Em — Weigh, heigh, and up she rises!   D — Weigh, heigh, and up she rises!

Em — Weigh, heigh, and up she rises,   Bm D — early in the   Em — morning!   :‖

© 2014 Faber Music Ltd
All Rights Reserved.

Whiskey In The Jar

Words and Music by Barney MacKenna, Ciaran Bourke, John Sheahan, Luke Kelley and Ronnie Drew (professionally known as THE DUBLINERS)

♩ = 105

Verses

1. As I was going over the far famed Kerry mountains, I
2. I counted out his money and it made a pretty penny, I
3. I went up to my chamber, all for to take a slumber, I
4. 'Twas early in the morning, just before I rose to travel, up

met with Captain Farrell and his money he was counting, I
put it in me pocket, and I took it home to Jenny. She
dreamt of gold and jewels and for sure it was no wonder, but
comes a band of footmen and like - wise Captain Farrell. I

first produced me pistol and I then produced me rapier, saying
sighed and she swore that she never would deceive me, but the
Jenny drew me charges, and she filled them up with water, then
first produced me pistol for she'd stolen away me rapier, I

"Stand and de - liver" for he were a bold deceiver.
devil take the women for they never can be easy.
sent for Captain Farrell to be ready for the slaughter.
couldn't shoot the water, so a prisoner I was taken.

Chorus

Mu - sha ring dumma doo damma daa. Whack fall the daddy - O',

Whack fall the daddy - O', there's whiskey in the jar.

Verse 5
Now there's some take delight in the carriages a rolling
And others take delight in the hurling and the bowling
But I take delight in the juice of the barley
And courting pretty fair maids in the morning bright and early

Verse 6
If anyone can aid me 'tis my brother in the Army
If I can find his station in Cork or Killarney
And if he'll go with me, we'll go rovin' in Killkenny
And I'm sure he'll treat me better than my own a-sporting Jenny

© 1967 Carlin Music Corp., London NW1 8BD
All Rights Reserved
Used by Permission

Traditional

Wild Mountain Thyme
Words and Music Traditional

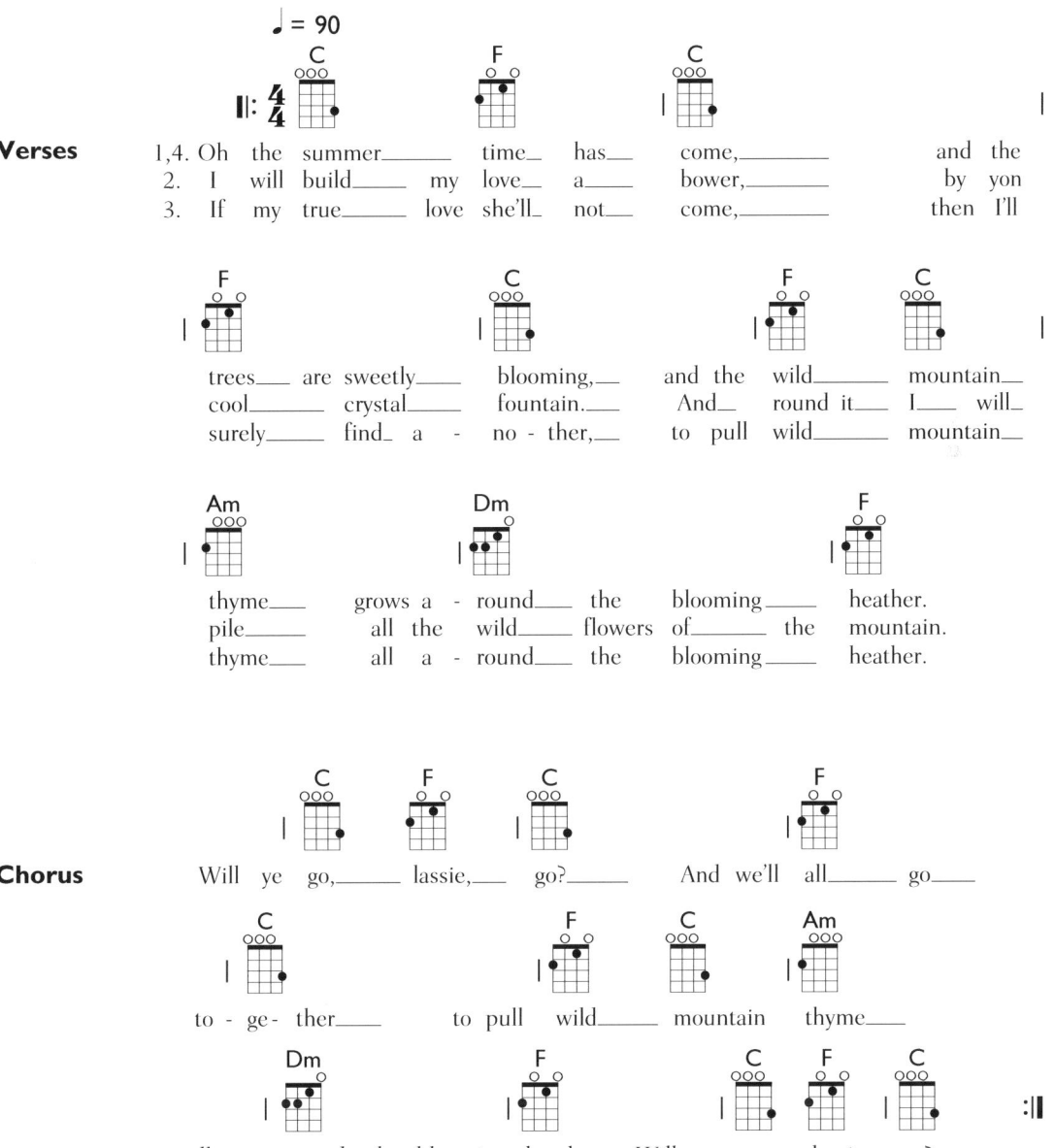

Verses:
1,4. Oh the summer time has come, and the trees are sweetly blooming, and the wild mountain thyme grows a-round the blooming heather.
2. I will build my love a bower, by yon cool crystal fountain. And round it I will pile all the wild flowers of the mountain.
3. If my true love she'll not come, then I'll surely find another, to pull wild mountain thyme all a-round the blooming heather.

Chorus: Will ye go, lassie, go? And we'll all go together to pull wild mountain thyme all a-round the blooming heather. Will ye go, lassie, go?

© 2014 Faber Music Ltd
All Rights Reserved.

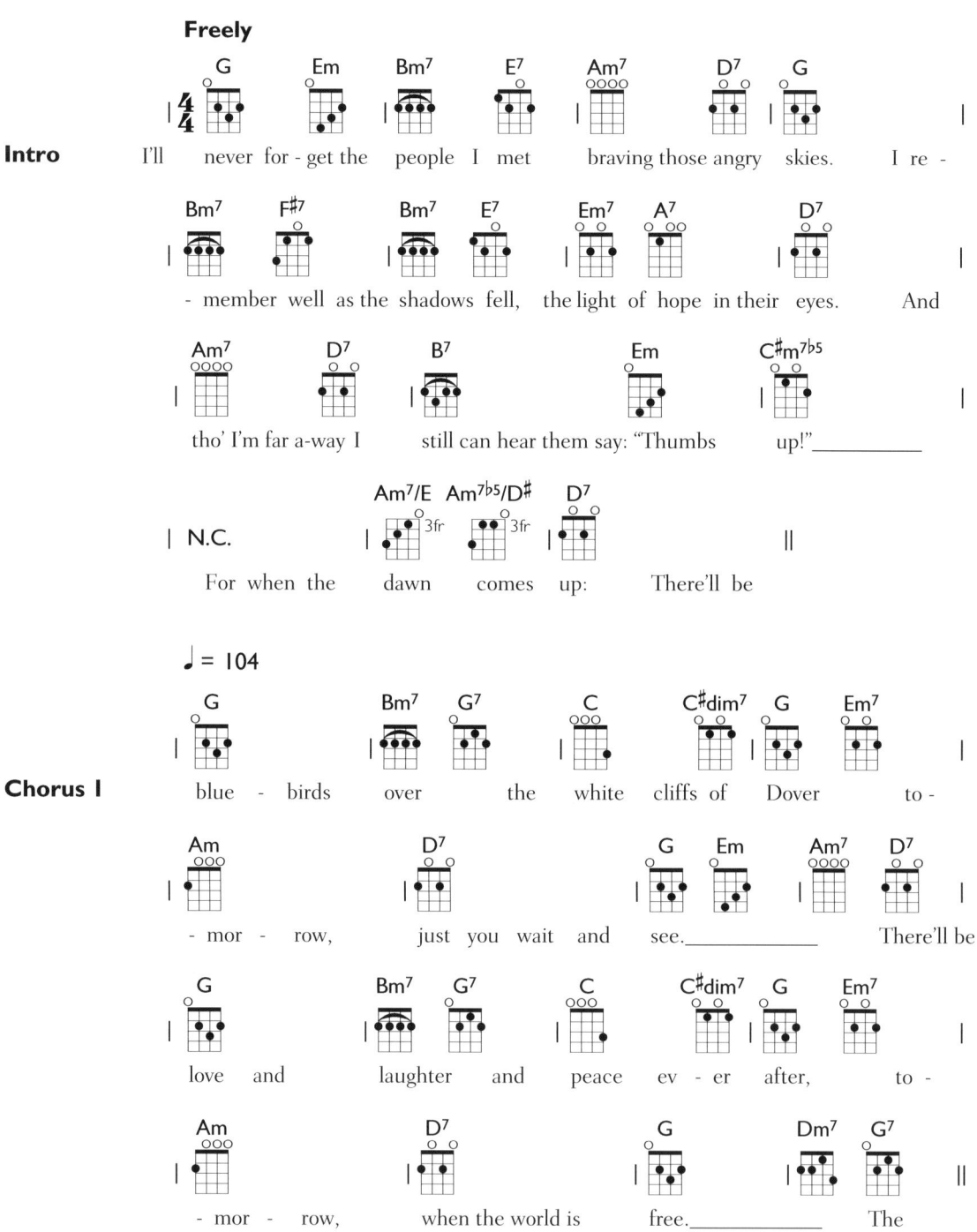

Verse

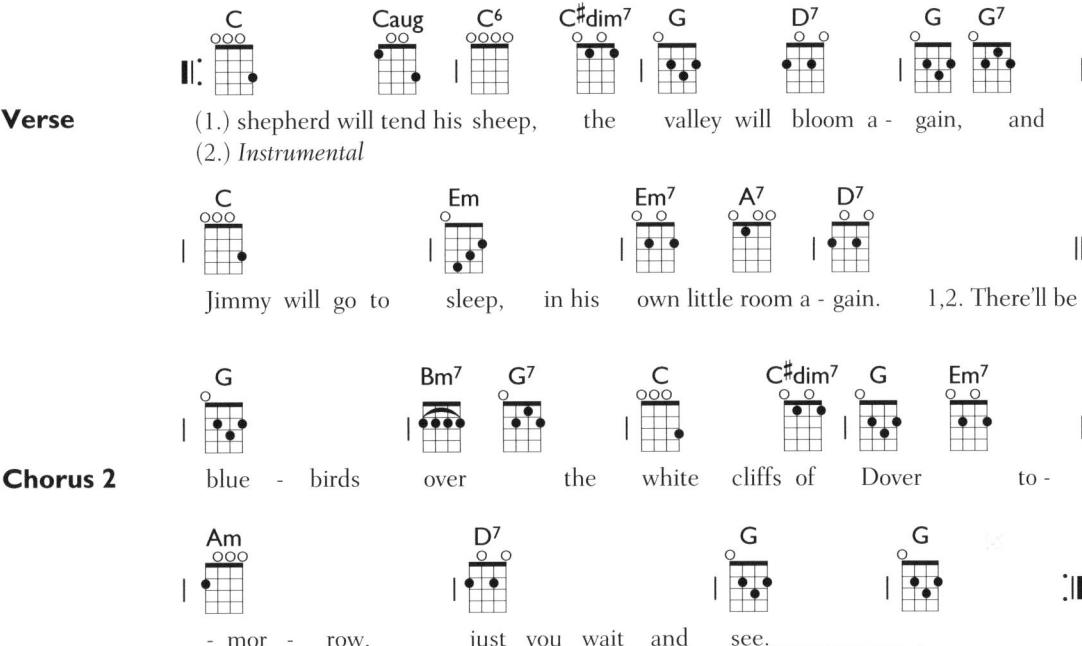

(1.) shepherd will tend his sheep, the valley will bloom a - gain, and
(2.) Instrumental

Jimmy will go to sleep, in his own little room a - gain. 1,2. There'll be

Chorus 2

blue - birds over the white cliffs of Dover to - mor - row, just you wait and see.____

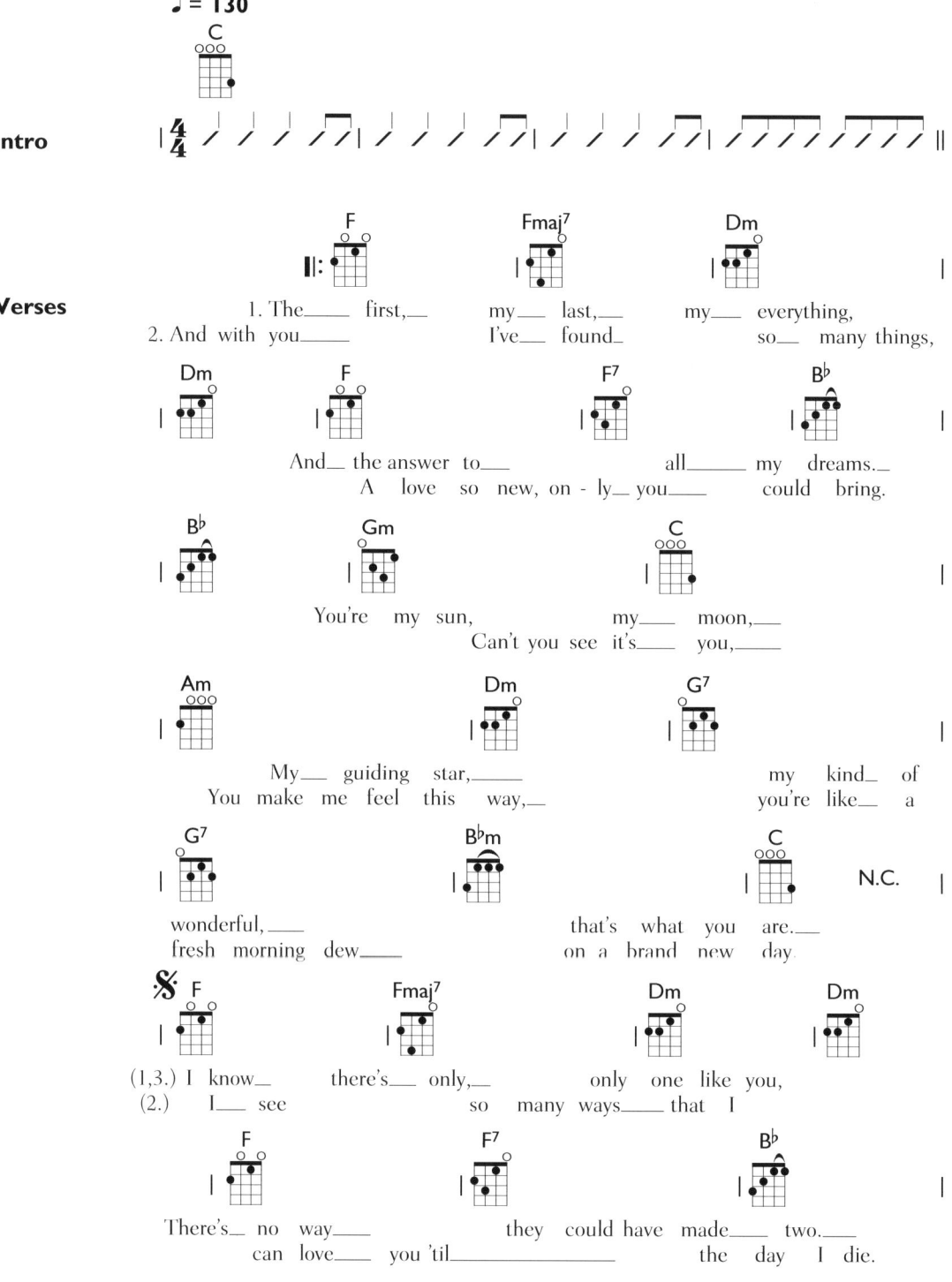

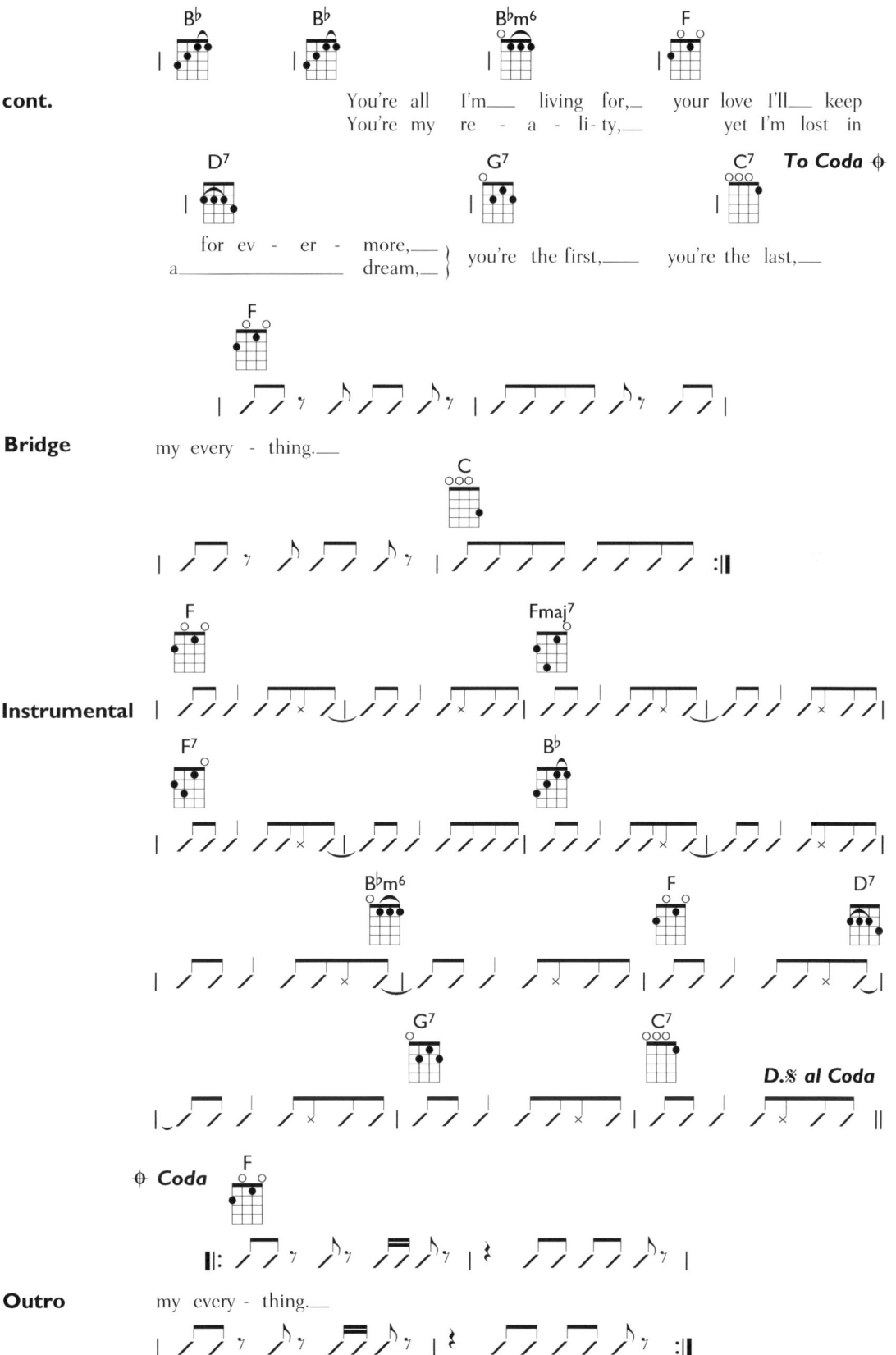

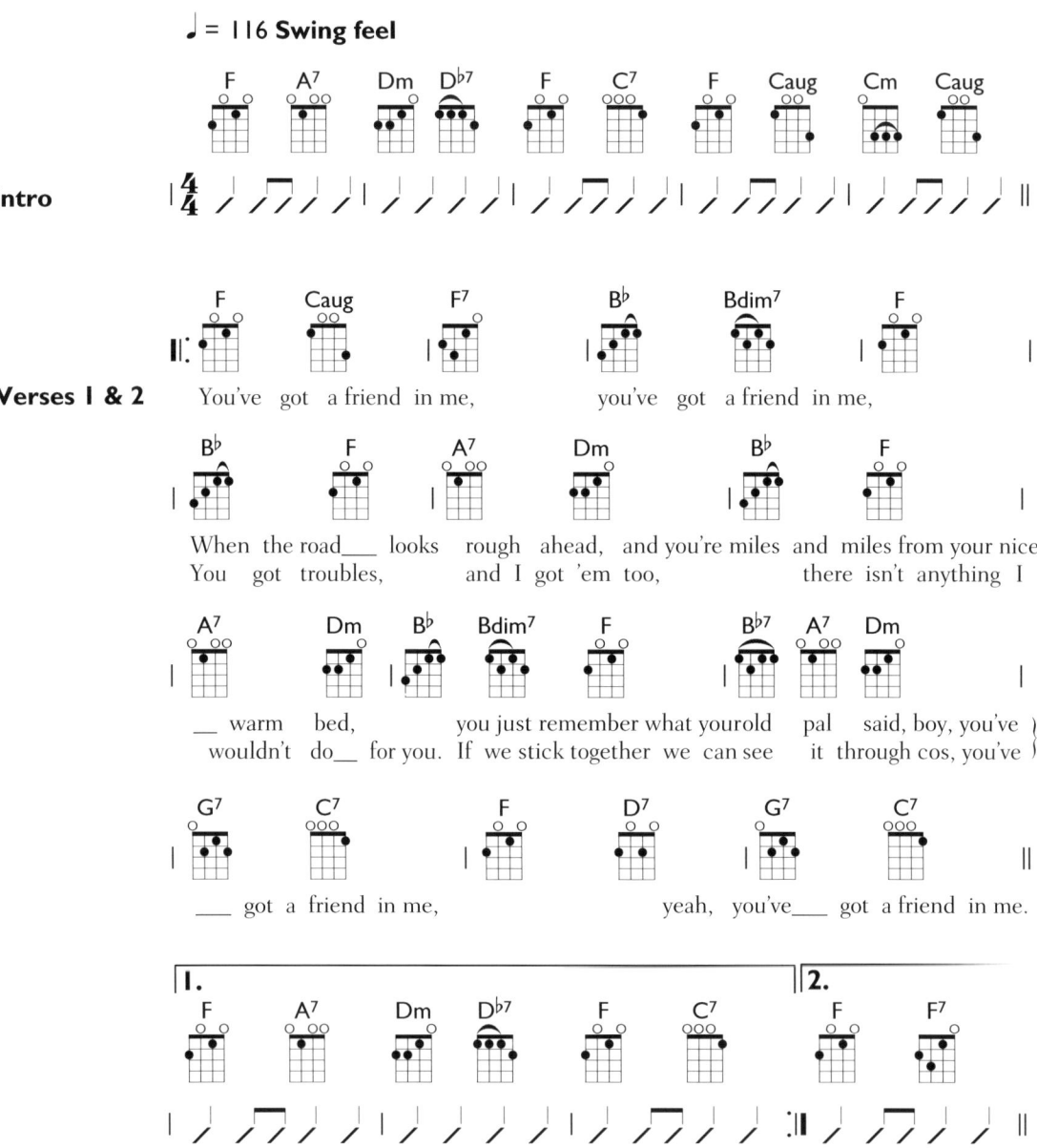

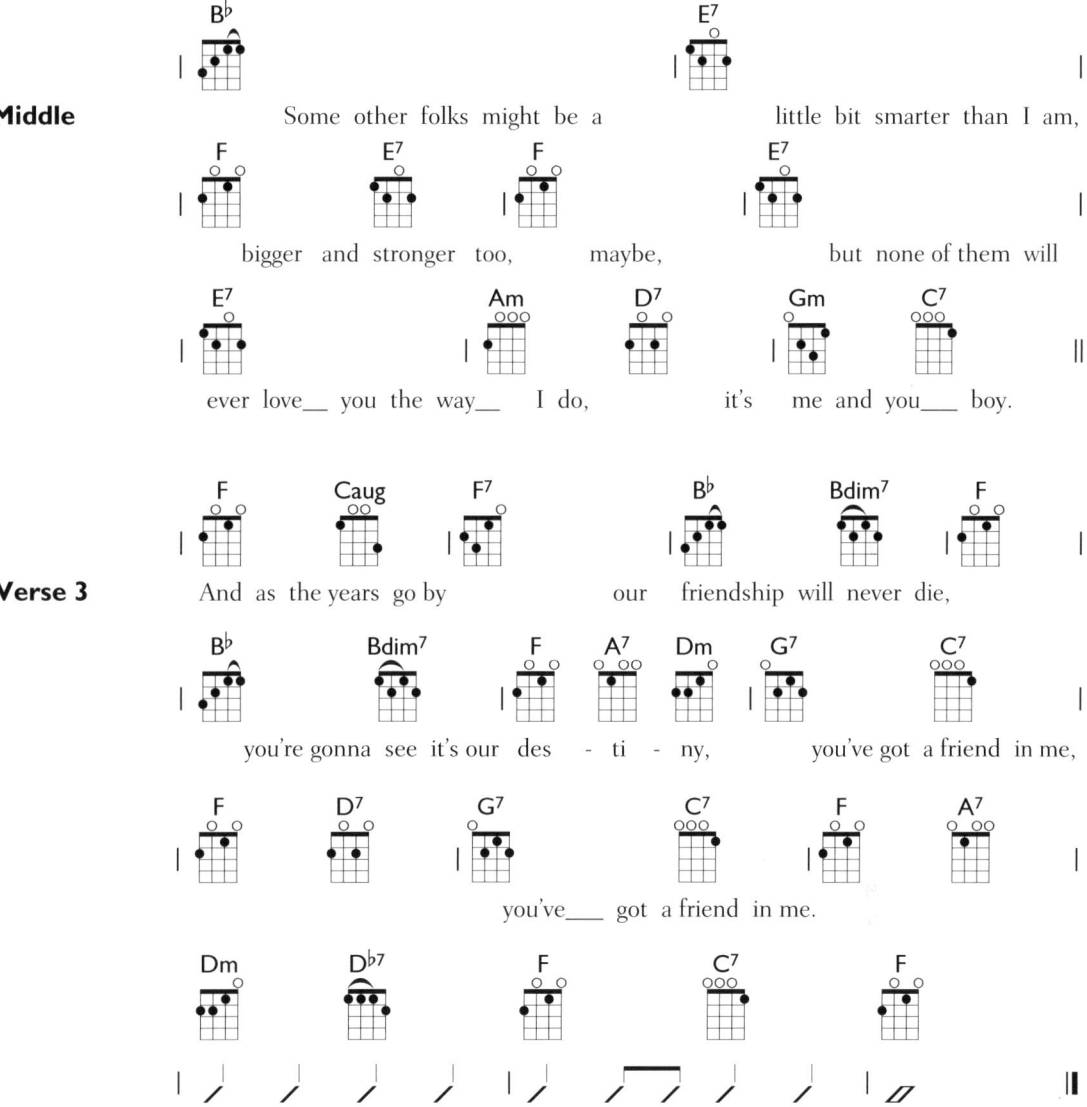

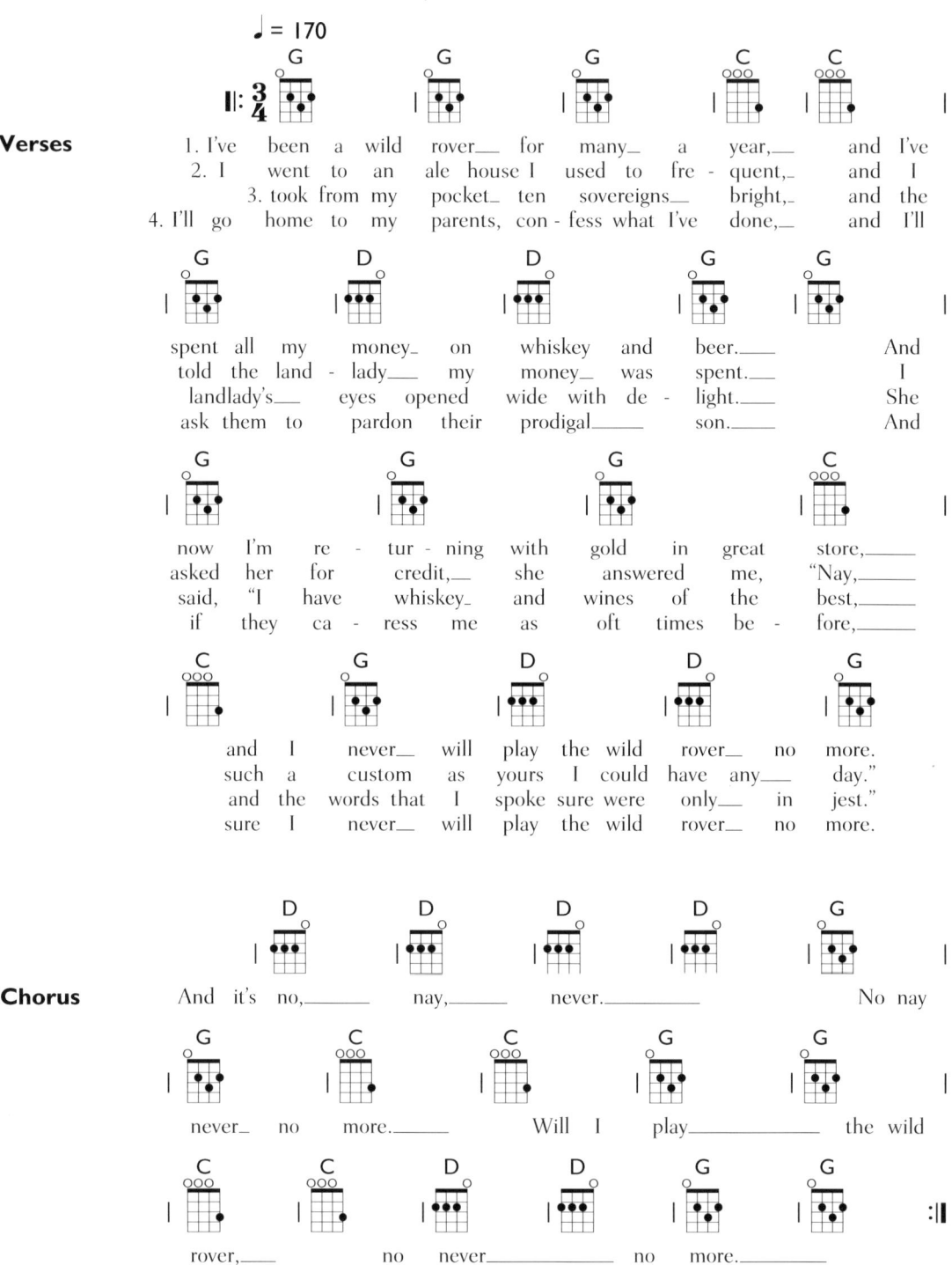